FOR GOD AND RACE

FOR GOD AND RACE

The Religious and Political Leadership of AMEZ Bishop James Walker Hood

Sandy Dwayne Martin

University of South Carolina

©1999 University of South Carolina

Published in Columbia, South Carolina, by the
University of South Carolina Press

Manufactured in the United States of America

03 02 01 00 99   5 4 3 2 1

Library of Congress Cataloging-in-Publication Data

Martin, Sandy Dwayne.
  For God and race: the religious and political leadership of
AMEZ Bishop James Walker Hood / Sandy Dwayne Martin.
    p. cm.
  Includes bibliographical references and index.
  ISBN 1-57003-261-0
  1. Hood, J. W. (James Walker), 1831–1918. 2. Afro-American
clergy—Biography. 3. Afro-American clergy—Political activity.
4. African Methodist Episcopal Zion Church—History. I. Title
BX8459.H66 M37 1999
287'.8'092—ddc21
  [B]

                                                          98-25444

This book is dedicated to the loving memory of
The Reverend Benjamin J. Carter—

former pastor of Johnson Chapel African Methodist Episcopal Zion Church in Courtland and other congregations in Mississippi, and family friend—in appreciation for all the years that he labored for Zion in the West Tennessee and Mississippi Conference, traveling unpaved roads, preaching in wooden and non-air conditioned churches, suffering and enduring misunderstanding, facing racial prejudice, and struggling with the weaknesses of humanity but proclaiming the love and grace of God.

Contents

Preface

Only in recent decades has sustained study been given to African American religious history. Not surprisingly, the lives and activities of many significant black religious leaders have thus far gone unexamined in scholarly circles. This is certainly the case with James Walker Hood (1831–1918) of the African Methodist Episcopal Zion denomination, one of the major black groups in the United States. Hood, unfortunately, left no extant, completed autobiography and there are no biographies of him. Nor is there any full-length critical article devoted solely to Hood's life or any aspect of it. This is regrettable, given the fact that Hood was one of the most dynamic, colorful, and influential African Americans in both the ecclesiastical and political realms during the nineteenth and early twentieth centuries.

Having long had an appreciation for the pivotal role that Hood played in American history, I have endeavored in the following pages to introduce him to religious and general historical scholarship. The thesis or objective of this study, therefore, is to recover for scholarly appropriation the highly influential religious and political (especially in racial matters) leadership of James Walker Hood, given his great neglect in scholarly circles. Available source materials demand that the focus fall on the public career of Hood. More attention will be devoted to the 1864–1872 era than to the earlier years; even greater attention will be given to the period 1872–1916, from the date of his elevation to the episcopacy of the African Methodist Episcopal Zion Church until his forced retirement as an active bishop in 1916. In addition to the greater availability of sources, Hood's greater impact upon the Zion denomination and American politics necessitate the ascending accentuation upon the 1864–1872 and the 1872–1916 periods.

A survey of Hood's life reveals the powerful impact he had on black American life in the context of the religious and political activities of the Zion denomination and the struggles of African Americans as they encountered new opportunities and new dangers offered by the Civil War, Reconstruction, and the white supremacist Redemption of the South. A perennial concern of mine has been exploring the relationship between black religion and social change, especially efforts to achieve racial justice and equity. James W. Hood, a mainstream black churchperson of the nineteenth and early twentieth centuries, presents himself as a worthy candidate through whom to pursue that interest. Others, such as the AMEZ Bishop Alexander Walters and the AME Bishop Henry M. Turner, played more open roles in "secular" organizations dealing specifically with the advancement of African Americans, especially after 1895. Yet even an analysis of the "moderate" denominational leader, Hood, demonstrates the profound seriousness with which the overwhelming majority of black denominational leaders took their obligations both to spread the word of God and to uplift the race. Although the present study focuses on Hood's public career as a religious and political leader, it offers, as well, a scholarly examination of the neglected AMEZ Church and a glimpse at how the independent black denominations carried forth both a spiritual and temporal message for African Americans during an era of crisis and change.

The reader will undoubtedly observe that there are relatively few secondary sources that refer to Hood's life and career, aside from those of his contemporaries. This fact simply underscores the vital necessity and contribution of this work in its collection of important primary and scholarly unexplored materials regarding Hood. And the reader should bear in mind that this work is a critical, scholarly introduction to Hood. Much still remains to be explored about the life of this fascinating leader in religion and politics. It is hoped that this work will engender enthusiasm for such undertakings.

A number of libraries, collections, and their staffs have proved instrumental in the completion of the present work: the Carnegie Library and the AMEZ denominational archives at the Bishop W. J. Walls Heritage Center, both located at Livingstone College in Salisbury, North Carolina; the Woodruff Library of the Atlanta University Center in Atlanta, Georgia; the library of the University of Georgia in Athens; and the microfilmed papers of Carter G. Woodson, available from Auburn University in Alabama. Important works and documents pertaining to the life of Hood and/or the history of the AME Zion Church and Methodism are also available at the Schomburg Collection of the New York Public Library and the library and archives of the Union Theological Seminary, both in New York City; the Divinity School Library of Vanderbilt University in Nashville, Tennessee; and the State Archives of North Carolina in Raleigh. Most of the denominational newspapers, church minutes, and related information used in this study are located at the Carnegie Library and the Walls Center. The Atlanta University Center contains a number of important books and documents dating back to the nineteenth and early twentieth centuries, including Bishop Hood's classic history of the denomination. The Carter G. Woodson Collection has a portion of Hood's unfinished autobiography and other papers, including correspondence from religious and political leaders of his day. Many items highlighting history and biographies of Hood's times are located at the University of Georgia Main Library, including the collected papers of Booker T. Washington and a number of Methodist histories. In addition, the University of Georgia's fine interlibrary loan department helped immensely with accessing vital resources located elsewhere.

Many individuals provided crucial information concerning Hood and the history and operations of the AMEZ Church, including Bishop J. Clinton Hoggard (Retired) of the AMEZ, concerning the family and descendants of Bishop Hood; Mrs. Louise Roundtree of Salisbury; Mrs. Minora Hicks, former librarian, and current head librarian Mrs. Elizabeth Mosby, and Mrs. Shirley Frost and Ms. Yalonda Carson, librarians, of Carnegie Library; the Reverend Mrs. Willie Aldrich, director of the Walls Heritage Center; the Reverend Cynthia D. Keever, library director, and the Reverend Scott C. Girard, technical services librarian of Hood Theological Seminary; Ms. Mary Love, editor of the AME Zion's church school literature and professor at Hood Theological Seminary; Dr. Dennis Dickerson, professor of history at Williams College and AME historiographer; and Dr. Thomas Slater, Methodist minister and colleague in the University's department of religion. Mrs. Catherine McNeil, archivist of the historic Evans Metropolitan AMEZ Church in Fayetteville, North Carolina, provided crucial information concerning Hood and his activities in and around Fayetteville. I also extend heartfelt thanks to Dr. H. H. Grier, the pastor of St. Peter's AMEZ Church in New Bern, North Carolina, for information on the history of his congregation, recognized as the mother church of Zion Methodism in the South. Mrs. Louise Everett, my cousin by marriage and the secretary of St. Luke AMEZ Church in Wilmington, North Carolina, provided comparable material on Hood's role in the history of that congregation. Dr. Hayward Farrar of the history department of Virginia Polytechnic Institute and State University provided great assistance by answering questions, providing critiques, and suggesting resources—all of which helped to place Hood in wider historical context.

The University of Georgia has been very supportive of my research. I thank the University for its Senior Faculty Research and Humanities Center and travel grants that permitted me to make a number of research trips to Livingstone College and other points. Dr. George Howard, head of the Department of Religion, has been supportive and encouraging, not only of this present enterprise, but also of all my professional activities. Mrs. Zinetta McDonald, departmental office manager, provided valuable and immeasurable technical information and assistance at all stages of this enterprise. Mrs. Ange Colson, her assistant, also provided valuable assistance. The Louisville Institute in 1995 funded summer research on a topic growing out of the Hood project and, consequently, occasioned my discovering information that proved helpful to me in better comprehending the leadership of Bishop Hood.

And there are other colleagues and friends who have me in their intellectual debt: Robert T. Handy, professor emeritus, and the late James M. Washington, professor of church history, both of Union Theological Seminary, and both of whom read and commented on portions of this manuscript; Lawrence N. Jones, former dean of Howard University School of Divinity, Washington, D.C.; Albert Raboteau, professor of religion at Princeton University; David Wills, professor of religion, Amherst College, Amherst, Massachusetts; Randall Burkett, associate director of the DuBois Institute, Harvard University, who provided important critiques to a portion of the manuscript; Will Gravely, professor of religion, University of Denver; Milton C. Sernett, professor of religion and African American Studies, Syracuse University; Lillian Ashcraft-Eason of Bowling Green University; Alonzo Johnson of the University of South Carolina; Phillip McGuire, professor of history, Fayetteville State University; Earl Sheridan, chair and professor of Political Science, University of North Carolina–Wilmington; Moses Moore of Arizona State University; and Lewis V. Baldwin of Vanderbilt University. Thomas Brown, dean of Phillips School of Theology of the ITC in Atlanta, and Louise Brown, an Atlanta area public school teacher, have been both intellectual and personal friends. I must add that Drs. Handy, Washington, Dickerson, Johnson, and McGuire have read and/or heard portions of this book in various forums and offered valuable comments and suggestions.

I am grateful to staff at the University of South Carolina Press for encouragement and support. I have had the pleasure of working with Joyce Harrison, former editor who at the earliest stages of this enterprise saw the merit of this work, and Fred Kameny, editor-in-chief, who has continued the Press's support of the project. Furthermore, I thank the University of South Carolina Press for permitting the republication of my "Biblical Interpretation, Ecclesiology, and Black Southern Religious Leaders, 1860–1920: A Case Study of AMEZ Bishop James Walker Hood," pp. 110–38 in Alonzo Johnson and Paul Jersilds, eds., *Ain't Gonna Lay My 'Ligion Down: African American Religion in the South,* copyrighted

(1996), and the *Journal of the Interdenominational Theological Center* for permission to republishing its copyrighted "The AMEZ Church and the Women's Ordination Controversy: A Case Study of the Value of Racial Inclusivity in Religious Studies," (Fall 1993/Spring 1994): 105–26.

Friends and family have provided emotional and social support of my professional endeavors through the years, directly and indirectly, including the Reverend James Kendrick and the membership of East Friendship Baptist Church in Athens, Georgia; the members of Johnson Chapel AMEZ Church and their former pastor and presiding elder in the West Tennessee and Mississippi Annual Conference, Reverend Fred Shegog; the Reverend Eugene Marizett and the Shiloh Missionary Baptist Church, in Courtland, Mississippi; and the Macedonia Missionary Baptist Church and its former pastor, the Reverend Aaron McCrae, of Wilmington, North Carolina. Family members have been a constant source of encouragement, including my brothers, Walter, Wesley, Teddy (church steward), and John Lee, my sister-in-law, the Reverend Mrs. Sarah Martin, former pastor and current presiding elder in the West Tennessee and Mississippi Annual Conference, and three wonderful aunts, Hattie and Adlena Martin and L. V. Rogers. These connections to Zion and the Baptist traditions undoubtedly strengthened my commitment to pursue this project to its completion. I am also appreciative of my mother-in-law and sister-in-law, Mrs. Linda Whitaker Green Lloyd and Mrs. Karen Green-Brown of Wilmington, North Carolina. I faced some very difficult days at one point during the execution of this enterprise. Through it all, Danita Danette Martin, my wife, friend, a good person, and a fine mother of our two sons, Terrance Ladale Purnell and John Wesley Michael, stood by me.

Finally, I am profoundly grateful for James Walker Hood. I have some serious differences with him, but he left a great and noble legacy of love for and dedication to God, church, and race, which the following pages will demonstrate.

All defects and shortcomings in this work are my own.

Chronology

ca. 1792 Levi Hood, the father of James Hood, is born.

1796 A group of black Methodists establishes Mother Zion Church in New York City, the oldest, or mother congregation, of AMEZ Church. The AMEZ dates its origin to this year.

1813 Thirteen black families, including Levi and Harriet Walker Hood, withdraw from the Methodist Episcopal Church in Wilmington, Delaware, and establish the first black denomination, the Union Church of Africans.

1816 The African Methodist Episcopal Church organizes denominationally in Philadelphia, with Richard Allen as its first bishop. The American Colonization Society, dedicated to placing African Americans on the continent of Africa, is established (1816–1817).

1821 The African Methodist Episcopal (Zion) Church organizes denominationally in New York City and selects James Varick as its first superintendent.

1828 Christopher Rush, originally from the area of New Bern, North Carolina, is ordained superintendent in the AMEZ Church.

1829 David Walker first publishes his *Appeal,* calling upon enslaved blacks to assert their moral right to overthrow (violently) their slaveholding oppressors.

1830 Black leaders begin the National Negro Convention Movement with the first meeting held in Philadelphia. Among other things, they protest vigorously the aims of the American Colonization Society to place free blacks in Africa.

1831 James Walker Hood is born in Kenneth Township in southeastern Pennsylvania, near Philadelphia and the Delaware state line. Levi and Harriet Hood parented a total of twelve children, six males and six females, but it is unclear where James Hood falls relative to birth order. Bishop Richard Allen of the AME Church dies. Nat Turner leads a slave revolt in Virginia. William Lloyd Garrison, a white abolitionist, begins publication of *The Liberator*.

1834 Henry McNeal Turner, future AME minister, bishop, and church rival of Hood's, is born in South Carolina.

ca. 1842 James W. Hood is converted.

1848 The term "Zion" is officially added to the name of the denomination, hence, the African Methodist Episcopal Zion Church, making it easier to distinguish this denomination from the larger and rival AME group.

ca. 1849 Hood is finally convinced of his salvation.

ca. 1850 (or at some point during the preceding few years) Hood, while a teenager, gives a public speech predicting the end of slavery.

ca. 1852 Hood experiences a calling to preach the gospel. Hood marries Hannah L. Ralph of Lancaster City, Pennsylvania.

1853 The AMEZ denomination divides into two factions: the Wesleyan Methodist Episcopal Zion Church, located primarily south of New York and the African Methodist Episcopal Zion Church, located primarily in New York, New England, and Nova Scotia. The breach, after a court fight, is amicably healed in 1860.

1855 Hood moves to New York City. Hannah Ralph Hood dies.

1856 Hood is licensed to preach in a branch of the Union Church of Africans in New York City.

1857 Having moved to Connecticut and finding no branch of the Union Church of Africans, Hood affiliates with the AMEZ denomination. The United States Supreme Court rules that an enslaved person's escape to free soil does not guarantee his or her freedom. Indeed, the Court rules that the U.S. Constitution does not understand blacks as citizens with rights that whites are liable to observe.

1858 Hood and Sophia J. Nugent of Washington, D.C., marry. Hood temporarily pastors a church in Connecticut. He is appointed as a missionary to Nova Scotia.

1859 A Quarterly Conference in New England receives Hood on a trial basis.

1860 Hood receives ordination as deacon. Now having accumulated sufficient funds by means of savings from his work as a headwaiter in New York City, Hood heads for Halifax, Nova Scotia. The breach dating back to 1853 between the two factions of the AMEZ is healed, and three bishops are elected as equals, the original position of the Wesleyan faction. There are fewer than five thousand members in the AMEZ.

1860–1861 Hood finally secures sufficient funds to begin his missionary sojourn to Nova Scotia. Abraham Lincoln is elected and assumes the presidency of the United States.

1861 The Civil War begins. Having settled in Nova Scotia, Hood invites his family to join him.

1862 Hood is ordained an elder by the New England Conference and returns to Nova Scotia.

1863 Hood assumes the pastorate of a congregation in Bridgeport, Connecticut. After six months Bishop Joseph J. Clinton appoints him as a missionary to the freedpeople in the South.

1864 Hood arrives in New Bern, North Carolina, and begins his organizing and missionizing work. The church recognized as the "Mother Zion of the South," Saint Andrews, affiliates with Zion. The name is changed in 1879 to Saint Peter's AMEZ Church. The AMEZ is in serious negotiations with the AME to consolidate the two churches. The AMEZ officially begins calling its chief officers bishops.

1865 Hood is selected as president of the first convention of free blacks in North Carolina, perhaps in the entire South. The convention meets in Raleigh, North Carolina, and calls for full citizenship rights for blacks.

1867 Congressional, or Radical, Reconstruction begins at the national level. Hood assumes the pastorate of Evans Chapel in Fayetteville, North Carolina. Hood participates with more than a dozen other blacks in a state convention to redesign North Carolina's constitution.

1868 The state constitution is ratified. The Third Episcopal District, composed of North Carolina, South Carolina, and Virginia, is organized and placed under the episcopacy of Bishop James J. Moore. Hood becomes the assistant superintendent of public instruction of North Carolina with special duties for black children. He also serves temporarily as a magistrate.

1869 After two years at Evans Chapel in Fayetteville, Hood is transferred by Bishop Moore to Charlotte. He remains at this post until his elevation to the episcopacy.

1870 The state Democrats, having control of the legislature, eliminate Hood from his education post. The Colored (later Christian) Methodist Episcopal Church, composed chiefly of black members who remained with the Methodist Episcopal Church, South, rather than uniting with either the AME or AMEZ, is organized as a separate denomination.

1872 Hood's father, Levi Hood, dies. Hood is elevated as the seventeenth bishop of the AMEZ Church. Hood gives some political speeches and serves as delegate to the national Republican convention but withdraws from any further active office holding in political and governmental affairs. The Reconstruction era comes to an end in North Carolina.

1875 Sophia Nugent Hood, Hood's second wife, dies.

1876 The presidential election is held. It results in the election of Rutherford B. Hayes, who agrees to begin withdrawing federal troops from the South. This signals the conclusion of Reconstruction in other portions of the South. Hood and other Zion leaders in North Carolina lay the foundation for what would become the official denominational newspaper, the *Star of Zion*. The church discipline is amended to grant women equal rights in the denomination.

1877 Keziah (or Kezia or Kizziah or Katie) Price McKoy, a Wilmington, North Carolina, widow, marries Bishop Hood.

1879 Hood plays an instrumental role in establishing Zion Wesley Institute, eventually Livingstone College, the denominational school later moved to Salisbury, North Carolina.

1880 Church rules are amended: Bishops are now elected for life conditional upon proper behavior and discharge of duties.

1881 Hood and the AMEZ Church participate in the first Ecumenical Conference of Methodists meeting in London, England.

1884 Hood plays an instrumental role in having William H. Hillery removed from the episcopacy because of charges of intemperance and immorality. Hood publishes his first book, *The Negro in the Christian Pulpit,* a collection of sermons, most of which he wrote and delivered himself.

1886 The AME and the AMEZ are in intense negotiations to achieve a merger of the two denominations.

1890 Mississippi ratifies a constitution that effectively disfranchises the overwhelming majority of its black citizens, who constitute the majority of Mississippians.

1891 Hood attends the second Ecumenical Conference of Methodists held in Washington, D.C.

1894 J. Paschal Thompson, senior bishop of the AMEZ Church, dies in December. Hood now becomes senior bishop.

1895 Booker T. Washington gives his Atlanta Exposition Address, in which he stresses conciliation between whites and blacks at the expense of the political rights of African Americans. Black Baptists organize their forces into the first, permanent nationwide organization, the National Baptist Convention. Hood publishes *One Hundred Years of African Methodist Episcopal Zion History*.

1897 The Church of God in Christ, a Holiness denomination, is organized in Memphis, Tennessee. In 1907 most of the members of this group agree to a re-organization that makes it a Pentecostal denomination.

1898 The Spanish-American War begins. Mary J. Small is ordained an elder in the AMEZ Church. This ordination sets off a storm of controversy over the ordination of women as deacons and elders in Zion. Hood concedes that the probability is extremely low that there will be further ordination of women as elders, given the lack of available candidates.

1899 Hood reasserts his progressive views on gender issues; for example, he felt that, as a matter of principle, women should enjoy the same religious rights as men.

1900 Hood publishes his commentary on the Book of Revelation, *The Plan of the Apocalypse*. There are approximately 500,000 AMEZ members.

1902 The AMEZ and the CME are engaging in intense negotiations toward the merger of the two denominations.

1908 Hood publishes his second book of *Sermons*. As in some previous presidential elections, some Zionites, such as Bishop Alexander Walters, endorse William J. Bryan, a Democrat, for President; Hood and other bishops lead a successful fight to keep Zion in the Republican column.

1912 With the support of some (but not most) Zionites, Woodrow Wilson, Democrat, is elected president. His presidency becomes the worst disappointment to African Americans since that of Andrew Johnson in the 1860s. Mrs. Keziah P. McKoy Hood, president of the Woman's Home and Foreign Missionary Society and wife of Bishop Hood, loses her reelection bid to the Reverend Mrs. Mary J. Small, also wife of a bishop.

1914 Hood publishes his second volume on AMEZ History, *Sketch of the Early History of the AMEZ Church*.

1915 Booker T. Washington and Bishop Henry M. Turner die.

1916 Bishops James Hood and C. R. Harris are forcibly retired as active bishops. The mandatory retirement age for AMEZ bishops is set at seventy-four. The AMEZ, at the conclusion of its General Conference, has approximately 700,000 members, 3,000 ministers, 30 general denominational officers, 10 active bishops, and 2 retired bishops.

1917 The death of Bishop Alexander Walters early in the year brings Hood back into active episcopal service.

1918 James Walker Hood, having served as active bishop for forty-four years and as minister for approximately sixty years, dies in Fayetteville, North Carolina.

1992 The AMEZ has 1.2 million members, twelve active bishops, and five retired bishops.

Abbreviation and Identification Table

AME or Bethel African Methodist Episcopal Church

AMEZ Zion African Methodist Episcopal Zion Church. Like the AME, it broke decisively and completely from the Methodist Episcopal Church in the early 1800s.

Annual Conference Representative meetings of church leaders and membership within a given geographical area. As the AMEZ grew, a number of annual conferences composed an episcopal district. A bishop presides over the annual conference and the episcopal district.

Church Depending upon context, this term refers in this study to a local congregation, an entire denomination, or the whole institutional Christian movement.

Deacon A ministerial office in the American Methodist traditions that is an intermediate step between a licensed preacher and an elder.

Discipline A guidebook or commentary in the Methodist tradition that focuses upon the meanings, rules, rights, and regulations governing membership and the affairs of the denomination.

Elder An ordained clergy who has full rights to pastor and administer the sacraments. Elders are eligible candidates for the episcopacy.

Episcopal District The collection of annual conferences under the authority of a bishop.

General Conference The quadrennial (i.e., every fourth year), representative meeting of the clergy and membership of the whole denomination. This body or assembly has ultimate legislative and judicial authority. It elects the general officers and bishops according to the rules of the church.

ME or MEC The Methodist Episcopal Church, the major forerunner of the United Methodist Church and from which the AMEZ Church seceded. Between 1844 and 1939 this appellation applied principally to the denomination that was headquartered in the North.

ME-S The Methodist Episcopal Church, South. This was a collection of churches in the South that organized in 1844 because of the dispute over slavery. It, the northern branch, and the Methodist Protestant Church united or reunited in 1939 as The Methodist Church. This latter Church consolidated with another tradition in 1968, becoming The United Methodist Church.

Presiding Elder A number of these officers assist a bishop in the oversight of churches in the annual conference. The annual conference is normally geographically divided among them. In the United Methodist Church these officers are designated district superintendents.

Quarterly Conference A quarterly (four times a year) meeting of the bishop with a local congregation's pastors and officers.

Superintendent The chief executive officer in the Zion Methodist tradition prior to 1868. Early Zionites referred to this officer as superintendent and, some have argued, bishop interchangeably. In 1868 the AMEZ officially changed the title to bishop, no longer using the title of superintendent.

UM or UMC The United Methodist Church. This body emerged in 1968 as a consolidation of The Methodist Church and the Evangelical United Church. It is thus the descendant of the Methodist Episcopal denominations of the 1800s and early 1900s.

PART I

Laying the Foundations of Zion

Introduction to the Study and Life of a
Neglected Religious and Political Leader

INTRODUCTION

Rediscovering James Walker Hood

His [Hood's] intimate friends and sincere admirers hoped that he would prepare and publish his Autobiography before his health became impaired or his passing would make it impossible for him to perform this very important service which would have proven a fountain of information and a means of inspiration to this rising generation.

Let us hope that he has left sufficient matter so arranged that a full story of his great and useful career can be published and read in the years to come.

—Bishop George Wylie Clinton, Eulogy for Hood, *Star of Zion*

This study recovers for religious and general historical scholarship the public career of one of the most dynamic and influential individuals in American history: James Walker Hood (1831–1918). The aim, theme, and purpose of this present endeavor may be succinctly stated thus: James W. Hood, though long neglected in scholarly circles, was one of the most significant and crucial African American religious and race leaders during the nineteenth and early twentieth centuries. James Walker Hood, who has been largely overlooked except in African Methodist Episcopal Zion (AMEZ) history, first and foremost considered himself a religious leader within the context of independent black Christianity and American Methodism. Yet intimately tied to Hood's commitment to the church was his concern for the temporal uplift and advancement of African Americans. Indeed, Hood represented those black Christian leaders of his day who saw the expansion of the African American church as a means of uplifting the race from economic and political proscription. For the most part, these black denominational leaders believed fervently that Christianity, practiced faithfully, was inseparable from a commitment to obliterate oppression and establish justice. The long public lives of Hood and these others provide us with a window through which to observe the nineteenth- and early-twentieth-century black religious and racial leadership and the growth, struggles, and accomplishments of independent black denominations during this era.

What can we say about Hood, a leader whom the renowned black historian, Carter G. Woodson, in his classic *History of the Negro Church* labeled as "in his day one of the most influential men of color in the United States"?[1] From the beginning of his public career as a minister in 1856 until his death in 1918, Hood was a major player on both the ecclesiastical and political stages. Among the highlights of Hood's years as a religious and political leader, he opposed slavery with abolitionist fervor; received full ordination in the AMEZ church; journeyed south to North Carolina from the Northeast during the Civil War, accompanying Union forces as a Zion missionary to former slaves and as a church organizer; participated in the state Reconstruction Convention and the emerging black leadership in North Carolina; established the first order of Masons among blacks in North Carolina; became a forceful advocate for public and private education; served actively as an AMEZ bishop for forty-four years, from 1872 to 1916, half of that time as senior bishop; strongly advocated temperance and prohibition; participated in ecumenical activities involving black- and white-controlled Methodist bodies; helped establish the denominational newspaper, the *Star of Zion;* cofounded the denominational Livingstone College, now located in Salisbury, North Carolina; authored two book-length histories of the AMEZ Church; published two book collections of sermons; wrote a commentary on the New Testament book of Revelation; authored numerous articles that appeared in denominational and other contemporary periodicals; continued to speak out on political issues and communicate with elected officials even after his withdrawal from public office in 1872; and advocated equality for women within the church. Thus, Hood played a tremendous role in American and African American life in religious, economic, political, and social arenas.

This study has six major divisions. Part I elaborates on the nature, purpose, and significance of this work, places Hood in historical and religious context, examines Hood's youth and early years as minister, and gives an overview of his public career and religious beliefs. Part II highlights Hood's religious and political leadership in the South during the period 1864–1872 covering the closing years of the Civil War and the age of Reconstruction in North Carolina. In Part III we observe the rise of Hood to the episcopacy and his religious leadership during the early years of the bishopric (1872–1885). Hood as political leader (especially in racial terms) and thinker during a period of increasing racial proscriptions against African Americans in the South, from 1872 to 1916, is the focus of Part IV. Part V provides an examination of Hood's episcopal leadership on a number of intra- and interdenominational issues facing the AMEZ and other black churches during the 1872–1916 era. Part VI concludes this study with a summary of Hood's religious and political leadership along with an analysis of his legacy. The remainder of this chapter falls into two main divisions: the first section dealing with scholarly significance and methodological concerns and the second division setting forth Hood's religious and historical context and his overall view of church and ministry.

I. SIGNIFICANCE AND METHODOLOGICAL CONCERNS

Significance of this Study

The present study throws light on a significant leader in both the religious *and* political realms. Had Hood merely labored successfully for the advancement of Zion Methodism and served as bishop in one of the major black religious denominations for forty-four years, that alone would merit this biography of his public life. Likewise, had Hood only been instrumental in North Carolina Reconstruction politics and government during the 1860s and 1870s and thereafter continued his position of speaking out for the interests and advancement of the race, that too would necessitate a book-length treatment of his career. Hood, of course, accomplished both of these feats, but there is a dearth of scholarly material devoted to Hood. Joyce D. Clayton's 1978 master's thesis focusing on Hood's political and educational leadership during the Reconstruction and immediate post-Reconstruction periods provides significant information on the Zion leader.[2] But there is no book-length biography of Hood, scholarly or hagiographic, not even by someone connected with the AMEZ tradition, and Hood apparently left no completed autobiography. Furthermore, many contemporary studies of black politics, history, and religion covering the nineteenth and early twentieth centuries do not even make reference to him, though there are significant exceptions, such as Hildebrand, Angell, and Dvorak.[3] For this study I have had to rely mainly on primary sources written by Hood and contemporary articles and references about him. This biography, thus, fills a significant gap in our knowledge of both religious and general history, particularly among African Americans.

A number of points emerge as important reasons to recover the career of Hood. First, Hood embodied the independent black Christian tradition. His life story reflects the origins of independent denominations in the Northeast, their extension in the South during and following the Civil War, their further institutionalization during this era, and the manner in which they responded to the tremendous economic and political challenges and barriers facing African Americans, particularly in the arena of racial justice and equity. Second, it is important to note that the African Methodist Episcopal Zion Church has been one of the major independent black religious traditions in American history. As C. Eric Lincoln and Lawrence H. Mamiya point out in their excellent *The Black Church in the African American Experience,* the AMEZ is still one of the major seven black denominations. Comprising at least 1.2 million members in 1989, it is the second largest black Methodist group.[4] Perhaps because comparably little scholarship has focused on the Zion church, some might consider it a minor denomination. The AMEZ, however, has a comparable membership to the Episcopal and American Baptist denominations and greater than the Unitarian-Universalists, to provide only a few examples. It would be difficult, for example, to read the history of the larger and perhaps better known African Methodist Episcopal Church (AME) and miss the significance of the Zionites for African American religious and American Methodist history, if for no other reason than the intense rivalry that often ensued between these two great bodies of black church members. The AME Church hardly considered the albeit smaller AMEZ as a minor and irrelevant player in American religious history. Although little scholarly research has been done on Zion, its leaders, and the impact they have had on American religion and history, this situation is rapidly changing with the work of authors such as Johnson and Williams, McMurray and T'Ofori-Atta, Thompson and Galloway, and the continued productions of Speaks.[5] By examining the life of Hood, someone who played a crucial role in moving the organization from a largely northeastern-based regional group in 1860 to a truly national body even before his death in 1918, we shall comprehend more thoroughly the significance of the Zionites.

Third, Hood was a mainstream African American religious and race leader. That is not to say that none of his views were outside mainstream black thought, as far as we can identify such a consensus. Fundamentally, however, Hood, despite his crucial role as a race spokesperson, considered himself primarily a Christian minister and a shepherd of God's people, who participated in community, educational, and political leadership as an extension of that vocational commitment; who was fervently orthodox in his religious thinking; and whose political views generally fell between those advocating racial emigration and renunciation of citizenship, on one hand, and those who adopted an accommodationist or otherworldly perspective that removed them from boldly challenging expressions of racial domination, on the other hand. Thus, a study of Hood will reveal much about African American political and denominational leadership during this era. Contemporary students of African American history do Hood and the legacy of the black freedom struggle a grave injustice if they simply dismiss Hood as a "conservative." When Hood and others termed themselves "conservatives" they certainly sought to distance themselves from the "radical" politics of a Henry M. Turner, the great AME leader and race spokesperson. But more important, they were placing emphasis on an interracial, moderate approach characterized by an attitude of hope, as August Meier points out in the classic *Negro Thought in America.*[6] While many undoubtedly find Turner's approach more in tune with their own political and historical analyses of late-nineteenth- and early-twentieth-century American life, they should be careful not to overlook the originality, courage, and the indispensable contributions to the freedom struggle of mainstream leaders such as Hood.

Finally, it is generally recognized that no understanding of African American (or American) history is complete without an understanding of the role of black religion and its leaders in matters that are not usually understood as strictly religious. Whatever criticisms of the role of the black church in the freedom struggle of African Americans might be advanced, it is generally accepted that much of the thrust for social and racial reform derived from the black church or from individuals intimately connected to it. Black Methodists and Baptists during the era following the Civil War constituted the overwhelming majority of black church members. A study of James W. Hood, therefore, will illuminate our understanding of a great segment of the African American community during the nineteenth and early twentieth centuries.

Methodological Concerns

It is my hope that the present study will break new ground and pave the way for scholarly exploration. Rather than providing an overview of every event in his life, this book identifies certain major events and situations that characterize the religious and political Hood and reflect important points in the religious and racial lives of African Americans during the nineteenth and early twentieth centuries. With such an approach, we are able to gather a firmer grasp of Hood and his impact on church and society. Regarding chronological scope, this study will examine the early years of Hood from the time of his birth in Pennsylvania to his ministry in New England and Nova Scotia (1831–1863). But a greater emphasis falls upon Hood's religious and political activities during the 1864–1872 period and the greatest emphasis upon his activities and thought after 1872, that is, during the term of his episcopal service. One could posit several reasons to pinpoint the 1872–1918 years, including the power and influence that Hood as bishop had during these years. Principally, however, this focus in this study rests upon the greater availability of sources by and about Hood during this period.

Hood's life span of eighty-seven years covers a significant corpus of general and religious history, including the early growth and development of independent African American denominations, conventions, and associations; the rise of abolitionism and the woman suffrage movement; the depressing decade of the 1850s that witnessed the passage of the Fugitive Slave Law (denying that one's presence on "free soil" could guarantee freedom) and the Dred Scott Decision by the United States Supreme Court (virtually stripping American citizenship from African Americans); the advent of the Civil War; Emancipation, Reconstruction, and the constitutional recognition of black freedom, citizenship, and suffrage; the extension of northern-based black denominations into the South; the "marrying" of southern, largely ex-enslaved, black Christians with northern black church people; the solidifying of black churches' institutional bases and the reconfirmation of their mission; efforts at ecumenical union and cooperation on intraracial and interracial terms; the spread of racial terrorism in the South as represented by the Ku Klux Klan; the adoption of Jim Crow measures of segregating blacks and whites; successful efforts in southern states to disfranchise black voters by both unlawful and "legal" means; the rise of the accommodationist philosophy of Booker T. Washington of Tuskegee Institute that minimized emphasis on black political activity and liberal arts education and maximized the focus on industrial or vocational education, self-help, racial solidarity, and economic betterment; the emergence of the National Association for the Advancement of Colored People (NAACP) as an advocate of political activism in the search for racial equity and freedom; and the advent of World War I. In the following pages we will observe the manner in which Hood's leadership, reflecting the AMEZ and independent black Christianity, operated in response to most of these momentous events.

Some Clarifications and Disclaimers Concerning the Methodology of This Study

In order to minimize confusion and misunderstanding concerning the purpose and general directional bent of this project, it is necessary to make some statements about what this study does *not* seek to accomplish. First, this is a biography will devote relatively little attention to the personal life of James W. Hood for the simple reason that I have found comparatively little material that reveals his private conversations and actions among family members, friends, politicians, or even fellow church leaders. Where I have located such or similar information I have endeavored to incorporate it into this text, especially if it bore relevance to comprehending the Hood accessible in public records. Mainly, therefore, this will be a study of the *public* leadership of Hood. The interested reader, as the author, may console him/herself with the realization that at this point in the study of the interplay between African American religion and society during this period the impact of the public Hood is of premium importance. Second, this study is not intended as a hagiographic portrait of Hood or as an uncritical encomium of Zion Methodism. The canons of critical analysis will apply. By the same token, this critical analysis of Hood and Zion Methodism will occur within the broader framework of the actions of other personalities and groups.

Third, one may conclude from this work that James Hood reflects a basic character of the black church during the 1831–1918 period, that independent black Christianity, like Hood, envisioned itself as having a divinely appointed responsibility for the race in both spiritual and temporal domains. It is *not* my argument, however, that the independent black denominations were primarily or merely political and economic institutions or social protest movements led by their leaders for the sole purpose of politically liberating the black masses. It seems to this author that the black churches by and large served a similar role or function vis-a-vis the African American community as German Lutherans, Irish Catholics, and others served relative to their communities. While working to reconcile humanity with God and with the neighbor, black churches also served as a significant avenue by which the faithful sought to become members of the often hostile majority society or as a means to escape from it. I agree with the proposition that the positions of black church leaders and laity fall on a continuum extending from those who focus on the church in largely otherworldly or "spiritual" (instead of temporal) terms to those who indeed come very close to identifying the church in effect as a protest movement.[7] As this study will reflect, few denominational leaders during this era embraced the "otherworldly" or "spiritual" dimension to the exclusion of concern for the immediately temporal and material concerns of life, however "weakly" or ineffectual those concerns sometimes may have been expressed. Likewise, those who worked tirelessly to nudge the church to embrace much more boldly its temporal, even protest, obligations very seldom did so without a clear, sharp, and recurring insistence on the overriding significance of the Holy.

II. Independent Black Christianity, American Methodism, and Hood's Religious Worldview

In order to place Hood in historical and religious context, it will be helpful to examine Methodism and the rise of independent black churches during the late eighteenth and early nineteenth centuries as well as the Zion leader's own religious worldview, especially as it involved a synthesis of Methodism and independent black Christianity.

American Methodism and the Rise of Independent Black Christianity

Some scholars of religion note the presence of Africans in the Jewish and Christian scriptures and point out that certain African peoples have ties to Christianity stretching back to the earliest days of the Christian movement.[8] In North America individual blacks and their families have associated with Christianity from the earliest days of colonial history. It was not until the evangelical awakenings of the middle and late eighteenth and early nineteenth centuries, however, that a significant portion of Africans in North America embraced the faith.[9] Evangelicalism is a type of Christianity that emphasizes the individual's personal relationship with God, private and public Bible reading, prayer, and spreading of the faith, the importance of the power of the Holy Spirit as it visibly operates on the individual, the priority of personal spiritual experience over doctrines and rituals, and the preeminence of a personal calling to the ministry or religious leadership over formalized training as evidenced by academic degrees. Methodists, Baptists, Congregationalists, and many Presbyterians might be classed generally as evangelicals, particularly during the eighteenth to the early twentieth centuries.

Reasons provided for the success of evangelical Christianity among African Americans vary: evangelicalism's spiritual and emotional character; its similarity in some respects to traditional African spirituality; greater willingness of white evangelicals (as opposed to nonevangelicals) to spread the faith among African

Americans; greater opportunities for leadership and participation for enslaved and poor people in this form of Christianity; and the often greater antislavery and humanitarian concerns demonstrated by evangelical leaders. Whatever the reasons or combination of reasons, blacks in greater numbers embraced this form of Christianity and by the mid-1700s had begun to establish independent black congregations, especially among the Baptists. In subsequent decades independent black Methodist congregations also emerged in cities such as Philadelphia, New York, Wilmington (Delaware), Baltimore, and Charleston.

It is imperative at this point to provide some brief historical outline of the white-controlled Methodist tradition from which some independent black groups, such as the African Methodist Episcopal (AME) and the AMEZ, sprung in the nineteenth century. To place Hood in religious and historical perspective we must discuss the general context of Methodism, and more specifically, the American Methodist tradition.[10] Methodism began in the 1730s as a revivalist, evangelical movement within the Church of England. Its founders and shapers included John and Charles Wesley and the renowned preacher George White-field. The chief individual personality behind the organizational development of Methodism was John Wesley, an Anglican priest, and, significantly, a fierce, un-relenting foe of slavery and proponent of racial equality.[11] In 1784 the American Methodists, like most other religious groups whose roots lay in the British Isles or continental Europe, moved to Americanize, or create national autonomy for their denomination at the conclusion of the Revolutionary War with Great Britain and thus founded the Methodist Episcopal Church. Although John Wesley had no desire to establish a separate or new religious denomination and although he died a priest in the Church of England, he consented to appointing "superintendents" for the work in the United States so that the Methodists there might have valid access to the sacraments, consistent with the "catholic," episco-pal tradition, and have general spiritual and organizational supervision. Soon the American Methodists designated two individuals, Francis Asbury and Thomas Coke, both ordained by John Wesley, as bishops. Though the American Methodists emphasized a greater liberty within their organization, they by and large continued to have deep respect for the advice, counsel, and labors of John Wesley, and the church in the United States was patterned to a considerable ex-tent after the model of British Wesleyan societies.

In the first half of the nineteenth century there were significant divisions in the family of Methodist Episcopalianism. Some of these secessions involved African Americans: the Union Church of Africans, organized as a denomination in 1813; the African Methodist Episcopal Church, organized in 1816; and the African Methodist Episcopal Zion Church, which made a decisive break with the Mother Church sometime between 1821 and 1822. All of these denominational groupings were preceded by black congregations founded in the latter half of the eighteenth century, although the earliest congregations were Baptist and located in the South.[12] Though particular circumstances differ, black denominations originating in the North separated from white-controlled Methodism for a combination of reasons: responses to continued racial segregation and discrimination against black laity and clergy within the Methodist Episcopal Church; search for settings where blacks might worship God in their own style and manner, which were generally more exuberant than those of their white counterparts; the desire for greater focus on evangelizing African Americans, whom they believed had been often overlooked by white-controlled churches and clergy; and an intent to utilize their resources for humanitarian, including antislavery, concerns of their race. During this era many white Methodist leaders actively fought the efforts of African Americans to achieve greater denominational autonomy. The reasons vary: plain racial prejudice that disrespected the abilities of African Americans to control their own affairs; a commitment to the principle of unity in the Body of Christ, a commitment that looked with horror on religious schism; and perhaps a feeling of guilt that stemmed from the correct perception that the secession of black congregations and denominations were judgments upon the failure of white Christians to treat their black siblings with fairness, Christian charity, and evangelistic concern. Likewise, some whites supported the secession efforts of African Americans. Principally, these white sympathizers were alert to the shortcomings of the white-controlled churches and agreed with the positions of the black groups.

What often escapes observation is that a majority of African Americans decided to remain with the predominantly white MEC.[13] Of course blacks in the southern states could expect little support or tolerance for independent racial denominations in the context of a system of chattel slavery predicated on the notion that blacks were incapable of independence. In the North and border states blacks remained with the Mother Church for a variety of reasons. Some supported the theological principle of unity in the Body of Christ. Many believed that remaining within the racially mixed denomination while protesting for greater liberties was a more effective means of dismantling racial discrimination and segregation than complete separation. Many did not know or trust the independent black leaders. In actual practice, many blacks, especially as time passed, were members of mainly or all-black congregations within the larger MEC. Thus, they already had a good bit of congregational autonomy. In later years the presence of independent black Methodist denominations criticizing racial proscription in the ME church encouraged the church to provide greater opportunities and autonomy for African Americans in the Mother Church in order to forestall other secessions and defections.

Like the African Methodist Episcopal Church or AME, the Zion Church has independent congregational roots going back to the latter part of the eighteenth century. The significant lay leader for the AMEZ was William Miller of New York City. Indeed, the Zionites, like their sister African Methodists, have traditionally traced the origins of the denomination to the late eighteenth century; for Zionites the year is 1796. Also like the AME, various independent black Zion congregations in the early part of the nineteenth century (1821 for Zion), gathered from a number of states and organized what would shortly become a separate, independent, black denomination of Methodists. The Zionites were fewer in number than the Bethelites, as the AMEs were often called, but the two were similar in many respects. On one hand, they both adopted the basic church structure, policies, rules, and regulations from their parent body and even had the same title, the African Methodist Episcopal Church, until 1848, when the smaller body added *Zion* to its name. On the other hand, both black groups ardently and uncompromisingly adopted or continued an earlier rule in American Methodism against members holding people enslaved, a rule that the parent body, like some other white-controlled groups such as the Baptist associations and the Presbyterians, had progressively softened and by 1816 had basically disregarded because of the opposition of slaveholders in the membership. Both the AMEZ and the AME clearly stipulated that no slaveholder could join or retain membership in their fellowships.

Many clergy and lay members in black Methodism worked to eradicate slavery by moral persuasion, legal and constitutional petitions to governmental bodies, joining the antislavery network that hid those escaping slavery and provided them with basic necessities, participating in other abolitionist endeavors, and striving to improve the usually poor and oppressed lot of "free" blacks. The Zion Church was well represented as a fierce opponent of slavery and a firm advocate for the empowerment of African Americans by denominational founders James Varick and Christopher Rush, abolitionists who were either lifelong Zion members or united with the group for at least a portion of their lives (as were Harriet Tubman, Sojourner Truth, Frederick Douglass). Entire congregations provided havens for refugees from slavery and permitted their houses of worship to serve as meeting places for antislavery activities, and there were other efforts as well that focused on enhancing the condition of blacks, whether enslaved or "free."[14]

African Americans, however, were not the only group to secede from the Methodist Episcopal Church. In the early part of the nineteenth century the predominantly white Methodist Protestant Church seceded when a number of Methodists grew restless and dissatisfied under the "authoritarian," episcopal structure of the MEC Church; they wanted a greater "republican" structure. In 1843 a number of mostly white members, particularly in the northern states, withdrew to form the Wesleyan Methodist Church. These Methodists believed that Christians should not be in fellowship with other so-called Christians who held people in bondage. Of course, they argued vigorously for the elimination of slavery in the United States

In 1844 came the most wrenching division of all in the MEC. Southern white Methodists felt that they were being treated as second-class citizens in the MEC because of their support of slavery, believing that the denomination should have silenced the Methodist abolitionists who remained within the ranks. White southerners also wanted firm approbation on the part of the national church that holding slaves was not sinful. When a fellow southerner was put forward as a candidate for the episcopacy over a nonslaveholding jurisdiction and was turned down by the national church, the southern dissenters organized the Methodist Episcopal Church, South. The division in the ranks of this major national denomination, as well as that among the Baptists a year later, signaled the ominous future for the unity of the nation as a whole, as many observers have noted. In many quarters vigorous disputes ensued over the legal control of church properties, particularly in the border states. The coming of the Civil War and the suppression of the rebellion by Union forces only aggravated the tensions in a number of places, with the northern-based church claiming church properties and congregations that the southern church believed lay within its sphere. In 1870 leaders in the white-controlled ME-S set apart its black membership of less than eighty thousand and ordained bishops for the Christian (originally Colored) Methodist Church, to the disapprobation and protest of the independent black Methodists who wished this body of African Americans to be united with their respective groups. All three black independent Methodist groups—the AMEZ, the AME, and the CME—continue to exist.

Methodists in America, consistent with the theology of John Wesley, have always placed great emphasis on the unity of the church and the obliteration of schisms. In the history of American Methodism both whites and blacks have attempted both intra- as well as interracial mergers and reunions. During the Civil War period serious talks and moves were made by the MEC to woo black independents back to the fold; and the latter seriously entertained reunion. In 1939 the ME-S, MEC, and the Methodist Protestant Church, after years of negotiation, succeeded in effecting reunion into a consolidated body known as The Methodist Church. The black membership associated with the MEC was placed in a separate, nongeographical episcopal district, known as the Central Jurisdiction, over which presided black leaders. In 1968 The Methodist Church merged with the United Evangelical Church, itself composed of consolidated Methodistic bodies, and formed The United Methodist Church. The Central Jurisdiction was abolished, an act that pleased most black Methodists in the denomination. As recently as spring 1991 the three major black Methodist bodies, the AME, the CME, and the Zionites, agreed to participate in discussions pointing toward organic unity. Despite attempts in both the nineteenth and twentieth centuries and ongoing efforts, black independent Methodists as of the late 1990s have been unable to effect interdenominational mergers among themselves. Nevertheless, the United Methodist Church and its three historically black counterparts, the AME, AMEZ, and CME, during the spring of 1994 began official talks that many hoped would lead to a union of the four groups.[15]

A Sketch of Hood's Religious Views—An Overview

By way of historical background, an overview of Hood's views on the church and ministry will prove helpful as we explore his public career of leadership. Let us, then, briefly explore Hood's understanding of the nature of the church and ministry, particularly as they relate to the black church and to the quest for racial justice and equity in American society, his approach to African missions, his views on ecumenicity, his understanding of temperance and sanctification, and, finally, his views on critical, scientific, and nontraditional approaches to religion. Hood was basically orthodox or traditional in his understanding of Christianity, the Church, Methodist doctrine and polity, and Zion Methodism in particular. As such, he represents an important key to understanding mainstream American Protestantism and Methodism, evangelicalism, and black Christianity, particularly during the years of increased urbanization, immigration, increasing religious pluralism in the United States, the advent of new scientific theories on the nature and origins of humanity and the world, and the emergence of critical studies of the Bible and Christian tradition.

The Zion leader envisioned Christianity as the only true religion revealed by

God to humanity, and thus it was incumbent on the faithful to disseminate the gospel so that all believers would enjoy eternal life of bliss rather than the endless torments of a fiery hell.[16] In addition to such spiritual benefits, Hood believed that Christianity brought to the individual and to the social order freedom from backwardness and corruption and gave them the benefits of an improved life in this world. In the last decades of the nineteenth century, when some questioned the logic and rationality of the religion, Hood insisted that the Christian faith was not contrary to true reason, reason built on the principles of the Bible rather than on faulty thinking that sets itself against the Divine Word.

According to Hood, the black church in the United States had a providential role to play in the economy of things. Indeed, the rise of black denominations was part of a collective movement from the white-controlled churches. In response to unambiguous racial prejudice among white Christians, black churches in various places had simultaneously begun an exodus to form independent communities. Hood, in looking back on this phenomenon in the 1890s, avoided the long-standing debate between the AME and the Zionites concerning which of them constituted the first independent black denomination. More important than the origins of specific black denominations was the general *racial* movement for independence. Interestingly, whereas most black Christians and many white churchpeople understood the Civil War, Emancipation, and black enfranchisement as a set of current developments analogous to the biblical Exodus event, Hood stated that the exodus of blacks from white controlled churches in the eighteenth and early nineteenth centuries was paralleled in momentousness only by the biblical Exodus event itself, when God liberated the enslaved, oppressed Hebrews from bondage in Pharaoh's Egypt!

One might say, then, that African American Christians in some significant sense constituted a chosen people, in Hood's view. Hood specifically placed the black church at the heart of God's liberating activity in the world. The coerced departure of blacks from white institutions (because they clearly could not remain in such racially inhospitable and uncharitable environments) actually fitted into the divine plan of God relative to developing the black race. First, the black church through its various abolitionist activities worked to overthrow the system of slavery. Second, the black church was God's instrument in preparing African Americans to practice leadership in nonchurch areas. While the heavy participation of black ministers in civic affairs during the Reconstruction era caused dismay for some observers, Hood stated that there were few "intelligent leaders" in the race besides the Christian minister. Though he was a conciliator and a moderate race leader, Hood was not naive about racial prejudice during this era. He entertained no fanciful idea that the great majority of whites were at that time prepared to overlook color and invite blacks into their religious or nonreligious circles on a plane of equality. Independent black Methodism, however, had elevated black men to the episcopacy, a status or achievement not fully duplicated in white-controlled Methodism. When these bishops conducted themselves well with the opportunities presented to them in religious circles, they demonstrated the capacities of the black race to a skeptical world.

As bishop, Hood set a high standard for those who ministered to the churches.[17] Consistent with the Methodism of the era, Hood insisted on a holy ministry, free of scandal, avoiding even the semblance of evil. The bishop often spoke out boldly against licentiousness, intemperance, and adultery. Though he demonstrated leniency and mercy as he saw the need, Hood was not beyond taking action to eliminate from the ministry those who violated their sacred trusts. More positively, Hood insisted that the minister's primary obligation was to the church, not to political office-seeking. While the minister must remain a valuable repository of political and civic knowledge for the benefit of his people, teaching them to be cognizant of their civic and religious obligations to advance the race, the clergyperson should avoid the role of a politician, who seeks to further his or her own personal political ambitions. The demands of the church precluded such endeavors. Hood encouraged ministers to acquire formal education and practice a ministry characterized by personal involvement and mutual sharing with the congregation.

A major area of black evangelistic involvement during the nineteenth and early twentieth centuries focused on missions in Africa, particularly during the post–Civil War era. Consistent with this tradition, Hood embraced foreign missions, particularly in Africa, but apparently not with the equal intensity of his AMEZ colleague Alexander Walters or his AME counterpart Henry M. Turner. Perhaps Hood's lack of intensity regarding Africa is attributable to his dedication to evangelizing African Americans. Hood was clearly less pan-African in his thinking than Turner and Walters. In some instances African missions were associated with African emigration and colonization, particularly during the 1870s and 1880s. Hood encouraged missionaries who would "go to that far off, pestilential land, . . . but any general colonizing of our people, I shall oppose."[18] Apparently, Hood never visited the African continent, but he stated publicly that God had called Zionites mainly for two major areas of work: the evangelization of African Americans and the redemption of "the Dark Continent."

Like most Methodists during this period, Hood was evangelical in outlook.[19] He relished an approach to Christianity that involved the individual's having an immediate, direct experience with God, often (but for Hood not necessarily) denoted by dramatic, emotional religious expressions; he favored the use of revivals to convert sinners and backsliders and a strict code of ethical and moral conduct. As the nineteenth century progressed, a number of Methodists, black and white, grew weary with the increasing worldliness of church people as their communion abandoned earlier, stricter codes of conduct. Not only had many Methodists relaxed the traditional stand against attending theaters, ballrooms, circuses, and other places of amusement, and against the wearing of fancy clothes, and the use of makeup, they also neglected the Methodist doctrine that Christians should strive to live free of all known sin. Incorporating these concerns, some Methodists organized "holiness" movements, especially near the turn of the century, that sought to return Methodism to its earlier religious positions.

Hood represented that general holiness movement within Methodism that sought to retain earlier emphases on religious strictness without breaking away to form separate holiness denominations. Hood's 1884 book, *The Negro in the Christian Pulpit,* a collection of sermons mainly by Hood that includes selections from at least four other bishops, exemplifies this stress on the holiness position, or complete sanctification, once promulgated by the founder of Methodism, John Wesley. Whereas Wesley taught that some Christians would only attain this state of complete freedom from all known sin at the point of death, Hood and contemporary holiness advocates insisted that such was clearly attainable in this life for every Christian and taught that it was the obligation of each Christian to strive accordingly. Not all Methodists, clergy or lay, shared this belief in the possibility of sanctification during the earthly life. Thus, Hood and other bishops made a point of questioning ministerial candidates very closely concerning this teaching, insisting that their adherence to this doctrine was an essential part of their vocation. By encouraging ministers to preach and pursue holiness, Hood and other Zion leaders, arguably, saved the AMEZ from increased defections to the growing holiness denominations.

Additionally, Hood steadfastly opposed all changes in traditional or orthodox Christian doctrine or the understanding of the Bible as literally accurate in all respects.[20] The Zion leader in the post–Civil War period opposed Darwinian scientific theories that raised serious challenges to the accounts of the origins of humanity and the universe based on a literal interpretation of the Bible; the literary, historical, and critical study of Scripture that rejected many traditional claims about the authorship and accuracy of portions of the Bible; and the idea that salvation was attainable by means other than Christianity, an approach accepted by some that resulted from significant new studies of other religious traditions such as Buddhism and Hinduism. Concerning this last point, Hood had an especially low opinion of Islam, viewing it as the religion of the false prophet that had persecuted Christians and was preventing the spread of the gospel.[21] There were also issues raised by the developing fields of sociology and psychology, issues that interpreted religion in more natural rather than supernatural terms. Basically, Christian America divided into three main camps in response to the above-mentioned developments: liberalism or modernism, which sought in varying degrees to utilize these ideas and findings and to attempt a reinterpretation of the traditional faith; fundamentalism or conservatism, which rejected these new ideas and reaffirmed the traditional faith; and the moderate stance or Christocentric liberalism, which sought to forge a middle ground between the other two positions.

Though we must be careful with labels, Hood was essentially a religious conservative in his response to these intellectual challenges to traditional religion. This is not to say that Hood did not tackle many of the issues of the time; he did not ignore significant developments. But the bishop employed his understanding of Methodism and Christianity and his American and African American experience to respond to these challenges in such a fashion that he was progressive on social concerns while being theologically conservative. Hood represents many black denominational leaders, and the black church generally, who embraced social activism as a corollary and mandate of evangelicalism and fundamentalism, just as some of them or their black and white spiritual forebears had done vis-a-vis the struggle against slavery. In other words, Hood and others read the Bible conservatively and literally, but their interpretations were in the tradition of liberation. Sometimes this literal reading of the Bible proved quite useful in formulating a liberationist perspective on events. For example, at a time when even respectable white scholars either ignored black and African history or denied the existence of it, some conservative readers of the Bible used the genealogical tables of Genesis to argue that not only the ancient Egyptians and Ethiopians, but the Assyrians and Babylonians as well were black or African peoples.[22]

Though Hood was not receptive to the idea of people finding salvation in non-Christian religions and while he was a staunch Methodist in doctrine and polity, he was not a narrow sectarian or denominationalist. The Zion leader accepted the validity of all Christian groups that adhered to the basic, mainline doctrinal principles of the faith, consistent with the general Methodist tradition. In a period when Protestants and Catholics held harsh opinions regarding the authenticity of one another's faith, Hood was not rabidly anti-Catholic. Unquestionably, he believed that Protestantism was the better reflection of biblical principles. Also, Hood believed that the pre-Reformation Roman Catholic Church embodied the beastly spirit (cf. New Testament Book of Revelation) that set itself up in a dominant and even idolatrous position, persecuting genuine Christian believers and perverting the true gospel. But Hood made it clear that many denominations, in his opinion, had pursued this same ambition to dominate other groups. While Catholicism had had greater opportunity to oppress other Christians, conflicts between the Wesleyan Methodist and Primitive Methodist churches in England, the Methodist Episcopal and the Methodist Episcopal, South, and the AME and the AMEZ pointed to the reality that the inclination to dominate other groups is found in a number of denominations. Hood insisted that no denomination had been more domineering toward the AMEZ than the AME. Relatedly, Hood shared in the Methodist principle of dealing ecumenically with other Christian denominations, particularly those of evangelical character. Within Methodism Hood participated in world ecumenical conferences on Methodism, was involved in ecumenical talks between the AMEZ and the AME and later the CME regarding possible merger, and was a supporter of the Federal Council of Churches, an interdenominational federation of churches organized in the early twentieth century and a forerunner of the current National Council of Churches.[23]

During the latter part of the nineteenth century a number of prominent church persons, males and females, blacks and whites, across the denominational spectrum began to insist that the former individualistic, charity approach to the solution of social ills did not suffice, that the churches should adopt more social approaches to interpreting the gospel and remedying the ills in society. These Christians were dismayed by crowded slums in the larger cities caused by the influx of poor European immigrants, the low wages and horrible working conditions of many employees, child labor, racial injustice, and other social maladies. Some individuals and churches began to advocate systematic expositions of "social gospel," "social Christianity," "practical Christianity," and in some instances "Christian socialism" as keys to establishing a just society. While he did not expound a formal social gospel, and though his economic views were clearly not socialistic, Hood shared with the socialists and the social gospelers the hearty expectation that an era of perfect peace, justice, and righteousness was about to dawn upon humankind as a result of the successful efforts of the faithful to convert the world to Christianity. This postmillennialist perspective, that Christ's Second Coming to Earth would occur after this golden age, was the favored view of many social reformers dedicated to evangelizing the world, confident that God's servants would successfully convert humanity to divine righteousness.[24]

CONCLUSION

This work reveals James Walker Hood of the AMEZ Church as a major religious and political leader of the nineteenth and early twentieth centuries. His public career offers the reader a valuable prism through which to study the growth, struggles, and accomplishments of independent black Christianity during this era. Examination of this highly influential leader is significant because of the absence of any book-length biography and a dearth of scholarly articles regarding him. The preceding pages outlined the purpose, theme, and scope of this enterprise: demonstrating the neglected but deeply significant religious and racial leadership of Hood during the nineteenth and early twentieth centuries. In order to place Hood in historical and religious perspective, the preceding pages also provided background information on evangelical Christianity, independent black denominations, the Methodist denominations, and an overview of Hood's religious views. The following pages demonstrate Hood's significance by focusing on his religious and political leadership in four main areas. Chapter 1 explores the early years of Hood and his ministry and offers an overview of his public career. Subsequent chapters treat his journey to the South and the exercise of religious and political leadership during the Civil War and Reconstruction eras, his early episcopal leadership, his political leadership after his elevation to the episcopacy, and his active role in debates and controversies involving the Zion church while he served as bishop. The book concludes with an assessment of Hood's public career and his impact on African American religious life.

Chapter One

JAMES WALKER HOOD

The Formative Years of a Leader (1831–1863) and an Overview of His Public Career (1864–1918)

I am not a self-made man, nor a school-made man. I am just what the good Lord made me.

> —James Walker Hood, *Sketch of the Early History of the African Methodist Episcopal Zion Church*

This chapter examines the formative years of Hood, focusing on Hood's early life and ministry, from his birth in 1831 to 1863, the year that the Zion Church appointed him missionary to the newly freed people in the South. Examining his early life, we will observe how certain influences in southeastern Pennsylvania impacted this future religious and racial leader, factors such as: evangelical Methodism, abolitionism, and Quakerism. His early years in the ministry included activities of preaching in New York City, pastoring in New England, and serving as a missionary in the religiously challenging environment of Nova Scotia, Canada. These early years were also marked by his association with some of the early, great leaders of Zion, such as Christopher Rush and J. J. Clinton. This combination of factors undoubtedly contributed immensely to the spread of the independent black church, his zeal for the temporal uplift of African Americans, and his unswerving confidence in diplomacy and interracial cooperation as vital factors in advancing the cause of God and the race. Even during his early years Hood demonstrated traits of a strong and effective leader, whether working with churches in the northeast, pioneering the Zion movement in Nova Scotia, or assuming roles of leadership in the fledgling AMEZ. Exploring these early years, the reader should bear in mind that this period, 1831–1863, is also a formative period for the independent black denominations, associations, and conventions. In addition, this chapter provides an overview of Hood's career during 1864–1918, noting significant aspects that space will not permit us to explore in great depth.

The Early Years

In 1813 Levi Hood, a young African Union Church minister in Delaware, married Harriet Walker, a member of Bethel AME Church in Philadelphia. Within three years her pastor, Richard Allen, became one of the founders of the African Methodist Episcopal Church, or AME, an independent black Methodist denomination, agreeing to serve as the first bishop of the group when Daniel Coker declined that honor. Like her future husband, Miss Walker, a woman of keen intellect and profound interest in ecclesiastical affairs, was concerned about matters relating to African Americans, sometimes delivering antislavery speeches. She was among the earliest American women to make public speeches, even though such activity ran counter to the idea of acceptable behavior for women of that era. Carrying certificate proof of her church membership, Harriet Walker transferred her affiliation from the AME Church to the Union Church of Africans, the very first black denomination organized, under the leadership of Peter Spencer and others in Wilmington, Delaware. Her great love for Bethel Church, however, never died. Even later in life, Harriet Walker Hood attended church services at the AME congregation when visiting Philadelphia. Of the six daughters born to her and Levi Hood, four became members of the church. Apparently one daughter left the AME for another denomination, while another was listed a member of the AME when she died. As late as 1895 two of Harriet Walker Hood's daughters remained members of Bethel. Despite her love for Bethel, Walker decided to join her husband in a newly constructed "pigeon box" church, as it was termed by Spencer's critics.[1]

After Spencer's death, this newly created black denomination split into two factions. Levi and Harriet Hood remained with the original Spencerite group and at some point relocated to Kennett Township in the largely Quaker Chester County, Pennsylvania. Kennett Township, now Kennett Square, was located in the southeastern portion of the free state of Pennsylvania, near the boundary of the slave state, Delaware. Thus, the Hoods lived close to both Wilmington,

Delaware, and the Pennsylvania cities of Philadelphia and Lancaster. Indeed, the Pennsylvania-Delaware state line ran through the farm where the family resided, so that Hood slept in Pennsylvania and drank water from a Delaware spring. It was in this section of the state that the greatest number of Pennsylvania African Americans lived. In this small town and rural section of the state the Hoods raised corn on a farm rented from a Quaker named Jackson. Levi Hood pastored a Union Church of Africans for a period of forty years, until his death in 1872. Though Harriet Hood was never an ordained minister, her roles as minister's wife and mother of the church constituted a de facto ministry. During their marriage Harriet and Levi Hood produced twelve children, six boys and six girls. On a spring day, May 30, 1831, James Walker Hood was born on the rented farm about a quarter of a mile from a main thoroughfare. Based on available information it is impossible to identify all of the Hood children or to place James Hood's order of birth relative to them, though John and Charlotte were older than James. I have located the names of only two of Hood's brothers: John, who served as a minister in the Pennsylvania area, including the pastorate of Union AME Church in Westchester; and Levi, a shoemaker and captain in the Delaney Guard, a black Pennsylvania company that served during the Civil War.

I have found sparse information on two of his sisters, Susan and Charlotte. The only information I have uncovered regarding Charlotte is her influential role in Hood's early spiritual development. I have more information concerning another sister of James W. Hood's. The Reverend Mrs. Susan Walker Blackson died January 12, 1900.[2] This sister, who had converted to Christianity during her seventeenth year, had lost her husband, the Reverend L. D. Blackson, a Zion minister in the Philadelphia and Baltimore Conference, five years before her own death. Only a few months prior to his death, the Reverend Mrs. Blackson had accepted her call to the preaching ministry, received her preaching license from her then Philadelphia pastor, and become an evangelist in Philadelphia and Asbury Park. She died in the home of her daughter, whose husband, J. S. Eaton, was an AME minister. Susan Blackson requested that the Reverend C. W. Simmon of the AMEZ and the Reverend W. S. Lowery of an AME church in Washington, Pennsylvania, conduct the funeral. Services were held in the Wright's Chapel AMEZ Church. Surviving Susan Blackson, in addition to her daughter, a Mrs. Eaton, were one sister and three brothers. In addition to the ministries of Susan, John, and James, three of James Hood's sisters married ministers, though I was unable to locate the names of two of them. Two first cousins of Hood, including Solomon Hood, who pastored in either the AME or AMEZ (it is unclear from available sources), and one unnamed nephew, who pastored a Presbyterian church in New York City, were also ministers.[3] These facts about the Blackson and Hood families demonstrate the frequent interchanging between the AME and the AMEZ memberships during the nineteenth century, even within a single family.

James Hood, then, was born into and matured in a strictly religious family. As early as the age of four, he began to think of his responsibility toward God, with his parents predicting his entrance into the ministry. He was converted at the age of eleven. I have not located information relating to the circumstances surrounding his personal embrace of religion. The young Hood struggled greatly until he was eighteen years old over doubts about the authenticity of his conversion. He grew up in an era when many evangelicals placed heavy emphasis on dramatic religious conversions. The testimonies or comments of others may have caused Hood to question the validity of his own experience. Haygood, in his introduction to one of Hood's books of sermons, suggested that Hood was fortunate to have parents who provided him with wise counsel and direction so that he eventually accepted his salvation.[4] Hood's comments along these lines, not necessarily contradictory of Haygood's, credit his sister Charlotte as the one who led him to spiritual peace of mind.[5] His coming from a family environment where his mother and sister were such strong religious influences might help explain why Hood was more open to the ordination of women as elders in the church than many of his contemporaries, black or white. Later in life Hood would also speak about having been raised by a Quaker family, the Jacksons, approximately fifty miles outside of Philadelphia. Evidently, he spent considerable time among members of this primarily white religious group that was, comparably speaking, more supportive of black civic rights and gender equity than most other denominations. He claimed to have learned from them the discipline of quietness and moderation.[6] The future bishop also stated that he read a very influential book, *A Kiss for A Blow,* when he was thirteen years old, that counseled returning good for evil and that that principle too had become a portion of his life[7] (although during the 1880–1916 era some fellow Zionites found him all too ready to respond to charges and attacks made upon him).

Growing up in Pennsylvania, Hood experienced racial prejudice early in his life. As a state, Pennsylvania reflected an attitude of ambivalence toward African Americans.[8] Slavery, while not as brutal there as in other places, did exist in the state. On the other hand, it was in Pennsylvania that the first recorded protest against slavery was lodged by the Quakers in 1688, and as early as 1780 it was the first state to set in motion a mechanism for the gradual elimination of the practice. By the time of Hood's birth there were about 38,000 free blacks compared to a white population of approximately 1.3 million. There were probably no more than 400 enslaved blacks; and by the time Hood reached twenty years of age, there would be no enslaved persons in the state. Owing no doubt to the very strong influence of the Quakers, the feelings among the white populace against slavery and sympathy for those fleeing bondage ran high. On the other hand, during Hood's early life, Pennsylvania blacks were effectively disfranchised of voting rights, segregated in public life, the victims of occasional riots and mob actions, and some whites strongly supported colonization of free blacks elsewhere, which most African American leaders vehemently opposed.

In addition to the racial climate of Hood's native Pennsylvania, adjacent Delaware was a slave state. As stated previously, the Hood family lived near the state boundaries of Delaware and Pennsylvania, with boundary line passing through the farm. The family's home was a part of the Underground Railroad, the secret network provided for refugees fleeing to the northern states and Canada to escape enslavement. Young James frequently heard of and saw escaped bondspeople fleeing to free territory. Not surprisingly, Hood very early in life developed an intense hatred for slavery and a deep love for the African race, traits that shaped his entire life and leadership.[9] Like most free blacks, especially those residing so near a slave state, Hood's family also lived with the strong possibility that some member of the family might be kidnapped and taken into slave territory. Indeed, Hood reported one such attempt on his life, though he did not provide much detail of the episode beyond simply mentioning it. It is no wonder, then, that Hood kept and cherished a copy of a song written from the perspective of one who had escaped slavery. Hood encountered a young woman singing the piece during his missionary service in Nova Scotia during the early 1860s. Approximately forty years later (1901) Hood could still recall the music and the words to this song that touched him deeply. The song grippingly described the hard toil and the brutal beatings an enslaved man had endured, broken promises made by the slaveholder, the joy of having found asylum in Canada, and the determination to remain a free person.[10]

Even free blacks in nonslave states had to struggle to maintain self-respect and pride in the midst of a majority white society that often considered them de facto slaves or at best second-class citizens. Thus, it must have been a great struggle for Levi and Harriet Hood to support twelve children. While Hood grew up doing farm work in Pennsylvania fields, his father, Levi, was determined that none of his children be bound out to farmers, as were many other free blacks, because that arrangement smacked too much of slavery itself. Instead, Hood's father agreed to his son's working for Jackson, the Quaker farm owner, with the verbal guarantee that his son would receive food, clothing, and six weeks of education each year. This latter work arrangement involving young blacks was a custom among Quakers in that portion of Delaware and Pennsylvania as part of their effort to support black aspirations. Hood performed chores for the Jackson household for twenty-four months.

During his childhood, Hood received only a small amount of formal education. Sources differ as to the extent of Hood's schooling. One source places the amount of formal training at three months, the twelve weeks received as payment for Hood's service on the Jackson farm. According to Hood's account, he acquired one year and eight months of training in a rural school between ages nine and thirteen. This formal training consisted of arithmetic and reading. Mostly, though, Hood taught himself with available textbooks and utilized the services of individual tutors when possible to acquire additional knowledge, including Greek. His mother, Harriet, provided grammar instruction and taught him the art of public speaking. As early as fifteen, Hood gave his first public abolitionist address, predicting the demise of slavery. Newspapers and journals also occupied a great part of his education, especially as he became an adult. As a child Hood cherished books, and he collected them throughout his life.[11] His speeches, sermons, books, and other writings abundantly reflect the breadth of his knowledge in both ecclesiastical and nonreligious areas. Later in life Hood received the honorary Doctor of Divinity (D.D.) and Doctor of Letters (L.L.D.) degrees from Livingstone College and Lincoln University (Pennsylvania) respectively.

Hood, the Minister

At the age twenty-one, around 1852, the younger Hood felt called to the ministry, yet he delayed quite a while because he felt unqualified for the task.[12] It is not clear whether Hood's understanding of being qualified referred to educational attainment or spiritual experience or both. At any rate, after his twenty-first year the young man began to study even harder to acquire knowledge. One account placed Hood in Canada, probably Nova Scotia, when he first experienced a call to the ministry. But this is highly unlikely since there is nothing in Hood's writings or any other available source to suggest that Hood lived in Canada prior to his entry into the ministry.[13] There were two other significant developments in Hood's life during or near his twenty-first year. He married Hannah L. Ralph of Lancaster, Pennsylvania, in September 1852. She died of consumption in 1855. Also, Hood moved from Kennett Township to Philadelphia, where he found successive employment as drayman, porter, and steward for a school for the mentally ill.[14] He also worked at the Cape May Hotel in New Jersey as headwaiter.

Hood's delay in entering the ministry was probably reinforced by the lackluster manner in which a minister in his quarterly conference, who was also Hood's class leader, responded to his ministerial leanings. After informing the minister that he felt the call to preach, the young man found to his surprise that the veteran minister did not inform the quarterly conference. Indeed, the minister was so confident that Hood had not received a call to the ministry that he implied that the young man perhaps had intercepted God's call directed to someone else! Evidently, the minister's lack of enthusiasm or outright opposition did not upset Hood. Like many nineteenth-century ministers, male and female, black and white, Hood did not rush into the ministry, which was considered a truly awesome and demanding profession. Indeed, he appears to have been rather relieved by the veteran minister's actions, content that he, Hood, had discharged all responsibility in the matter.[15]

In 1855 James Hood traveled to New York City, where again he found employment as a waiter, and there joined a small congregation of the original Union Church of Africans that held its meetings in a Twenty-eighth Street hall.[16] Perhaps he decided to relocate based in part on the fact of his first wife's death, assuming she died prior to his move. At any rate, Hood continued to feel the call to minister. The Reverend William Councy, pastor of the congregation, granted Hood a preaching license in 1856.[17] During the autumn of 1857 Hood relocated once again, to New Haven, Connecticut, but this time he was unable to locate a branch of the African Union Church. So he joined a quarterly conference of the Zion connection, which accepted his license to preach. Hood did not provide a reason why he chose the AMEZ rather than its rival AME, given his mother's earlier association with the latter and its stronger presence in Pennsylvania. Perhaps he found the AMEZ more willing to accept his ministerial license obtained from the Union Church. Maybe Hood's choice reflected the influence of the Reverend Samuel Giles, the pastor of the local Zion congregation. Hood greatly admired him as a "useful," "pious, progressive and intelligent" minister, teacher, and role model. "I regarded Rev. Giles as one of the best preachers I have known and one of the best preachers the Church has produced. I owe much to him for my success in my calling."[18]

Most black ministers of that period, and many evangelical pastors in general, could not depend on the small salaries that their parishioners were able to provide. Besides, at this point Hood had not received a pastorate. To support himself the young minister worked as headwaiter at the Torntine Hotel in New Haven. Even this early in Hood's ministry he had the opportunity to operate as de facto episcopal officer. As headwaiter he had supervision over a number of young male coworkers. Some of these joined him in an evangelistic effort, which resulted in seventy-two conversions. His coreligious workers and employees must have been impressed with Hood or the Zion Church or both. Almost all of them followed Hood's example and united with the AMEZ.

In June 1858 the New England Annual Conference made an appointment to a Zion Church in New Haven, Connecticut, but the pastor selected never assumed his post. Upon learning that the given congregation did not desire his services, the minister was determined to convey to them that he did not feel obliged to accommodate an unreceptive church. It is not clear how many churches of Zion were located in New Haven at this time, but apparently, there was only one. If that is the case, the pastor mentioned above, Samuel Giles, had either taken another parish or left because of sickness. What is clear is that the bishop of the New England Conference assigned Hood this responsibility for the remainder of the conference year. Interestingly, Hood did not receive reappointment to this church, apparently because he had not yet received ordination as either a deacon or an elder.

The following conference year, nearly two years after his affiliation with the New Haven Quarterly Conference, that body recommended to the June 1859 New England Annual Conference meeting in Hartford, Connecticut, that it accept the young minister on a trial basis. The annual conference consented to this request and gave Hood an appointment of two stations in Nova Scotia, Canada, within forty-five miles of each other: Bridgetown and Kentsville. Robert T. Handy, the eminent American church historian, has pointed out that the distinction between Canadian and American church history is often too sharp, that some of the same trends and activities operative in the American theater also have transpired in the Canadian sphere.[19] The New England Annual Conference's appointment of Hood to the Canadian mission illustrates the truth of that observation. During this era many blacks in the northeastern and New England states had strong bonds to their counterparts, and even relatives, in Canada. This bond was strengthened by the fact that the 1850s represented in many ways the most distressing time for those hoping and working for the elimination of American slavery. With attempts by the federal government to enforce fugitive slave laws, that is, the retrieval of enslaved blacks who had escaped bondage, many recently escaped as well as veteran escapees fled farther north into Canada, joining other African Americans who had migrated there in the eighteenth century. The independent African American churches took a keen interest in the spiritual and temporal conditions of these black Canadians, just as they also expressed concern for their racial siblings in the Caribbean and the African continent. It is certainly possible that Hood, acquainted with the Underground Railroad and having himself been the victim of an attempted kidnapping for enslavement, might have requested appointment to the Canadian field. On the other hand, ministers in the Methodist traditions often received appointments based on seniority. Conferences generally assigned persons new to the ministry, and even the bishopric, to missionary fields as opposed to more established ones or, in the case of pastors, to less prestigious churches. At any rate, we see how Hood's biography reflects a larger reality of the independent black denominations and associations during these years: even in the earlier, formative period of their existence, these groups took keen interest in the international extension of their churches and the salvation of African kin wherever they were found.

While the annual conference made the Canadian assignments, it could not provide the requisite funds. With the authority of the conference to do so, Hood set out to secure the funds through solicitations. This approach, which often elicited rude rejections, proved entirely unsatisfactory to the young minister.[20] Hood then returned to New York to secure more palatable employment. While walking Nassau Street one day he found a hotel soon to be opened that required a headwaiter. According to Hood, he secured employment without any letters of recommendation. The employer simply looked at his face, took Hood at his word, and awarded him the job. Of course the owner might simply have been desperate for an employee.[21] Yet this experience adumbrates the fact that Hood during his life secured many advantages because of generous benefactors. Understandably, then, later in life the older Bishop Hood had tremendous difficulty comprehending why younger men wished to campaign for ministerial appointments, such as the bishopric, rather than allowing the positions to find them. These early experiences also contributed to Hood's views of race relations and racial advancement. He firmly believed that hard work and good character would find recognition and reward by the better elements of any people, including whites.

Having worked at the hotel for thirteen months, the young minister now had sufficient funds both to support his family and to journey to the Canadian mission field. Between his arrival in Connecticut in 1857 and his appointment to the

Nova Scotia in 1859 Hood entered his second marriage in May 1858, this time to Sophia J. Nugent, the daughter of Deacon Eli Nugent, of Washington, D.C. I have not been able to locate any details of the courtship between Hood and Nugent, his second wife, including where or how they made acquaintance or where she was living during the pre-engagement period. Sophia Nugent Hood died in September 13, 1875, survived by four children: Gertrude, Lillian, Maggie, and Joseph. Two years later Hood married Keziah Price McCoy of Wilmington, North Carolina. The third Mrs. Hood, Keziah—also called Kezia and Katie—along with their two biological children, Maude and James, Jr., and their four children from the previous marriage, survived Hood's death.

In early September 1860 the New England Conference convening in Boston, Massachusetts, ordained Hood a deacon, one step away from the final ministerial appointment of elder. Three days later, a Wednesday, Hood journeyed alone to Halifax to inaugurate his Canadian missionary work. In 1861 Hood sent for his family, who were still in Washington. In 1862 Hood came to the meeting of the annual conference in Hartford, Connecticut and received ordination as elder.[22] Three of Zion's superintendents were present at this conference: William H. Bishop, superintendent, and Peter Ross and Christopher Rush, assisting him as associate superintendents. Besides Hood there were nineteen other persons in attendance: twelve elders, two deacons, three preachers, and two lay delegates. In a conference session that prohibited absolutely the use of tobacco by any in attendance, Hood received appointment as assistant secretary. Reflecting the high standards attached to the ordained ministry at the time, Hood appears to have been the only one of three candidates ordained as elder. Abraham Robinson asked that consideration of his ordination be deferred until the next conference. William B. Smith was then examined "and found rather deficient."[23] The problems encountered by these two apparently revolved around matters unrelated to their spiritual characters, because all three were deemed "eligible to [worthy of?] Elder's Orders." Hood also provided leadership in worship in song and prayer.[24] After the conference, Hood returned to Nova Scotia for his third and final year's service there.

HOOD IN NOVA SCOTIA AND CONNECTICUT, 1860–1863

Hood's three-year missionary work in Nova Scotia had mixed results. Because he had almost no financial assistance from the small and struggling Zion denomination in the United States, the young minister was unable to establish a great Zion presence there. According to Hood, the only funds he received from Zion amounted to six dollars paid to help his wife leave Washington during the Battle of Bull Run as she traveled to New Bedford, Massachusetts. Obviously, the money he had saved from his New York employment was not enough to live on because Hood had to get a job digging potatoes, work that brought him a salary of approximately forty cents each day.[25]

Hood's relative lack of success in building up a strong Zion presence in that portion of Nova Scotia did not derive from a lack of enterprise and commitment on his part. Hood labored intensely, tirelessly, passionately, and with great commitment in the Canadian cities of Kentsville, Bridgeton, and Englewood.[26] During his three years in Canada, the Zion minister walked approximately fourteen hundred miles, preaching in more than two dozen places, in homes, schools, and churches, to white and black congregations.[27] The "Hardshell" or Primitive Baptists, who dominated the area, were strongly denominational and simply refused to unite with Methodism. Undoubtedly, the Methodist practice of infant baptism, the existence of the episcopal form of government, and the Arminian theology (with its emphasis on free will and opposition to predestination) discouraged the interest of these Baptists. Though area Baptists were forthright in their rejection of Methodism, they were not rude or mean to the young missionary. Indeed, they responded to Hood's preaching and to the young Methodist preacher personally with amazing courtesy and respect. "Personally I was never better treated." Later in life Hood lamented that still Zion had done so little to build on the earlier foundation he had laid. "We have almost ceased to make any effort in that field now."[28]

These evangelical activities, whether in Connecticut or Nova Scotia, were typical of Christian ministries at the time. People were in real danger of having their souls eternally lost if they did not embrace the Christian gospel. Out of their love for human souls and obedience to God's will, these evangelical ministers endured great hardships, trials, and even outright hostility in order to carry out the Great Commission, the spread of the gospel to all humanity. Although Hood did not encounter outright hostility in his preaching, he did undergo tremendous hardship. He accepted an appointment in Nova Scotia that had no denominational financing, experienced separation from his family for a considerable period, walked tremendous distances, and watched as persons converted under his ministry affiliated with other churches.

In 1863 Hood and his family returned to the United States for the assembling of the New England Annual Conference in Boston.[29] The Reverend Peter Ross now had the superintendency of this annual conference. Both Superintendents

Rush and Bishop, unable to attend because of serious illnesses, sent their regrets. The conference's strong stand against any alcohol consumption for nonmedicinal purposes points out the ardent view of temperance that prevailed during Hood's early life and ministry. This strict attitude characterized many, if not most, members of Zion, including James W. Hood, throughout the period of this study.[30] Hood was even more active at this conference than at the previous one, demonstrating his capacity for leadership and a keen understanding of human relations. The conference or superintendent selected Hood to be statistical reporter and to serve on the Committee on Complaints with Dempsey Kennedy and G. A. Spywood. Hood also served as president of the Board of Officers of the Home and Foreign Mission Board for 1863–1864 and addressed his fellow Zionites concerning the advantages of Sunday school.

In addition, Hood had the opportunity to exercise his diplomacy, a quality that throughout his public career characterized his approach to church and political matters. The Reverend S. M. Giles, the pastor who so greatly impressed Hood during his early ministry, raised controversy in the annual conference when he brought up the question of the payment of expenses of a Zion minister stationed in Liverpool. Full details of the problem faced by the conference are not available. It appears that the New York Annual Conference demanded that the missionary report to it, regardless of his specific membership. On the other hand, the New England Conference had decided in 1862 that it would not pay the expenses of the missionary. Apparently, there were issues of accountability and payment of salary. Hood's proposal resolved the controversy that erupted at the conference because of Giles's comments. The conference members agreed that they and their New York counterparts would share equally the expenses of the missionary.[31] Hood also presented Nathaniel Stubbs for ordination and assisted with a number of other candidates. The conference selected Hood as a conference delegate for the Southern Conference, which was probably the conference created out of the Philadelphia and Baltimore Conference.[32]

Hood, president of the Board of Officers of the Home and Foreign Mission Society, made a report lamenting the loss of a congregation in Halifax, Nova Scotia, that had dissolved its connectional ties. But the committee held out hope that the situation might be rectified. Turning most specifically to the mission of the connection in the South, Hood's missionary society called attention to what they, like many other Christians, black and white, interpreted as a prophetic development. There was a huge need for missionary workers to serve the newly emancipated people in areas captured by Union forces in the South. Hood saw the opportunity to bring more African Americans into the church as a fulfillment of Psalms 68:31, which he and many other Christians of the era interpreted as a prophecy of the African race's acceptance of the gospel and rise to temporal power.[33]

The board recommended that the conference, if necessary, should release a pastor from a present obligation and send him to work in the South, filling the resulting vacancy temporarily until the next meeting of the conference. This report reflects the future duties of Hood, who was actually removed from his post for the duty. One might wonder if Hood already knew in taking the Connecticut appointment that Bishop Clinton would later appoint him to go South. Also, this report reveals the theology of many black and white Christians of the time. Providentially, God was moving in human history through the agency of the Civil War to end slavery and to evangelize the many African Americans held in bondage who had not embraced the gospel. Interestingly, no extant materials document Hood's stance on the involvement or noninvolvement of African Americans as soldiers in the military conflict, particularly during the early years of the war, when there was lack of unanimity in the black community concerning this question. This silence regarding military service stands in marked contrast to the position taken by at least two outstanding ministers of the rival AME connection: Henry M. Turner played a key role in organizing black soldiers for the Union; whereas Daniel A. Payne counseled blacks to praise God, rather than being resentful over their early exclusion from military service because others (whites), but not they, were fighting a war that would result in freedom for their African American enslaved siblings.[34] Though Hood clearly did not eschew civic involvement, his active, vocal commitment to the ministry as operative within the church body and the expansion of Zion took first priority for himself and other Christian ministers. Given the considerably smaller size of Zion in comparison with the AME at the time (approximately twenty thousand members compared to fewer than five thousand), such a priority made practical sense.

HOOD'S APPOINTMENT TO
BRIDGEPORT, CONNECTICUT, 1863

In 1863 many of Hood's earlier hardships experienced in Nova Scotia were alleviated by the appointment he received at the New England Annual Conference. The conference appointed Hood to pastor a congregation in Bridgeport, Connecticut. For Hood and his family the difficulties of this situation, where the church had long remained without a pastor because of its perceived inability to support one, must have seemed small compared to the Hoods' experience in Nova Scotia. Hood, sensitive to the limits of the financial resources of the congregation, entered an agreement with church officials to accept their best efforts in collecting for him a salary of four hundred dollars. The church's contributions combined with the fruits of his own collections resulted in the amount of six hundred dollars in salary for Hood by the end of six months. Furthermore, upon Hood's departure, the Bridgeport church was financially stable and enjoyed an increase in membership under the leadership of his successors.[35]

Hood toward the end of his long life still cherished fond memories of that appointment.[36] Of course some of these pleasant memories might have been influenced by the possibility that he and the church shared a "honeymoon" period during his relatively brief, six-month stay there. Perhaps this was insufficient time to witness the many disputes, disagreements, and other difficult situations that often arise during a pastor's tenure. After six months, Bishop Joseph J. Clinton, who had episcopal oversight of the New England Conference, appointed Hood for missionary work among freed people in the South. Hood's congregation resented this removal of their pastor by Clinton. According to Hood, he was able to calm his parishioners by sharing his conviction that such was the providential will, that God had specially called him for the missionary work delegated by Clinton. At the end of his life, Hood expressed absolute, continuing confidence in that earlier conviction of God's purpose.

HOOD AND INFLUENTIAL ZIONITES

During his childhood and the early years of his ministry, Hood felt the influence of significant black leaders who contributed to the development of his own skills as a race and religious leader. At the risk of appearing to digress from a discussion of Hood, brief biographical details about a few of these leading Zionites will show how they influenced Hood's leadership style. A concise treatment of these individuals helps to place Hood in historical and religious context, helping us to understand the challenges that the young minister and Zion faced in the early 1860s. By means of a devout and serious mother and his other childhood experiences, Hood felt the influence of Richard Allen of the AME, though Allen died during the year that Hood was born. Through both of his parents, Hood gained deep appreciation for Peter Spencer, pastor of their Union Church of Africans congregation in Wilmington, Delaware. Spencer's emphasis on freedom for the laity undoubtedly influenced Hood throughout his life. Even in later years as Hood defended the episcopal nature of Zion Methodism, he continually insisted on the rights of the laity.

Hood encountered, and at times interacted with, some individuals whose names will live forever in Zion tradition, such as Peter Ross, Christopher Rush, and J. J. Clinton. One of the great early leaders of Zion was Peter Ross (1809–1890), a native New Yorker who was ordained deacon and elder in 1840 and 1842 respectively.[37] In 1852 a denominational schism over the episcopacy occurred in Zion. It had been the custom of Zion to elect one superintendent and two assistants. When the superintendent died in 1852, a dispute arose as to which of the assistants had superior authority. This dispute resulted in the division of the church into two groups: one, the Wesleyan Methodist Episcopal Church, centered in Pennsylvania and areas to the west and south, placed strong emphasis on the episcopal character of Methodism; the other, the African Methodist Episcopal Zion Church, centered in New York and the Northeast, placed emphasis on congregational polity. In 1860 that schism was healed, and from that time forward all bishops were elected on equal terms. The 1860 General Conference selected, first, Peter Ross, then Joseph Clinton, and later William H. Bishop. Highly respected throughout his life, Ross held episcopal jurisdiction with the two other bishops over all three districts on a rotating basis. Because he found that the connection was unable to support him in a sufficiently financial manner to keep him free of debt, Ross later resigned the episcopacy and pursued his own secular business. He remained a faithful minister of the gospel for Zion, however. By the time of his death in 1890, Ross was the only surviving retired bishop and had been retired so long that some Zionites did not know of his episcopal record. Hood recorded that at the time of his episcopal consecration, he was among the best preachers of the denomination and a person of frank and clearly expressed beliefs. Hood's concluding comment, however, suggested that he was not very close to Ross: "So much I have felt to say, others who knew him better may say more."[38]

Hood's memories of the great Zion leader, Christopher Rush, suggest a closer relationship than that between Ross and Hood. They also offer an insight into the contributions the superintendent made to Zion's early growth. In his 1912 quadrennial report on the First Episcopal District, Bishop Hood spoke of the tremendous respect that Rush, by then deceased, commanded among Zionites. Some had even begun looking on him as more influential than the first superintendent, James Varick. Hood did not take sides in that debate, but he insisted that Rush was highly deserving of the highest praise. Bishop Hood related the manner in which Rush, a native of North Carolina, worked to extend the church from New York City into areas such as Massachusetts, upstate New York, Pennsylvania, and even as far into the South as possible during the pre-Emancipation era. Hood, noting Rush's twenty-four years of episcopal service, regarded him as pious, full of energy, and widely respected. According to Hood, Rush cherished "pious young men," and Hood was one of his favorites. Interestingly, the aging superintendent, who had ventured north, lived to see a future bishop, perhaps one who would become even more influential in Zion and American history, journey to the very area of Craven County, North Carolina, where he was born and reared. Greatly rejoicing in Hood's appointment to his home town, the elder Zionite gave the future bishop his blessings and prayers.[39]

Hood's closest association and mentoring relationship, however, was with a Zion superintendent who was to eclipse Rush in terms of organizing new Zion conferences, Joseph Jackson Clinton. It was this bishop who appointed Hood to his mission field in the South. Clinton (1823–1881) was a native of Philadelphia who eventually made his home in Atlantic City, New Jersey. He was ordained deacon, elder, and bishop (for the first time) in 1845, 1846, and 1856 respectively. A few months shy of being thirty-three years old when elected bishop, Clinton has kept the distinction of being the youngest person ever selected to that post in Zion. Clinton married Letitia Sisco, with whom he had ten children, one of whom became a presiding elder in Florida. Having episcopal charge of the entire South but no established base of operation, Clinton organized a great number of conferences, incorporated a hundred thousand Sunday school students, and seven hundred traveling preachers.[40] Hood believed firmly that had Clinton's episcopal colleagues "possessed the forethought and energy that he [Clinton] possessed" the AMEZ would have accomplished even more than it had by the second decade of the twentieth century.[41] Hood praised the late bishop for his unrelenting efforts on behalf of Zion, considering him as the most effective bishop Zion had produced; he spoke highly of their close personal association, and held Clinton as his ministerial and episcopal model.[42] At least one source suggests that Hood's admiration extended to the naming of one of his two sons, Joseph Jackson Clinton Hood, after the this episcopal leader.[43]

Hood claimed that he made an appeal to the General Conference of 1864 that Clinton be granted a northern conference to support him in the missionary field of the South. But Hood's efforts in that direction collapsed when he made a crucial (though unspecified) remark that shifted the conference's attention away from Hood's proposal to Hood himself. For this remark the superintendent chairing the session, as well as some very influential ministers, sternly rebuked Hood.[44] This episode illustrates that even at this early date Hood's sometimes acerbic tongue was counterproductive. But the above account also explains the closeness between Clinton and the young minister. Hood climbed the ecclesiastical ladder because of both his own hard, dedicated, organizing work and the favor of Bishop Clinton.

Hood, reflecting on Clinton's work in the South during the 1860s, also described him as a creative, energetic individual who would adopt rather unorthodox methods in pursuit of his task. Given the fact that Clinton was receiving no financial or personnel assistance from his episcopal colleagues and given the large missionary field, the bishop had to work with haste and to improvise. In some instances, for example, Clinton requested young men in an assembly to preach on the spot and if satisfied would then order the pastor to ordain them—and rarely was he wrong about the potentials and future ministerial success of such persons![45] Sometimes, however, Clinton's procedures and unorthodox methods spelled trouble for himself and Zion. The connection lost a large congregation in Augusta, Georgia, because the bishop had no solid Zionite minister to leave in charge of the work, and, thus, upon Clinton's departure the church changed affiliations; presumably joining the AME, a rival of Zion. Because Clinton traveled alone and needed travel expenses, he often had to request money for himself. Sometimes he sold photographs of himself to raise the necessary funds. His "enemies" in rival Methodist denominations probably portrayed Clinton as greedy and/or vain because of these actions.[46] There was never a suggestion on the part of Hood or any other church leader, as I have been able to determine, that Clinton was dishonest. Indeed, he was, despite these irregularities, highly lauded for his sacrificial work in successfully spreading the denomination throughout the South.

OTHER SIGNIFICANT DETAILS ABOUT HOOD, 1864–1918

In addition to his religious and political activities, Hood played a significant role in establishing black Masonry in North Carolina. Indeed, the Zion leader played a number of key Masonic leadership roles, as the "Grand Master of Masons of N. C. for 14 years, Grand Patron Order of Eastern Star 19 years, Grand Chaplain of the Grand Lodge of World of Good Templars."[47] Hood, in a sense, introduced black Masonry into North Carolina. Given the secret nature of Masonry, it is not surprising that Hood left few comments concerning his activities in this area.

Hood's leadership in religious and connectional matters, however, is very well documented. The Zion leader was a key founder, trustee, and supporter of the denominational newspaper, the *Star of Zion,* which began operation in North Carolina in the late 1870s. He was also instrumental in the establishment of Zion Wesley Institute, later Livingstone College, that found its permanent home in Salisbury. Hood served as president of the board of trustees of the college from its founding in 1879 until his death in 1918. In addition, it was he who discovered the dynamic and eloquent Joseph Charles Price, who became the cofounder and legendary first president of the school. Bishop Hood commissioned Price to campaign for funds in order to establish and operate the institution. As a Methodist bishop, Hood participated in the World Methodist Ecumenical Conferences, attending the 1881 assembly in London and the 1891 meeting in Washington, D.C. In 1891 he became the first African American bishop to preside at one of these meetings, which was a source of pride throughout the Zion connection.

Hood's voluminous publications did much to convey his knowledge, wisdom, and sense of history. During his life he was probably the most prolific writer of the Zion bishops in the columns of the denominational *Star.* But the prelate also wrote articles for other newspapers and publications. He published five major books. His first was *The Negro in the Christian Pulpit: Two Characters and Two Destinies,* published in 1884, a collection of sermons, most of them authored and originally delivered by Hood. In reading these sermons, one is struck by the strong emphasis on holiness flowing from the pages of the book. His great historical work was *One Hundred Years of the A. M. E. Zion Church,* published in 1895. This book is a classic and is still useful as a reliable guide to early Zion history.

In 1900 Hood published a significant commentary on the biblical book of Revelation, *The Plan of the Apocalypse.* Hood did not make use of the historical-critical method in his exegesis of this New Testament work, but it is a well-researched work with deep insights by the bishop. One is struck with his strong belief in postmillennialism, the doctrine that a golden age of righteousness and justice is near and will precede the Second Coming of Jesus Christ, a belief shared by many Christians during this period. In 1908 Hood published another collection of sermons, simply titled, *Sermons.* In 1914 the aging bishop published his last major work, *Sketch of the Early History of the A. M. E. Zion Church,* sometimes referred to as *Hood's History, Volume 2.* At the time of his death the bishop was writing his autobiography. Unfortunately, it was never completed, or if it was, I have been unable to locate it. A portion of this work, located in Hood's Papers in the Carter G. Woodson Collection, covers the period from roughly 1868 until the early 1880s. Regrettably, the portions dealing with his childhood, early adult life, and his last years are missing.

Finally, something should be said concerning Hood's personal characteristics, physical traits, and family. According to one commentator, Hood's family tree represented African, Native American, and Caucasian lineage. "He was of rugged build, tall and stately with an imposing and impressive presence and picturesque stature, and of a regulation motion in his movements."[48] From the available black and white photographs of Hood, he appeared to be medium brown in skin color with light brown or grayish eyes. The constant traveling and other exertions associated with the ministry and the episcopacy exacted great tolls on his health. As an adult, Hood suffered from various illnesses: yellow fever, rheumatism, strokes, and influenza. During his missionary activities in the South, Hood grew a full beard, which he kept for the rest of his life. Intellectually, he was brilliant and an avid reader, traits that reveal themselves in his many debates, sermons, addresses, and newspaper articles. In debates he was usually well prepared and sharp, marshaling facts from history and contemporary life. Persistent in and eager to debate, Hood sometimes did not recognize the opportune moments to withdraw from confrontations, with the result that having presented a very strong case he sometimes damaged it by sinking to the level of personal attacks and pettiness. "He always met criticism with a strongly opposing argument or reason sometimes savoring of deeply biting irony or sarcasm." For the most part, he encountered few who disagreed with his opinions because of their logical constructions. Unfortunately, this fact might have reinforced the idea in Hood's mind that his views were always the correct ones and thus sometimes rendered him insensitive to the arguments of his opponents—incredulous that anyone who was well informed and well meaning could possibly not understand the wisdom of his (Hood's) viewpoint! As one editor of the *Star of Zion* stated, Hood was "self-confident and self-possessed[;] he knew just what he was going to do and did it having the utmost confidence in the wisdom of his action."[49] I must note, however, that this tendency to credit unworthy motives or ignorance to one's opponents in debates also characterized other church people during this era.

On the other hand, Hood, firmly committed to the AMEZ Church and evangelical religion, was admired deeply and even greatly loved by many. He was rated as an eloquent and popular preacher by many of his contemporaries, who often cited the fact that both blacks and whites invited him into some of the most prestigious pulpits in all sections of the country. Without detracting from his power as a preacher, it might be pointed out that many of these invitations were no doubt occasioned by his prominence as bishop and, from the mid-1890s, senior bishop of a major black denomination. Many observers credited him as a calm, deliberate, careful person in discourse. He seemed to have been particularly concerned for the rights of women and the laity in Zion. Despite his sometimes acerbic style of debating, Hood was generally warm, generous, self-sacrificing, and diplomatic in dealing with others. "While frugal he was distinguished for his public charity to his Church always maintaining meager circumstances on that account . . . and he was curiously sympathetic toward the unfortunate of his ministerial constituency."[50]

Contemporary observers also portray him as a committed, compassionate family man. As previously noted, Hood was born into a family with eleven other children, six sisters and five brothers. We have already discussed his two marriages to Hannah L. Ralph, who was childless, and then Sophia J. Nugent. After approximately seventeen years of marriage, Sophia Hood died in 1875 in North Carolina, leaving four children. Two years later Bishop Hood married Keziah P. McCoy of Wilmington, North Carolina, who survived his death. Hood spoke very warmly of the third Mrs. Hood's motherly care for her four stepchildren as well as for her two natural children with Hood, who survived infancy. As was customary during this era, Hood made few sustained references to personal, family matters.

There is, however, significant information about Keziah Hood. She was born in 1844, the child of a free Methodist mother. Having learned to sew at an early age, she later became a renowned dressmaker. Around 1867 she ventured to Baltimore, Maryland, to attend Frances Academy for more than a year. Her first husband died in 1871, only six months after their wedding. A hardworking and conscientious person, the future Mrs. Hood used her sewing skills to pay for the house that her husband had purchased. It is clear that Keziah Hood played an active role in church affairs and enjoyed the admiration of her contemporaries. Hailing from both Episcopal and Methodist backgrounds, she was nurtured by the Sunday school of the Episcopal Church and even received confirmation in that denomination after her conversion during a camp meeting run by Methodists. But Keziah Hood, like her late mother-in-law, Harriet Walker Hood, left her own chosen denomination to unite with her husband's.

Mrs. Hood earned high regard for both her personal demeanor and her activities in the church. As a free woman in Wilmington, the future Mrs. Hood carried herself with a demeanor that even Confederate and Union soldiers—and soldiers could often be quite crude and vulgar, particularly to women of color—paid her great respect during the military occupation of Wilmington during the Civil War. Later as a bishop's wife, she hosted a number of social and formal occasions involving the bishop and church affairs. In general, Keziah Hood was regarded as a compassionate person who shared her resources with members of the community. In addition, Mrs. Hood served a number of years as president and secretary of Zion's Women's Home and Foreign Missionary Society. Related to her duties with the missions society, she also published a column in the *Star of Zion,* the denominational newspaper.[51]

Hood fathered a total of ten children, six of whom survived infancy: Gertrude C. Hood Miller (the oldest daughter); Lillian A. Hood McCallum; Margrette or Maggie I. Loguen Hood Banks; Maude E. Hood (the youngest daughter); Joseph Jackson Clinton Hood (a physician and the older son); and James Walker Hood, Jr. Evidently, Gertrude and Maude spent their entire lives in Fayetteville, North Carolina, and died as members of the historic Evans Metropolitan AMEZ Church, with Gertrude serving as chorister for some time. Gertrude also served for a while on the faculty at Livingstone College, the denominational school in Salisbury, North Carolina, teaching dressmaking or sewing. She had learned her skills from study in Boston, Massachusetts, and her stepmother, Keziah. Maude accompanied and assisted Bishop Hood as his private secretary. Lillian McCallum and Maggie Banks made occasional contributions to the pages of the *Star of Zion.* Maggie Banks married James Campbell Banks and settled for a while in New Bern, North Carolina. It appears that the Bankses also lived in Winston-Salem, North Carolina, and Tuskegee, Alabama, during the period under study. Other than the fact that Joseph Hood was a medical doctor and married, I have little or no information on Hood's two sons. All six of Hood's children were educated at Livingstone College and lived into their seventies, eighties, and nineties.[52]

CONCLUSION

This chapter has traced the early life of Hood, from his birth in 1831 to the eve of his departure as a missionary to the freed people in North Carolina in 1864, and provided an addendum chronicling some of his most significant lifetime contributions. Hood grew up in an environment of evangelical Methodism and abolitionism, an environment characterized by Quakerism's overall positive concern for the well-being of blacks. This period had a profound influence on the development of his own style of religious and racial leadership. Throughout his life the twin goals of propagating the gospel and uplifting African Americans remained mutually supportive objectives for Hood. Reared in the Union Church of Africans, Hood, upon moving to New England (via New York City), entered the northeastern-based African Methodist Episcopal Zion Church in the 1850s. After briefly serving as interim pastor in Connecticut, Hood became a missionary to Nova Scotia. Though the fierce loyalty of the black Canadians to the Baptist tradition prohibited him from winning many converts to the cause of Zion, Hood did gain some converts to Christianity. These early years reveal an energetic, dedicated Methodist minister who was already a leader in Zion and who learned from some of the major luminaries of the connection, such as Christopher Rush, the second general superintendent of the denomination. Concomitant with the growth, increased institutionalization, and expansion of the independent black Methodist denominations and the Baptist conventions and associations, Hood was maturing as a leader and expanding the geographic reach of his ministry.

PART II

Zion Goes South

Hood's Religious and Political Leadership, 1864–1872

Chapter Two

HOOD'S RELIGIOUS ACTIVITIES
IN THE SOUTH, 1864–1872

When the history of the great men who have done the constructive work
of the Negro churches in the South is written, we will find J. W. Hood's
name among the great and good.
　　—C. W. Winfield and M. N. Levy, Part IV, "The Hood Golden
　　　Jubilee," in Hood, *Sketch of the Early History of the African
　　　Methodist Episcopal Zion Church*

Hood's skillful and passionate leadership manifested itself during his early life
and ministry in the Northeast and in Nova Scotia prior to 1864, but his most outstanding contributions and notoriety derived from religious and political activities in the South during the Civil War, Reconstruction, and post-Reconstruction
years. When Hood came South, he came as more than an individual religious
and political leader, reflecting the expansion of northern-based denominations,
particularly independent black organizations. In this chapter we explore Hood's
missionary, organizing, and other leadership activities specifically on behalf of
the Zion Church and symbolically on behalf of the independent, northern-based
black denominations, conventions, and associations that extended themselves into
that region of the country where the overwhelming majority of blacks lived until
around the 1920s. Most particularly, the following pages focus on Hood's church
activities in the North Carolina town of New Bern, Beaufort, Wilmington, Fayetteville, and Charlotte as representative instances of Hood's leadership style and
examples of how the independent, northern-based, African American religious

bodies penetrated the South, uniting forces with their Southern racial siblings. Hood's leadership in the South represented the continuity of the spiritual-temporal tradition within black Christianity during this era. That is, black religious leaders propagated the gospel and expanded church parameters to accomplish both religious and "secular" or temporal objectives, to save both the souls and the bodies of a race of people. As we examine some specific, crucial missionary and church organizing campaigns by Hood during the 1864–1872 period, it becomes readily apparent how the young Zionite's activities in these areas helped to solidify the foundation of the AMEZ in the South and thus make Hood one of the most important religious leaders in the country. In these episodes are reflected Hood's sagacity, diplomacy, adroitness, ability to understand people, and his maneuverability. Facing stiff denominational competition from other Methodist bodies, armed with limited financial resources, attacked by illness, but empowered by his commitment to spread the gospel and uplift the race, Hood succeeded in helping to expand Zion in the South, and thus it became like its black counterparts, the AME and subsequently the Baptists, truly a national denominational body.

BACKGROUND AND RELIGIOUS CONTEXT OF HOOD'S SOUTHERN LEADERSHIP

As the fortunes of war leaned toward the Union cause, many black and white Christians in the North began missionary efforts to evangelize blacks in the South. Many of them saw the Civil War as the means by which God was acting in history to liberate the enslaved, perhaps even a second great Exodus. But the liberation of blacks from physical bondage was only one step, albeit a significant one, in God's providential plan for the formerly enslaved. God also desired their spiritual salvation. These Christians firmly believed that Christian conversion brought spiritual salvation and inculcated the moral and social values and ethics that would be instrumental in any people's striving toward temporal advancement.

These northern Christians, then, saw a great field of unclaimed souls, ripe for harvest for the Kingdom of God. On one hand, they correctly surmised that many of the approximately four million blacks in the South were completely unchurched. On the other, both African American and white Christians often questioned the quality of religious teaching that the enslaved had received from missionaries who were either explicitly proslavery or operating in restrictive environments relative to the liberation aspects of the gospel (although my reading of history convinces me that most southern enslaved and free black Christians received their faith from other black Christians). Thus, northern Christians sought to convert the masses of African Americans to Christianity and to purify current Christians from the distortions of southern white religion.

To a great extent the first impression, that there were a large number of unchurched African Americans in the South, was a correct one. Forest G. Wood, in his *Arrogance of Faith,* offers some revealing statistics.[1] Of the four million blacks in the South in 1860, only 468,000, or 12 percent of the enslaved population, were church members. Only 171,857, or 4 percent of the enslaved in the South, were members of Methodism. Methodists in the northern free states, on the other hand, represented 18 percent of the black population. I believe that Wood overstates the extent to which blacks were unchurched. He should provide corresponding data on the percentages of white Christians to the overall population. Low church attendance was not unique to southern blacks. Furthermore, to be unchurched was not necessarily synonymous with being non-Christian for either whites or blacks. Wood should call greater attention to black Christians who were members of the "invisible institution" but not the organized, official churches controlled by whites.[2] On the second issue, regarding the character of southern black religion, many white and black northern church workers during the 1860–1920 era once on the southern field found that these Christians, far from being ignorant of true Christianity, possessed a depth of spirituality and devotion that often far exceeded that of many northerners.

However we might disagree with Wood's interpretation of statistical data, he correctly points out that many blacks in the antebellum South remained either completely unchurched or, in any case, that their adaptation of Christianity required additional organization and structure in the postwar years, at least from the northern perspective. Indeed, it appears that during the first years of the missionary expansion into the South, northern churches gained most of their new membership from existing black communities of faith (whether or not they were meeting in church structures) than from the evangelization of non-Christians. One perspective of the northern missionary effort is that these white and black denominations were taking control from the southern white denominations relative to African American Christians, just as the military and political forces were depriving white southerners of control in secular spheres.

Recent studies by scholars such as Dickerson, Dvorak, Hildebrand, Montgomery, Washington, Johnson and Jersild, Angell, and Martin have provided valuable information on African American Christianity and its expansion in the South during the Civil War and Reconstruction eras.[3] As a northern missionary and church organizer, Hood operated in a milieu where most of the mainline northern-based denominations, either mostly black or mostly white, had representatives on the mission field, often occasioning fierce competition among the various parties for the ecclesiastical allegiance of southern African Americans. Black Christians in the South, however, tended to be most successfully wooed by northern black Baptists; the African Methodist Episcopal, or AME, Church; the AMEZ, or Zionites; and the northern, mainly white, Methodist Episcopal (ME) Church—and in that order. The AME Church was the most successful of *all* Methodist bodies in securing black members. This success might be partly explained by several factors: the greater size of the AME, which allowed it to field more workers; the fact that it was one of the first northern groups sending missionaries and workers South during the Civil War; a historical, pre–Civil War presence in a few areas, such as Charleston, South Carolina, and New Orleans, dating back to the early nineteenth century; more strategic planning of missionary and organizing activities; and in some instances the successful portrayal of itself as more genuinely Methodistic than the AMEZ, blacker than the ME, and bolder in political matters than the Colored, later Christian, Methodist Episcopal Church, or CME (organized from the membership of Methodist Episcopal Church, South in 1870). Nonetheless, the Zionites, under the leadership of dynamic individuals such as Hood and Bishop J. J. Clinton, made a highly impressive showing, increasing its membership from just under 5,000 members in 1860 to approximately 750,000 by the time of Hood's death in 1918. The membership strength and headquarters of Zion would shift from a few northeastern states to the South, particularly North Carolina and Alabama.

Hood and Bishop J. J. Clinton played pivotal roles in effecting that shift by their tireless, creative, and dedicated organizing of churches and conferences. As previously noted, Bishop Clinton, who had episcopal charge of the New England Annual Conference, appointed Hood as a missionary to the southern freedpeople in December 1863, only six months into his pastorate at the Bridgeport church in Connecticut. With the financial and fund-raising help of influential women and men in the connection, especially, for example, the Daughters of Conference of the New England Annual Conference, Zion moved to spread the gospel in the South. The very first missionary appointed by Clinton, John Williams, tarried in the north beyond the patience of the most fervent Zion mission supporters. Perhaps he felt that circumstances were still unsafe for a black person's travel into an area with a Confederate headquarters less than thirty miles away! Hood, however, responded more expeditiously and, by so doing, perhaps cemented a bond between himself and Clinton. By January 1, 1863, Hood and his family had come as far south as Washington, D.C., and would have traveled farther had not icy conditions prohibited travel. On January 20, 1864, at noon, Hood entered the city of New Bern, North Carolina, in the northeastern section of the state. Hood was within the very field of battle between Union and Confederate forces and was in serious personal danger. Twice the city of New Bern was attacked by the Confederates. As Federal forces fired cannons over New Bern into southern forces near the city on one occasion, Hood found himself "sitting in my room writing" and nearly fifty years later could not explain why he remained so calm amid the danger.[4]

THE COMPETITION FOR ANDREWS CHAPEL (ST. PETER'S)

Hood's first notable success, and perhaps the most significant one for the expansion of Zion, was Hood's victory in securing the denominational allegiance of a pre–Civil War black congregation in the city of New Bern, North Carolina. Around 1839 Andrews Chapel was organized in the city, apparently as a congregation of the Methodist Episcopal Church, South (ME-S). With Hood's arrival in the city, this church became a point of contention among the ME, the AME, and the AMEZ, and perhaps the Congregationalists as well. The Reverend J. E. Round of the ME Church first arrived in 1862 under episcopal supervision of that denomination. About one year later another white man, named Fitz, of the Congregationalist Church, arrived. He taught Sunday school for a period and eventually secured a preaching license from Round. His purpose, however, was to bring the church into the Congregationalist fold. On the same day that Hood arrived, two AME ministers from Norfolk came to New Bern and also began competing for Andrews Chapel. Consistent with the general preference of southern blacks during this era, the New Bern church people did not want to enter either of the predominantly white denominations. Thus, as far as the congregants were concerned, the real contest was between the two independent black groups, the AME and the AMEZ.

An area smallpox epidemic complicated matters. Hood contracted an illness on Thursday, the day after his arrival. Because of the smallpox plague, the Union military temporarily halted all church services. This order did not prevent the two AME ministers from conducting a door-to-door campaign, from the

Wednesday of their arrival until the following Sunday, to convince members of
the congregation to affiliate with their denomination. According to Hood, they
were spreading inaccurate information about the Zion Church, perhaps calling
into question its Methodistic validity. The young Zionite missionary, however,
had a strong advantage. The Zion bishop Christopher Rush, whom the towns-
people still remembered, hailed from the New Bern area (Craven County), having once lived in the city of New Bern itself. The citizens' fondness for Rush drew
these Carolinians to Zion and perhaps induced a number of them to keep Hood
abreast of the activities of the Bethel men.

Hood moved as quickly as his illness and circumstances allowed in his effort
to win the congregation for Zion. The New Bern congregation circumvented the
military order forbidding church services by assembling the trustee board the following Sunday. Of course there were forty persons serving on the board! Along
with the two AME representatives, the group assembled "in a private school-
house belonging to the wife of one of the members of the official board, namely,
Joseph Green."[5] Permitting the two Bethel men the opportunity to present their
case first, Hood listened attentively. In Hood's presence they did not repeat the
earlier alleged disparaging statements about Zion; Hood, however, raised the
issue and found the two representatives unable to defend adequately their positions. Hood quizzed them on a number of ecclesiastical points with the result
that the two individuals, who had really not ventured farther north than Norfolk, demonstrated not only their ignorance of the AMEZ but also superficial
knowledge of their own AME connection. The board then met in closed session
and voted unanimously to enter the Zion denomination. "The fare of the other
two brethren was paid back to Norfolk, and they were requested to return at
once and make no further effort. To this they agreed."[6]

Of course we must take care with this account of the AMEZ-AME competition for Andrews Chapel. First, I am drawing largely from the account provided
by Hood, which, though accurate in the details listed, understandably, places Zion
in a much more favorable light than Bethel. Quite possibly, the AME missionaries were spreading information about Zion that they considered to be accurate
and that might be so understood from an objective perspective, though Hood
took such statements as untruths and perhaps regarded them as intentionally so.
For example, if the AME representatives did indeed question the validity of the
AMEZ episcopal government because Zion required its chief officers to stand for
election or reelection every four years and designated them superintendents rather
than bishops, such practices were clearly contrary to the accepted customs and
definition of episcopacy of the AME, the ME-S, and the ME and, in the opinions

of these three bodies, could be considered un-Methodistic and non-episcopal. Second, while Hood and Zion secured victory in this instance and some others, Bethel had notable successes elsewhere, often outmaneuvering Zion. After all, the AME did grow at a faster rate in the South than Zion. Third, the departure of these two unnamed AME representatives from New Bern did not spell the termination of the AME's interest in New Bern. Dennis Dickerson points to the labors of George Rue. This northern Bethel missionary later succeeded in establishing a small AME congregation in New Bern. Rue, like Hood, entered the South from a New England pastorate.[7]

Nonetheless, Hood had secured a clean, clear-cut win in his competition with the AME representatives . Such would not be the case with the representatives of the ME Church. Hood's contest with the ME required even greater ingenuity and preparation. If Hood's characterization of the AME ministers was fundamentally correct, it is possible that they left with a marked sense of respect for an able, worthy ecclesiastical rival who understood the AME tradition better than these AME representatives. Besides, the trustee board, which was representative of the congregants, had spoken and granted Hood a well-deserved victory. For a number of reasons, the Methodist Episcopal representative, J. E. Round, on the other hand, probably saw Hood's AMEZ as an interloper in the legitimately acquired territory of the ME. First, Round had been working among the people as de facto pastor since 1862, nearly two years. Second, Round probably considered the ME as a more appropriate representative of Methodist episcopalianism than the AMEZ. Had not the latter church, like its counterpart the AME, broken away from the ME, the original Methodist church in the United States? Did not the Zionites, in clear distinction from the practices of the MEC, the ME-S, and the AME, quadrennially elect their chief officers (rather than elect them for life tenure) and designate them "superintendents" (rather than "bishops")? Furthermore, clearly the Methodist Episcopal Church's membership rolls, in terms of numerical strength and diversity of people (including a large membership of African Americans), undergirded their claim that it was the authentic and best Methodist body—from the perspective of the ME. Third, Round had the official appointment of the ME Bishop Baker, and the latter enjoyed the official sanctioning of his authority from Secretary of War E. M. Stanton.[8] The fact that the black church's former pastor had official ties with the "breakaway" ME-S placed Andrews Chapel legally under the ecclesiastical domain of the Methodist Episcopal Church. Round made it clear that, regardless of the wishes of the local people, he would protect the rights of the ME church in this matter.

Thus, the religious contest between Hood and Round became a legal battle

ultimately settled by the secretary of war himself. The basic question was reduced
to whether the ME Church's authority took precedence over the right of a local
congregation to decide its own affiliation? Both Round and Hood prepared their
respective cases and presented them to General B. F. Butler. Butler, who already
had granted official sanction to Hood's missionary activities among the freedpeople, agreed with the Zionite minister that the local people should have the
freedom to select their own denominational affiliation. "There is an old Church
maxim that a bishop cannot delegate his power."[9]

Hood, demonstrating his political wisdom and determination, left nothing to
chance. While the matter was under consideration by Butler and being forwarded
to Secretary Stanton, Hood worked on another front. Having conferred with
"the official members" of Andrews Chapel, he went straight to the source of
Bishop Baker's legal authority, Secretary Stanton. Traveling on his own expense
to Washington, he remained there for two weeks, making almost daily trips to
the office of the secretary of war to validate his own official commission to engage in military work. The adjutant general indicated to Hood that his original
papers had been misplaced and "suggested that Hood prepare another copy."
Hood was then told that "he could return to North Carolina and await the results."[10] The case was first presented to Butler around February 1, and Stanton's
final decision did not arrive until mid-March. But it was good news for Hood.
Stanton endorsed Butler's opinion by writing, "The congregation of the colored
Methodists worshiping in Andrew's Chapel, New Bern, N.C., shall have the right
to decide their own church relations, and select their pastor."[11] Hood's rendition
of Stanton's reply in his major historical work was more concise, "The congregation worshiping in Andrew Chapel are permitted to select their own pastor."[12]
Both versions make it clear that African Americans, having acquired physical
freedom by way of the war effort and the Emancipation Proclamation, were also
to have, for the first time in their or their American ancestors' lives, full religious
freedom as well.

Hood did not approach the expansion of Zion in incremental steps. As he
waited for a ruling on the legal appeals before government officials, and while
the smallpox epidemic still prohibited certain public services in New Bern, Hood
extended his missionary activities to the nearby town of Beaufort. Residing in the
area for several days, Hood preached at Purvis [or "Purvice"] Chapel, accepted
the congregation into the AMEZ, granted Enoch Wallace a preaching license,
and appointed him pastor.[13] Interestingly, Round permitted Hood to operate in
this area without any strong opposition. Round certainly claimed this congrega-

tion for the ME as well as Andrews Chapel and all the churches under Union jurisdiction. Perhaps the ME missionary was busy with other church affairs, was overconfident that the government officials would rule in favor of the ME Church, or underestimated the organizing skill and energy of the young Zionite. At any rate, Hood's efforts proved extremely beneficial to Zion. The Zion minister managed to bring about three thousand new church members into the connection, all of whom Round had claimed for his denomination. Hood mentioned that fifty persons in New Bern did not immediately connect with Zion, but did so eventually. Perhaps these individuals had chosen initially to follow the Congregationalist, Fitz.[14]

By the middle of March Secretary Stanton's decision, granting Andrews Chapel the right to select its own affiliation and pastor, reached Hood. Also, the smallpox epidemic had subsided so that public services could resume. Hood moved quickly, informing the parishioners that he would deliver the message on the upcoming Easter Day, an announcement made prior to Round's having received Stanton's decision. The young Zion minister realized that the trustee board's endorsement of his pastorate was not binding upon the body at large. Making sure that he first occupied the pulpit, Hood arrived early on Easter morning and preached a sermon that cemented the church's relations with Zion.

The occasion was one of great racial significance and huge excitement because a black preacher had journeyed to the city to work among his own racial siblings, had entered an ecclesiastical contest with a white person, and the black church members themselves had exercised the right to settle the matter. Large crowds gathered both inside and outside the church eagerly awaiting the sermon of the African American hero who had earned for them greater religious freedom. Having prepared himself with "several days" of prayer, Hood preached a sermon on Jesus's resurrection based on Matthew 28:6 and observed, "The presence of the Lord filled the house, and the people were truly joyful." After the services were closed, someone read the decision that Stanton had rendered, and the congregation, according to Hood, chose the AMEZ and himself as pastor without dissent.[15] Round, the white ME minister, retired from the ecclesiastical battle at that point. As late as the mid-1890s, Hood and his former rival had remained on friendly terms. In 1879 the New Bern parishioners adopted a new name—St. Peter's AMEZ Church. It is not clear whether St. Peter's or Purvis Chapel was the first church in the South to enter Zion Methodism. Apparently, Purvis was admitted prior to the resolution of the ecclesiastical contest in New Bern and, thus, should be designated the first Zion congregation in the South. At any rate, St. Peter's has been historically viewed as "the Mother Church of southern Zion Methodism."[16]

Hood's contests with both the unnamed AME representatives and the ME Round were direct, open confrontations. Fitz, however, received a more negative character appraisal from Hood. Unlike the other opponents of Hood, Fitz worked clandestinely and in a manipulative manner. First, according to Hood, Fitz's ultimate loyalty was to the Congregationalist church, not the ME, with whom he ostensibly aligned himself. Even had Round triumphed, the church might still have passed out of Methodism into Congregationalism because of Fitz. With the assistance of Chaplain James, superintendent of Negro Affairs, Fitz continued to oppose Hood. First, he reported to the post commandant that Hood had disobeyed military orders by holding religious services during the smallpox plague, a charge that, arguably, had some accuracy.

The commandant, General Palmer, summoned Hood, who was ignorant of these behind-the-scenes machinations. But upon examining the pass granted to the Zionite organizer by General Butler, Palmer took no action against Hood. Indeed, Butler's favoring of Hood had made him an object of respect within Union military circles around New Bern. Fitz was not to be so easily outdone, however. Hood's rival took further action to advance his cause by reporting to military officials, perhaps falsely, the presence of thousands of idle blacks in the city who should be relocated to work the Dutch Gap Canal. Fitz then submitted a list containing the names of almost all the main leaders of the New Bern congregation, including those who were, because of age or physical infirmities, clearly unsuited for the work in question, as well as other members who already had well-paying employment. Hood appealed to the post commandant, who in one instance accompanied Hood to the place of departure with the result that Hood was able to rescue many of his church members from relocation. In addition, Fitz's accomplice, Chaplain James, received such a strong verbal reprimand from the commandant that such activities launched against the AMEZ ceased for the duration of the war.[17]

In addition to securing the right to select their own denominational affiliation, the New Bern congregation had the pleasure of welcoming Bishop Clinton to the city in May 1864. This was the first time that the people had actually seen a black episcopal officer, and understandably, such an event created a sensation. Bishop Clinton had officially appointed four Zion missionaries in addition to Hood: William Ryle (or Rile), Isaac (or Enoch) Wallace, David Hill, and John Williams. Hill and Williams were northerners commissioned to work in the North Carolina and Virginia areas. Ryle and Wallace,[18] on the other hand, were local ministers, both at least seventy years old. They represented local southern black leaders who had worked for years, even decades, among their racial kin as ordained or nonordained clergy, probably under the authority of the ME-S. Now they were affiliating themselves with independent black denominations. As an indication of the difficulties and risks these pioneering ministers faced, three of these men (Hill, Ryle, and Wallace) soon fell victim to the yellow fever epidemic in the area. While Hood in later years spoke glowingly of all three men and felt the pain of their departure, he especially lamented the death of the approximately thirty-year-old Hill, a young man in "the bloom of youth," brilliant, self-taught, and who had mastered five languages. Hood correctly wondered at the strength that Hill might have brought to the denomination had he survived. Actually, the survivors, Hood and Williams themselves, did not entirely escape the yellow fever affliction that plagued that area of North Carolina. The disease was so terrible that the opponents of Zion expected all of its workers would die.[19] For example, the New Bern church had about four hundred members upon its joining the Zion connection. The smallpox epidemic nearly wiped out the church membership. After three years there, however, Hood had added another four hundred persons to the few remaining original members. Hood's outstanding leadership in religious and political affairs in New Bern merited the dedication of a highway marker in his memory at Broad and George Streets in the city in September 1972.[20]

Bishop Clinton returned to New Bern on December 17, 1864, for the organizing session of the North Carolina Annual Conference in Andrews Chapel. Along with J. J. Clinton, the presiding bishop, there were four elders present: E. H. Hill (not to be confused with David Hill), John Williams, Ellis Lavender, and Hood; six deacons: A. M. Ferribee, David Cray, Joseph Green, Sampson Coffer, W. J. Moore, and H. W. Jones; and one traveling preacher: Amos York. Actually, some of these titles were conveyed as a result of actions taken at the annual conference. Hill and Lavender were ordained to the offices of both deacon and elder on the same date, Christmas morning and afternoon. Cray, Green, Jones, and Moore were elevated to the diaconate on Christmas morning. These twelve members of the first conference, given the relatively short time of their labors in the field, made an astounding report. Ten Zion congregations reported over 1,800 members, nearly 300 probationers, ten local ministers, and twelve exhorters, for a combined membership of 2,197, not counting the five Sunday schools with over 1,200 members. The conference reported about $135 in collections.[21] Sixteen years later, in 1880, the ranks of this band of twelve hearty pioneer leaders of Zion

Methodism had dwindled to four persons still actively serving in the ministry. Five had died; one, John Williams, though living, had left Zion; Clinton suffered health problems; and Green no longer traveled because of his wife's illness.

Hood's Other Organizing Activities

With Clinton farther South doing organizing work, Hood effectively operated in the North Carolina, upper South Carolina, and southern Virginia areas as a de facto presiding elder or bishop during the 1860s, receiving a number of ministers into the church. In some instances, he granted licenses to preach; in other instances, he recognized or accepted the licenses with which black ministers had operated in the Methodist Episcopal Church–South during slavery. Many of these indigenous ministers were later elevated to the offices of deacon and elder based on recommendations at the quarterly and annual conferences. These southern ministers, whether selected by Hood or not, played a huge role in the expansion of Zion and included Ellis Lavender, William Rile (or Ryle), E. H. Hill, Bird Hampton Taylor, Thomas Henderson, William H. Pitts, G. B. Farmer, Daniel C. Blacknell, and Jeffrey Overton. These persons hailed from various portions of North Carolina and were incorporated into the connection as Hood operated in New Bern and other areas of North Carolina.

These ministers in turn went into various areas of the tristate area of Virginia and the Carolinas preaching and organizing churches. Jeffrey Overton deserves special mention. He had retained a preaching license granted to him in 1831, the year of Hood's birth and of Nat Turner's armed rebellion against slavery in Southampton, Virginia. Southern white-controlled churches generally imposed severe restrictions on the religious activities of black congregations and ministers because of this insurrection. In Overton's case Hood was unable to secure a renewal of his license from the ME-S.[22] As these ministers expanded their mission into other areas, they also licensed other ministers. The Reverend E. H. Hill, elder, journeyed to Charlotte, where he established the influential Clinton Chapel AMEZ Church. He later granted a preaching license to Bird Hampton Taylor and placed the church in his care.

Taylor proved to be a hardworking, committed Christian minister. In 1865 he came to the annual conference and so impressed Bishop Clinton that the prelate ordained Taylor deacon and elder at the morning and afternoon sessions, respectively, on the same day. The bishop then commissioned Taylor's return to Charlotte. According to Hood, Taylor literally killed himself preaching. In addition to his work in Charlotte, Taylor went in various directions, ventured fifty miles into South Carolina, and laid the groundwork for twenty new congregations. In Hood's estimation, the energetic minister accomplished more in one year than many other ministers did in ten.[23] Some southern ministers of various denominations coming out of the slavery era would advance to high positions in the church, acquire pastorates of large and influential churches, or even attain the episcopacy. Others, however, would die early in life, some of old age and broken health, and many largely forgotten, too little appreciated, financially destitute, insufficiently cared for by the connection, and the temporal needs of their wives and children largely neglected. They are the unsung heroes who built up Zion and other denominations, associations, and conventions in the South.

As for Hood, he remained in New Bern for three years, until 1867. Though maintaining his main residence in that city, Hood, as we can see in the case of Purvis Chapel, continued his organizing work elsewhere in the state, following the advancing troops of the Union Army.[24] In Edenton the Zionite missionary founded the Kedish A. M. E. Zion Church. The *Historical Sketch of St. Luke AMEZ Church* employs the term "established," but the word "organized" might be more appropriate, given the fact that in many locales of the South, African Americans had already achieved some type of ecclesiastical community and autonomy. In 1865 Hood journeyed into coastal Wilmington, then North Carolina's largest city, and there located thirteen black people who had met regularly since 1861 in the Old Fifth Street Methodist Episcopal Church. Like many other black religious communities during this period, the Wilmingtonians had achieved some degree of autonomy but were still legally and denominationally connected with the ME-S. Also like many other communities, they eagerly entered black-controlled communions once the opportunity presented itself. According to the *Sketch of St. Luke,* this community became a part of the AMEZ denomination on April 8, 1865, exactly one Easter-year following Andrews Chapel Church's union with the Zionites.

Though omitted in the official history of St. Luke AMEZ in Wilmington, a fierce competition ensued in the city between Zion and AME regarding St. Luke.[25] According to the AMEZ historian Bishop William Walls, in his exhaustive history of Zion Methodism, the AME, too, had followed Union forces into Wilmington and had enrolled two major Methodist congregations into its connection: this church, which became St. Luke, and St. Stephens, which remained with the AME. Hood, however, entered the picture and persuaded St. Luke to transfer its allegiance from the AME to the AMEZ. St. Luke's history and Walls's work are not necessarily contradictory. It is possible that the AME interlude was omitted from the official history of St. Luke because it was so short that the original recorders of the history did not deem the AME association as very significant. Indeed, the document is a *sketch,* not a comprehensive treatment of St. Luke's history. In addition, St. Luke has become the premiere AMEZ congregation in Wilmington. Rehearsing the account of its former denominational association with the premier AME congregation in the city, St. Stephens, might not have been deemed particularly useful. At any rate, St. Luke AMEZ Church has occupied a major role in the history of Wilmington. Some of Zion's most renowned and talented ministers have pastored this congregation, including George W. Price and Ellis Lavender, the first two pastors, both of whom eventually left the denomination. In addition, at least four of St. Luke's pastors during its illustrious history eventually ascended to the episcopacy: Thomas H. Lomax (1876), John Bryan Small (1896), L. W. Kyles (1916), and E. L. Madison (1936). Interestingly, a time span of exactly twenty years separates the elevation to the bishopric of each of these individuals.

HOOD MOVES TO FAYETTEVILLE AND CHARLOTTE, 1867–1872

In 1867 Bishop Clinton offered Hood the opportunity to remain in New Bern. Hood's response surprised the prelate. The young Zionite was interested in moving to the central and western portion of the state. Hood's account leaves the impression that he sacrificially left a pastorate with the pay of eight hundred dollars to take one in Fayetteville with a salary of only three hundred dollars. According to his account, Hood argued, and Clinton agreed, that some in the church would grow increasingly resentful should Hood, "the only Northern man down here," continue to retain such a prosperous appointment and that this disenchantment might harm the progress of the entire connection.[26] Hood had the reputation throughout his life of being sacrificial and benevolent; for some years he, like other bishops, did not receive full salary. One wonders, however, if Hood might have already encountered resentment.

In addition, Fayetteville, Hood's choice for an appointment, was closer to Raleigh, a larger city and the state capital, an area less isolated than New Bern. Hood was already emerging as a leader in the political life of the state. In 1865 he had been selected as president of the first black convention of freedpeople meeting in Raleigh. Shortly after moving to Fayetteville, Hood was chosen as a delegate to the State Reconstruction Constitutional Convention. In 1914, two years prior to the General Conference that forcibly removed him from the active episcopacy, then-Bishop Hood wrote about this move to Fayetteville. Hood may have had reasons for portraying his move from New Bern in as unambitious and self-sacrificing a light as possible. Already in 1914 suggestions were abroad that some bishops should be retired. It is possible that, by using this account, Hood sought to buttress his claim that individuals should not be ambitious for powerful positions such as the episcopacy but should willingly labor as the church saw fit. Those who have sacrificed for the cause of Zion should receive reward, not face removal from office. On the other hand, it is possible that any individual who had already attained the presidency of the first black convention of freedpeople would have little trouble getting elected to the constitutional convention should he so desire. Also, the possibility that Hood might have used this anecdote to make a point concerning the retention of episcopal officers and discouraging episcopal ambitions does not negate the possibility that, for whatever purposes, Hood the historian was recalling facts about the sacrificial nature of his move.

Hood offered as a reason for his selection of Fayetteville a concern over the attempt to remove Evans Memorial AMEZ Church from the connection. Evans Chapel, now Evans Metropolitan, was named for Henry Evans, the pioneer of Methodism among both blacks and whites in the city. Evans's preaching abilities were renowned, and he succeeded in enlisting many to the Methodist Episcopal connection prior to his death in 1810. Apparently, both black and white congregations emerged from Evans's work in Fayetteville. W. J. Moore was the first black pastor of the black congregation since Evans. The role of Evans and the biracial beginnings of the Methodist community in the city left most black Methodists there inclined to remain with ME-S. But the irresponsible and rather puzzling actions and mean attitude of the white pastor during the time of Union advancement in the area pushed the congregation into the Zion fold. The white minister could not reconcile himself to the idea of preaching to freed, rather than enslaved, black people. Prather, the minister in question, angrily advised the congregation of African Americans that since the Union forces had brought them freedom, they should seek a minister from that source. The disgruntled white preacher made it very clear that he would never again preach to the group—a promise he kept.[27]

This historical anecdote points out an interesting anomaly regarding race and religion during this period of religious history. In New Bern and Wilmington the black congregants eagerly embraced the opportunity to align themselves with black-controlled denominations. In Fayetteville African Americans affiliated with a black connection by default. In some areas of the South white Christian leaders struggled to maintain control over black churches or at least agreed to separate the races on relatively amicable terms. In Fayetteville the white minister was just as eager to be rid of the pastoral care for black Christians as black Christians in other places were eager for the elimination of white ecclesiastical control over their affairs! This anecdote is of great significance in that it warns us not to permit general trends to lead us into a simplistic, overgeneralized understanding of black and white ecclesiastical relations during this area.

As early as 1866 Hood had traveled to Fayetteville to assist the Reverend W. J. Moore in his efforts to retain Evans Chapel for the Zion connection. When Hood arrived that year, the leader of the Hay Street MEC-S had almost succeeded in restoring Evans Chapel to the white-controlled connection. Simmons, a North Carolina Zion minister and contemporary of Hood, credited Hood with skillfully retaining the congregation for Zion, but he did not elaborate on the specifics. Hood's contribution to the church during his three years of its pastorate was a boon, according to Simmons. An "excellent pastor" with the singing voice of "a Methodist preacher," Hood, by his faithful and evangelical ministry, brought hundreds of converts into the church.[28]

The Fayetteville area became quite influential in the AMEZ. Hood and his family settled in this community and connected with this church. Two of his daughters, Mrs. Gertie Hood Miller, the oldest, and Miss Maude Hood, the youngest, became actively involved in the life of Evans Chapel, remaining faithful members until their deaths. Hood and other family relatives were buried in Cross Creek Cemetery near this church. The original founder, Henry Evans, is entombed inside the church. Like St. Luke in Wilmington, Evans Chapel has a historical connection with the episcopacy. Two years after Hood left this post for one in Charlotte, he ascended to the bishopric. At least three Zionites from Fayetteville have entered the episcopacy: Thomas H. Lomax (1876), Cicero Harris (1888), and John Wesley Smith (1904).[29] Early in the 1990s, the Evans Church remained one of the outstanding churches of Zion Methodism and had been designated a national landmark.

Hood's subsequent move to Charlotte occurred as a result of a rivalry that had developed between two Zion superintendents, John J. Moore and Hood's supporter, Joseph J. Clinton. Bishop Moore now had episcopal jurisdiction over the Fayetteville area, not Clinton, and according to Hood, another minister, the Reverend G. W. Price, maneuvered him out of the Fayetteville station in 1869. Price raised suspicions concerning Hood in the mind of Moore by portraying Hood as a close ally of Clinton's and, therefore, presumably an enemy of Moore's.[30] The appointment in Charlotte carried a salary of only two hundred dollars. So, according to Hood, he had moved successively from eight-hundred- and three-hundred-dollar appointments in New Bern and Fayetteville, respectively, to a two-hundred-dollar position in Charlotte. The young Zion minister, however, did not face desperate financial straits. By the time Hood moved to Charlotte, he had served in the state Reconstruction Convention that rewrote the constitution; he was also engaged as the state Assistant Superintendent of Public Instruction and held a similar position with the federal Freedman's Bureau. From these two positions he gained a respectable salary. Nor did Hood have reason to regret his move as it related to building up the Zion connection. He continued his organizing work in seven counties in and around Charlotte. Toward the end of his life, Hood could point to Charlotte, Fayetteville, and New Bern as the greatest centers of Zionism in North Carolina, knowing that he had played a great role in these developments. After two and a half years in the Charlotte church, the Zion connection, while meeting in the city, elevated Hood as the seventeenth bishop of the African Methodist Episcopal Zion Church. His first episcopal work encompassed the North Carolina–northern South Carolina–southern Virginia area. Ironically, Price's maneuvering Hood to the Charlotte area proved favorable in terms of Hood's ecclesiastical accomplishments and career.

An Analysis of Hood's Organizing Activities

As we look back at Hood's organizing activities in North Carolina, South Carolina, and Virginia, we can make a number of crucial observations concerning the expansion of northern black and white denominations into the South during the Civil War era. In his struggle for Andrews Chapel, Hood won two important battles, one with the AME and the other with the ME. The outcome of these contests adumbrated later Zionite developments in North Carolina and offers lessons for black church expansion in the Civil and post–Civil War eras. First, Hood defeated the efforts of his unnamed rivals from the AME. Whereas Georgia became a stronghold for the Bethelites, North Carolina became a stronghold and even headquarters for the Zionites, largely because of Hood's untiring organizing activities.

Second, Hood triumphed over Round, the representative of the mainly white ME Church. This victory exemplified the reality that would prevail in North

Carolina and throughout the South during the Civil War and immediate post-war years: the predominantly white-controlled ME's successes among African Americans would trail that of the black Methodists, the AME, and the AMEZ. One could also draw this point from Zion's successful struggle with the ME-S over Evans Chapel. In addition, Hood's victory over the ME regarding Andrews Chapel was a significant *legal* precedent for the black churches of the South. No denomination to which southern black church people were not already members could enter the field and forcibly incorporate them into its fold. Rather, the local people had the right to make their own choice. This fact proved a boon for southern black Christians. It gave them the opportunity for ecclesiastical negotiation. Blacks, having suffered under the brutality and the proscriptions of a slave society, generally chose affiliation with independent African American denominations and associations with whom they had stronger affinity. These southern, and for the most part newly freed, people were insisting on both physical and ecclesiastical freedom from white domination and supervision.

Third, the victory of Zion Methodism within the first few months of Hood's presence in the South and under difficult conditions points to the dramatic growth in memberships that characterized northern black Methodist bodies as they expanded into this territory. As late as 1860 the AMEZ was more or less confined to the northeastern states, with fewer than five thousand members. Of course there had been an increase in membership rolls since 1860. But Hood and those working with him, in about three or four months during 1864, had brought three thousand new members into the connection, for a 60 percent increase over the 1860 membership of a denomination that traced its origins back over sixty years. At the General Conference of 1864 the North Carolina area mission fields reported a membership that equaled one-fourth of the overall connection. The membership statistics were no less dramatic and astounding for the AMEs and the black Baptist associations.

Fourth, this Zion missionary enterprise reflects the fact that the overwhelming majority of these early Zion affiliates in the South came from existing churches and Christian communities. In some ways we might more accurately speak of these northern workers as "denominational organizers" rather than "missionaries" in the strictest sense of the word. These northern workers in the southern field were to a great extent incorporating into their connections congregations and individuals already committed to the Christian faith, whatever prior assumptions about the purity of their religion might have been held by their northern counterparts. Fifth, we have also observed that much of the credit for the success for enrolling people into the Zion connection, whether as new Christians or as church members exchanging denominational affiliation, belonged to the local, indigenous preachers, many of them former slaves. Sixth and finally, the missionary and organizing work in North Carolina became the center for much of Zion's expansion in the South. Four conferences emerged from the North Carolina Annual Conference that organized in New Bern in December 1864: the Virginia Conference (1866), the South Carolina and Georgia conferences (1867), and the Tennessee Conference (1872). These four conferences in turn produced additional conferences so that by 1914 fourteen conferences had emerged, generating nearly one-half the general assessments of the entire AMEZ denomination.[31] For purposes of our study it is worth noting that James W. Hood played a major, if not the greatest, role in organizing—either directly by himself or indirectly by supporting and commissioning others—this vital section of AMEZ expansion.

CONCLUSION

Hood had a profound impact on, and played a key role in, the development of black independent Christianity in general and the AMEZ connection in particular in the South following the Civil War. He and Bishop J. J. Clinton led the forces that helped transform the Zion Church from a small, mainly regional organization of fewer than five thousand members to a major national religious body during the 1860–1920 period. Both Hood and his connection are emblematic of the advancement, challenges, opportunities, and rapid growth of the major black Baptist and Methodist, northern-based religious bodies as they followed the Union's occupation of the South during the Civil War and Reconstruction periods. Clearly Hood and independent black Christianity sought the salvation and spiritual strengthening of African Americans. This desire for spiritual uplift was intimately connected with the effort to uplift temporally, as subsequent chapters demonstrate. The success of Hood's missionizing and organizing efforts alone during the 1864–1872 period more than justify his classification as a major religious leader. The next chapter examines his political leadership during these years.

Chapter Three

HOOD'S POLITICAL AND EDUCATIONAL LEADERSHIP IN THE SOUTH, 1864–1872

Bishop James W. Hood, of the African Methodist Episcopal Zion Church, in his day one of the most influential men of color in the United States, found himself in the political world. . . . His very going to North Carolina, . . . , had a political setting."
—Carter G. Woodson, *History of the Negro Church*

Previous chapters have focused on Hood's leadership in building up the Zion church, but his legacy of leadership extended to the political realm, particularly as it related to the Zion leader's fierce dedication to securing and maintaining justice and equity for African Americans. This chapter demonstrates Hood's crucial political leadership in North Carolina during the Civil War and Reconstruction periods. Examining Hood's political leadership, like studying his religious prominence, is a prism through which we might observe the entire leadership of the independent black church, Methodist and non-Methodist, North and South, during these years. Hood's leadership, in other words, is representative of the independent black church's expansion into the political sphere of the South. Many of these religious leaders in the South, whether northern- or southern-born, did not recommend political involvement of the "radical" character of the Reverend (and eventually Bishop) Henry McNeal Turner of the AME Church or the black educator, race leader, and philosopher W. E. B. Du Bois. Nor for that matter did they imitate the obsequiousness of a Booker T. Washington, the leader of Tuskegee Institute. These black Christians, however, were predominantly and clearly committed to improving the temporal as well as the spiritual state of African Americans and hoped that the results of the Civil War would be full equality, economic advancement, and political freedom for all Americans, including blacks. By carefully, comprehensively, and meticulously surveying Hood's political leadership, one encounters one of the most consistent and indefatigable fighters for African American social and political freedom, whose story in this regard has hitherto remained basically untold beyond the walls of Zion and even within the AMEZ often appears in abbreviated fashion. James W. Hood was born, reared, and matured in a religious, cultural, and racial climate that predisposed him to a lifelong commitment to seek racial justice and freedom. Hood's writings, personal reminiscences, biographical sketches, and the remarks of reliable and influential black and white contemporaries of Hood reveal a young man reared in an atmosphere where family members and church people displayed strong abolitionist sentiments and actions and held freedom dear. As indicated in the previous chapter, the Zion minister himself delivered an abolitionist speech predicting the end of slavery when he was only fifteen years old.[1] In addition, Hood, from his late teen years to the time of his missionary journey south, refused to bow to the practices of racial discrimination in public transportation in the North. Many times between 1843 and 1863 Hood attempted (sometimes successfully) to integrate railroad cars and public transportation in northern cities. During one evening in 1857 Hood so vigorously challenged segregation that he required streetcar workers to remove him five times.[2]

This persistent fight against discrimination continued with Hood's relocation to the South. As a Methodist minister and especially as a Methodist missionary and church organizer covering southern Virginia, North Carolina, and northern South Carolina, Hood spent much of his life traveling, sometimes fifteen thousand miles annually. Like other southern blacks, Hood experienced efforts to impose segregation on public conveyances in the South, much like the attempts he had encountered in the prewar northern states. By his steadfast refusal to accept such treatment, he set a standard for resistance to racial injustice, placing his personal safety on the line, while living up to his rhetorical commitments and ideas. For example, on one of his many journeys on the Cape Fear River in eastern North Carolina in 1868 he successfully demanded the right to travel in the cabin aboard one of the steamers. The agents reminded him that only the presence of the federal military afforded him the opportunity to enjoy such service and that it may be wise to abstain from using the privilege, since the eventual removal of the military presence might place him at a disadvantage in the future. Characteristically, Hood responded that he would exercise the right as long as possible and trust God beyond that.[3] An examination of his role in the black state convention of 1865, the Reconstruction state convention of 1868, and other postconvention endeavors illustrates Hood's powerful impact on the southern political landscape during these years.

The Black or Freedmen's State Convention, 1865

Hood's involvement in political affairs transcended his own personal refusal to suffer racial indignity or his wish to set an example of resistance for others. In North Carolina, the Zion minister played a key role in the quest for the political advancement of his racial siblings. Like many free and newly freed blacks in the South, North Carolinians in the middle to late 1860s moved aggressively to voice their concerns that they, wholly and with equity, be included within the body politic of their state by holding freedpeople's state conventions to lay out those claims. The group of blacks meeting in Raleigh in October 1865 represented the first such meeting of free blacks in the state of North Carolina and probably in the entire former Confederacy. Understandably, ministers, who often had experience in the exercise of leadership skills, such as public speaking and literacy, figured prominently among those deemed qualified to serve in political leadership roles on behalf of fellow blacks previously marginalized and enslaved. These meetings of freed black people immediately following the Civil War occurred in various cities across the Old South, and many of the participants, such as Hood, emerged as leaders in the later Reconstruction era.[4]

In North Carolina this first assembly of 115 southern black people, mostly former slaves, convened a four-day meeting on September 29, 1865, on a back street of Raleigh in a wooden AME church structure filled to its 400-seat capacity in the sanctuary and gallery. Abraham H. Galloway, a mulatto and escaped slave, convened the meeting, but the assembly elected Hood as its permanent chairperson.[5] Interestingly, Hood emerged the victor in a first ballot vote involving three other candidates for the presidency of the assembled convention. This demonstrates that already the northeastern-born minister had attained a significant degree of respect within the state's African American population. In later years Hood, bemoaning the fact that many Zion ministers promoted themselves for various secular and religious offices, insisted that both his election as a delegate to this convention and then as its chair were totally unsolicited and unexpected on his part.[6] Nonetheless, some delegates took offense at the election of a native northerner to preside over a session composed principally of those who had been held in southern bondage. This fact amply demonstrates that while southerners appreciated the assistance of their northern siblings, they were not passive about determining their own political, economic, and ecclesiastical future. Hood defended himself by stating that North Carolina was his newly adopted home state. He would have resigned, but the majority of the assembly refused to permit him to step down.[7]

Hood's inaugural address, like the gathering itself, was politically moderate in tone, certainly if judged by the standards of racial protest of the last quarter of the twentieth century. In the historical circumstances of the times, however, it proved to be extremely controversial, causing quite a stir in the white press of the time.[8] According to Woodson, "On this occasion he advocated equal rights for the Negro so fearlessly that he was warned by the people around that his life would be in danger, if he did not desist therefrom."[9] For the first time in the history of the state, a black leader was publicly, boldly, and clearly expressing the simple position that blacks demanded treatment as equal persons before the law, a radical view for many whites at the time. Hood, like many antislavery and pro-black speakers prior to him, white and black, spoke of the principle of natural rights reflected in the Declaration of Independence. According to Hood, this cherished document stipulated that God or the Creator accorded every person, black as well as white, fundamental human rights. Whereas many white contemporaries evidently assumed that legal, physical freedom and the abolition of chattel slavery per se would completely fulfill the government's debt to blacks, Hood, in accordance with the consensus of the black community and many white progressives, spoke for the assembled group when he demanded that black Americans be guaranteed "a right to the jury-box, cartridge box, and ballot box" or full citizenship. This remark occasioned the rejoinder by some of the most established newspapers in the state "that he would get all these in one box," presumably the "coffin box."[10]

As convention president, Hood helped to set the moderate tone of the convention regarding cooperation between the races and appealing to the consciences of whites, an approach that would characterize Hood's philosophy throughout his life. Yet even judged by more "radical" standards, this tone did not convey an acceptance of white supremacy. In addition to receiving Hood's address calling for full citizenship rights for blacks, the assembly passed a resolution honoring

John Brown, the white man who plotted and attempted to execute a violent overthrow of the system of slavery prior to the Civil War, and also resolved appreciation for Radical Republicans, such as Charles Sumner and Thaddeus Stevens,
who had struggled aggressively in the U.S. Congress to extend citizenship rights
to African Americans. Even the symbolic nature of such a resolution would
hardly endear Hood or the convention to those determined to keep blacks sub-
servient. The fact that these blacks were not abdicating their rights to full citizenship is also demonstrated by the fact that about a year later a second
convention was held. It was apparent that the olive branch approach of a year
earlier had not worked, and thus this group much more aggressively and pointedly called for the end to racial violence perpetrated upon blacks and full inclusion within the body politic. At least three of the black delegates present at the
first convention were able to take their concerns to the second North Carolina
State Constitutional Convention in 1868, where they served as delegates there
also.[11]

The Reconstruction State Convention, 1867–1868

Hood's political contributions to racial progress were not limited to participation in the state black convention. The U.S. Congress set aside the more conservative Reconstruction approach of President Andrew Johnson, an approach
that focused its sympathy on the white South, and adopted "Radical Reconstruction," which set about the task of making African Americans not simply free
of chattel slavery but truly equal citizens. There were undoubtedly political advantages for the Republican-dominated Congress in enfranchising Republican
blacks and disfranchising Democratic former secessionists. But many in Congress sincerely believed that the Union victory over the Confederacy would ring
hollow should not blacks be accorded full citizenship rights. Thus, across the
South, state conventions were held to bring the former Confederate states into
accord with Congressional Reconstruction.

The Zion leader, as with the Freedpeople's State Convention two years earlier, made his presence felt in a profound manner at the 1867–1868 North Carolina Reconstruction State Convention. According to Du Bois, "The Rev. James
Walker Hood of Pennsylvania was the outstanding Negro delegate."[12] The work
of this assembly not only laid a foundation for black equality before the law, but
it also contained provisions that benefited nonblack citizens as well, such as those
promoting homestead laws, public education, and women's rights. According to

renowned historian Carter G. Woodson, Hood played such a pivotal role in framing the new state constitution, particularly with regard to education and homesteads, that the document bore the name "Hood Constitution" prior to its amendment by conservative forces in 1875.[13]

Of the 120 delegates to the convention, only 13 were black, and their power was offset by the presence of 13 "Conservatives." Some scholars suggest that as many as 15 of the delegates were African Americans. Even so, the black presence constituted a distinct minority of the delegates.[14] There were 94 white Republicans. Like James Hood, who represented Cumberland County, the twelve other African Americans represented counties in the eastern portion of the state, where the greatest numbers of blacks were concentrated. As far as I can determine, Hood was the only minister in the group of black delegates. He had in common with the others, however, that he would hold political office in the post-convention North Carolina. The one office that is most commonly cited is that of assistant superintendent of education, an office that appears to have had special authority relative to black children. But Hood's Reconstruction offices also include positions as magistrate, assistant superintendent of education for the Freedmen's Bureau, and at one time deputy collector for the Internal Revenue Service. Before the Democrats and the reactionary white conservatives regained complete control of the state, at least eleven of the other black delegates also enjoyed the spotlights in the political arena, with some serving in both houses of the state legislature, at least one in the U.S. House of Representatives, and one as a delegate to the 1875 state constitutional convention.[15] Two black delegates, James J. Harris and Abraham Galloway, had been active participants along with Hood at the Freedmen's or Black Convention held in Raleigh in 1865.[16]

The black delegates, including Hood, were quite active in the state convention. Sometimes they would unanimously agree on a given issue; other times, they split their votes. The delegates of color served on thirteen different committees of the convention. Hood in particular served on two committees: those dealing with education and homesteads. Hood stood out on a number of issues coming before the convention. He opposed "stay-laws" on the ground that they served the interests of the wealthy and harmed the poor; but given the mixed support of his black colleagues, Hood's position apparently was not a clearly established "black" stance. Hood took a keen interest in matters relating to homesteads, supporting efforts that prevented homesteads from being attached because of debt incurred before or after the convention.[17]

With the support of Hood and other African American delegates, the state convention's impact in the area of education was great. The body approved a system of education for the state that included free public education supported by public taxation; a provision that required local governments to provide primary schools that meet at least one-third of the year; made the University of North Carolina a part of the public education system and extended free education to those attending; established a state board of education composed of the highest officers of the state, including the governor, lieutenant governor, and auditor, to oversee the state educational program; and mandated that every youth between six and eighteen years of age receive at least sixteen months of education.[18] Provisions such as the above vastly extended public education in North Carolina, benefiting both whites and blacks.

Understandably, the issue of suffrage and the qualifications for it elicited a great deal of attention at the convention. Predictably, the black delegates were in favor of a wide extension of the vote to all citizens regardless of property background. Significantly, some free blacks in North Carolina had enjoyed the right to vote until the early to middle 1830s, when the white government—anxious over rebellions such as the one led by Nat Turner in 1831 in nearby Virginia, the publication of David Walker's *Appeal,* and the growing strength of the abolitionist movement—eliminated black voters from the rolls. Now there was the opportunity to place free black as well as formerly enslaved voters on the rolls.[19] Consistent with the thinking of the overwhelming majority of American blacks, Hood and his colleagues in the convention had no doubts about the absolute necessity of suffrage as a guarantee of freedom and racial progress, and they supported such measures vigorously. On the other hand, conservative convention leaders questioned why African American males should possess the right to vote when white women and children did not. Hood registered extreme opposition to these conservative sentiments. First, he made it clear that the real issue was not granting black males a new right but preventing the elimination of a right already recognized by the federal government. Second, it was common knowledge, said Hood, that males voted as representatives and protectors of the rights of women and female relatives, such as mothers, daughters, and wives. Denying the franchise to or withdrawing it from African American males eliminated representation and protection of a whole race of people. In later decades Hood and other Zion leaders would support the extension of suffrage to women, but in the immediate postwar period, Hood's views reflected the sentiments of most men and women of both races regarding the purpose of suffrage restricted to males.[20]

Hood and all other black delegates, except one, favored a section of the suffrage provision that required that anyone voting had to affirm by oath loyalty to the laws and the Constitution of the United States, a provision obviously aimed at ex-Confederates. Nonetheless, most black delegates, including Hood, opposed an attempt to eliminate ex-Confederates from the state franchise. Had eleven blacks changed their votes, the measure disfranchising ex-Confederates would have passed, a point that Hood would bring up near the end of the century when conservative forces succeeded in disfranchising the great majority of black voters. Black delegates also supported measures outlawing physical or economic harassment of voters, expressed personal opposition to "race-mixing" or interracial romantic alignments, supported the de facto, though not constitutionally mandated, separation of public schools for whites and blacks.[21] However one might explain these positions, it seems that interracial dating and marriage were not popular issues with African American leaders of this time, especially in the South, and that these leaders placed a greater premium on black access to education than on *integrated* education.

Furthermore, Hood, while opposing the introduction of racial segregation language into law, believed that whites and blacks would voluntarily elect to associate with their respective races. It was perfectly fine with Hood, even preferable, that blacks have schools and teachers of their own race. Obviously, said Hood, notwithstanding the noble sacrifices and the social ostracism suffered by white northern women for the cause of educating blacks, only black teachers generally could truly comprehend the needs of African American children and respond to them most appropriately. A law to segregate schools might work to exclude education for black children. By guaranteeing access to free, public education for blacks, the constitution would force local governments to provide schools for blacks to prevent racial integration. Thus, the separation of the races would exist without mandating segregation and guarantee schools for African Americans.[22]

During the state constitutional convention the black delegates faced opposition from within and without the convention. Outside the walls of the assembly, white newspapers treated the convention and its black delegates very contemptuously, considering the group a convention in name only.[23] In addition, the black delegates had to contend with chauvinistic and derogatory attacks from within the chamber, especially from the two ringleaders of the hard-core faction of thirteen conservative delegates, Plato Durham and John W. Graham. Time and again these two former officers of the Confederacy attempted to insert race- and class-restrictive provisions into the new Constitution and its Preamble. Furthermore, certain racists were not above outright, unambiguous racial insults.[24]

Of course black delegates eagerly and effectively defended themselves and their causes, sometimes going on the offensive by successfully ridiculing their racist opponents. For example, at one point, when a young white delegate declared that the white race had always been superior to other races, Hood replied with biting sarcasm, polite condescension, and humor, revealing a love for debate—all of which characterized his career as a community and religious leader. Hood reminded the young upstart that his British ancestors were once Roman slaves. Whereas some contemporary whites contended that the ignorance of blacks fitted them to be only slaves, Julius Caesar received warning that the British were too ignorant for even slavery, that the Britons could not even master music lessons. "Now I have never heard it said of colored people that they were too ignorant to sing . . ."[25] When conservative leaders foolishly asserted that African peoples had never created any worthy civilization, Hood decimated them with his knowledge of ancient history. Indeed, the Zionite insisted that the African race stood at the front ranks of the earliest civilizations of the world. Using the genealogical tables of the Bible, the Zion minister identified Ham as the ancestor of blacks, pointing out that the whole line of Ham was not cursed by Noah and even the Canaanites who were cursed by Noah proceeded to establish great civilizations (a fact that hardly limited them to the roles of slaves), and traced the origins of major, ancient civilizations, such as Egypt, Ethiopia, and Babylon, to Hamitic ancestry.[26]

Any doubt regarding Hood's uncompromising boldness on issues of racial equity and justice would quickly dissipate in the mind of anyone reading Hood's classic speech on suffrage for African Americans. The bluntness with which the young Zion minister defended the interests of African Americans combined with the fierceness of his attack on racism, expressed within and outside the convention, makes comprehensible the threats against his life by some of those committed to white supremacy. He vigorously defended black suffrage, as we have seen, as a necessary means to protect African Americans against the designs of those, who if they had their way, Hood claimed, would reduce the former slaves to a harsher bondage than they had already experienced. Of course the conservatives recoil at the idea of blacks voting. They remember well the inhumane and brutal manner in which they had inflicted chattel bondage on men, women, and children and worry about the possibility of black vengeance. Yet these white supremacists need not have anxiety about African Americans using political power to crush their former oppressors, stated Hood. Presaging an argument that the educator and race leader Booker T. Washington would use nearly thirty years later, Hood stated that when white males were away fighting the Civil War, the enslaved, though conscious of their oppressed state and their power to execute vengeance on defenseless women and children left behind, elected not to do so. Aware that his attacks on conservatives were harsh, Hood nevertheless stood his ground. "If my language seems severe the gentleman must remember that I speak in fetters of their own forging." Slavery had wreaked its horrible pain even on free blacks, since "colorophobia has pierced and rankled in my own soul."[27]

For the first time in the lives of many of the former Confederates and former slaveholders, they were encountering blacks on basically equal terms in situations where they had equal, if not superior, training, whether formal or self-taught. The keen intellect and rhetorical skill of men and women like Hood persuaded some whites to rethink their biased assessments of the capabilities of blacks. And for those who remained unalterably opposed to any semblance of equal treatment of blacks, encounters with intelligent, outspoken black people represented one of their worst nightmares.

HOOD'S POST-CONVENTION RECONSTRUCTION ACTIVITIES, 1868–1872

Like many black leaders of the time, Hood placed a great deal of emphasis on the power of formal education to uplift the race. After campaigning for the ratification of the new state constitution, he served briefly "as a magistrate under the provisional" state government, and some months as a deputy collector of the Internal Revenue Service. Hood then assumed the appointed position of state assistant superintendent of education with the specific responsibility for the establishment of schools for black children.[28] According to Hood, his service on the education committee of the state constitutional convention had brought him to the attention of persons connected with the State Board of Education, and these persons secured his appointment. Later General O. O. Howard appointed him to a similar position, assistant superintendent of education, in the Freedman's Bureau. Thus, Hood pursued the education of his race under three auspices: the federal government, the state government, and the African Methodist Episcopal Zion Church. It appears that the greater bulk of his salary was derived from the state government, $1,500 per year. From the Freedman's Bureau he received travel expenses of four dollars a day. During the high point of his tenure in office, he had supervised the placement of about forty-nine thousand black children in public schools. Hood was on the verge of establishing a state university in 1870, but the Democrats, having regained control of the state legislature, voted him from office. By that time, however, Hood had so established public education in the state, and more specifically among his people, that even the conservatives were not able to undo completely his work.[29] In addition to these contributions, Hood also "established for Negroes a department for the deaf, dumb, and blind and had about sixty inmates under care and instruction at the expense of the State."[30] Hood also played a great supporting role in the establishment of what is now Fayetteville State University, a public school in the University of North Carolina system, and Livingstone College, an educational institution in Salisbury, supported by the Zion Church.

Hood's achievements in the area of public education during the 1868–1870 period are even more remarkable given the fact that he did not surrender his pastoral obligations. While stationed in Raleigh, he continued to minister to the strong congregation he had built up in Charlotte, about 175 miles away. Weekends were particularly taxing to the young Methodist minister, who remained constantly on the go, at times preaching up to three sermons a day. The Zion minister exerted a great deal of drive, energy, and dedication as he strove to balance his church responsibilities with civil obligations of an office holder. In addition, Hood paid considerable respect to the principle of "separation of church and state" and ecumenism, since on some of his travels he would attend both Baptist and Methodist congregations, demonstrating that he was not using his secular office to favor Methodism.[31] The state superintendent of education extended generous praise for Hood's devoted and effective work.[32]

Hood's ejection from office in 1870 by a Democratic state legislature did not extirpate his involvement in political matters. By 1872 Reconstruction in North Carolina had come to a conclusion, but Hood had attained a prominence in the political field that exceeded that of all but few black people, clergy or lay, in North Carolina. Blacks constituted only about one-third of the population in the state and came nowhere near controlling the Republican party. Thus, the Methodist minister's election as temporary chair of the Republican State Convention in 1872 was a significant honor, especially for a person of color during this era. It was this body that produced the slate of nominees for state government. Also, the state convention determined the at-large delegates to the 1872 Republican National Convention, a body that nominated President Ulysses S. Grant for his second presidential term. Hood was also selected as one of those at-large delegates.[33] Based on Simmons's biographical account of Hood, it appears that Zion minister may have been rather modest about his political opportunities in 1872. For example, Hood declined to run for North Carolina secretary of state in 1872. Instead, he selected, presumably, a white candidate who ran successfully and later fulfilled a promise of appointing a black person as chief clerk. There are a number of contemporary accounts that speak of the high favor in which Hood was held not only by blacks but also by a significant portion of the white community. The stories provided by Simmons confirm those accounts.[34]

Perhaps the voluntary withdrawal of Hood from public political life compared with the forced removal of the AME's Henry M. Turner from the Georgia legislature helps to explain Hood's more moderate stance on racial matters. Of course one must also admit that Turner's fiery temperament differed from Hood's disposition. Furthermore, North Carolina during this era was much more racially tolerant than Turner's Deep South state of Georgia.

HOOD AND THE DANGERS AND REWARDS OF POLITICAL LEADERSHIP, 1864–1872

It would be a mistake to assume that during the 1864–1872 years North Carolina, or any state, was an oasis of complete and unchallenged freedom, opportunity, and equity for blacks, or that Hood did not face dangers. Indeed, the Zionite's political activities in North Carolina, especially during this period, carried with them some grave perils for the future bishop. It has been observed from earlier comments that some white supremacists threatened or hinted at physical danger or even death for blacks who dared to assert that African Americans should enjoy equal political rights with whites. R. H. Simmons, an AMEZ minister and presiding elder in North Carolina, spoke at the twenty-fifth anniversary celebration of Hood's episcopacy in 1897. Simmons's comments have special interest because there were times when he and Hood differed sharply over church matters, indicating that Simmons was not a "knee-jerk," uncritical supporter of Hood. In his speech, Simmons pointed out how Hood's political activities in and around Fayetteville during the Civil War and immediate postwar periods occasioned stiff opposition from racist forces in the form of slander and threats directed at the young minister. The Ku Klux Klan in particular made serious threats "and they would have killed him outright had it not been for the protecting care of Almighty God."[35] Simmons made it clear, however, that the divine protection was not only miraculous but involved determination and concern on the part of blacks who armed themselves to protect the young pastor. "I well remember those fearful days and nights of gloom and fear; how a large number of young men armed themselves with a few old shot guns and pistols, and many pocket knives, and brick bats and sticks, and guarded him night after night for a long time."[36] Simmons delivered this speech in 1897, during a time when lynch-

ing was rampant in many parts of the South. While some in the Zion connection
in the 1890s called for blacks to respond by arming themselves for self-defense,
others, like Hood, disagreed, believing that such efforts would lead to increased
racial violence. Thus, Simmons may have felt the need to emphasize that Hood
did not request this type of armed protection, that those who had taken such a
step did it of their own accord. At any rate, Hood remained calm and level-
headed in the face of the turmoil and life-threatening circumstances confronting
him, according to Simmons.[37]

As discussed in a previous chapter, Hood was elevated to the episcopacy of the
African Methodist Episcopal Zion Church in 1872.[38] In 1868 the Third Episcopal District of the Zion Church was formed, comprising Virginia, North Carolina, and South Carolina, the area in which Hood and other missionaries of Zion
were working. It was this district to which he was initially assigned in 1872 and
in which he maintained close contact one way or another for the rest of his life.[39]
Just as Hood had not actively sought political office, he claimed that he also did
not consciously seek the episcopacy. As far as he was concerned, he was selected
because of the earnest, faithful discharging of his duty as a Christian pastor, which
drew the attention of the appropriate persons. Notwithstanding this very prob-
able explanation, Hood's role as an active spokesperson for the rights of African
Americans and the respect that he had gained across racial and denominational
lines undoubtedly contributed to his visibility. Such an outstanding and tireless
fighter for Zion and the race would prove an immeasurable boon to a denomination in fierce competition with other black groups and the predominantly white
Methodist Episcopal Church for the allegiance of southern blacks inclined toward Methodism. Indeed, a church with strong bishops was in an advantageous
position in the eyes of many black Christians. His prestige and prominence
brought to a small northeastern-based, but rapidly growing and heavily southern, church a distinction that could not be easily overlooked within or without
the denomination.

Hood's election to episcopal office signaled the end of his active participation
in state politics, as far as office-holding was concerned. As Hood himself noted,
his attendance at the Republican National Convention in 1872 was the last such
attendance. "When I was set apart to the episcopal office, the senior Bishop[,] J.
J. Clinton[,] advised me that it would not be well for me to take a further active
part in politics."[40] Perhaps this advice reflected the practical wisdom that the hec-
tic schedule and travels of an episcopal leader prohibited political office holding.
In addition, Hood, as previously mentioned, considered his primary duty the

preaching of the gospel and the establishment and nurture of churches; he did not consider work for the state board of education a political appointment but more like community service. I have found nothing in my research on the life of Hood suggesting that he did not fully and unreservedly agree with Clinton's suggestion that bishops should abstain from holding political offices.

It would be a mistake to conclude that Hood completely withdrew from all political activity. Hood permitted his voice to be heard publicly on a number of significant issues facing black individuals or community when he registered complaints in 1880 regarding the insufficient number of blacks appointed to federal posts in North Carolina;[41] opposed the Republican state leader John J. Mott's effort in 1881 to position the party against the prohibition movement but rather favored the enactment of a state prohibition law;[42] recommended various individuals for governmental positions, such as E. E. Smith as minister to Liberia in 1888;[43] and spoke out vigorously against emigration schemes that would have removed blacks from the United States.[44] In addition, Hood's papers contain a number of items that reveal Hood's political interaction with U.S. presidents, governors, and other important leaders.[45]

CONCLUSION

Early on, Hood established himself as a political leader in North Carolina during the Civil War and post–Civil War eras, playing a crucial role that has been largely forgotten or ignored by more recent critical scholarship. Undoubtedly, Hood and many other ministers took such leadership roles because they were among the few qualified persons in the black community at the time. Furthermore, Hood, rightly or wrongly, saw his role more as one of ministry than as strictly political. But Hood's involvement in the Freedmen's State Convention in 1865, his participation in the State Reconstruction Convention in 1867–1868, and his office holding and other political activities after ratification of the state convention all point to the major role that the young Zionite played in the political arena of North Carolina. While his assumption of the episcopacy in 1872 marked his withdrawal from active office holding, Hood would remain involved in matters relating to the public good and the temporal progress of African Americans. Hood, in sum, exemplified those African American denomination leaders and workers who saw their mission as advancing the righteousness of God and justice for African Americans.

PART III

A STAR IN ZION

Hood's Early Years as Episcopal Leader, 1872–1885

Chapter   Four

HOOD'S EARLY EPISCOPAL LEADERSHIP, PART I

Ascending to the Bishopric and the Early Years, 1868–1880

This is a true saying, If a man desire the office of a bishop, he desireth a good work.

—1 Timothy 3:1, Holy Bible, King James Version

If Hood's entire career had been limited to his successes in pastoring, missionizing, and organizing churches, his contributions would have been very noteworthy. But the young Zionite's earlier career indicated that Hood, whether he wanted it or not, was headed for an even more pivotal role in religious leadership. In 1872 the Zion connection elevated him to the episcopacy, where he would remain in active service for the next forty-four years, nearly half a century and half of his life. Furthermore, half of his active episcopacy consisted of service as the senior bishop of the connection, that is, as the one with greatest seniority on the bench. As with the AME, CME, and the two mainly white ME churches during those times, seniority brought with it no greater legal authority, but it usually conveyed to the holder a greater level of influence, prestige, and often affection. Thus, Hood's extended service as bishop, and later as senior bishop of one of the major American and African American denominations, meant that he exerted a profound influence on Zion and American religion.

This chapter examines Hood's ecclesiastical involvement from 1868 (when it became clear that he was under consideration in some quarters for election to the episcopacy) to 1880 (the end of Hood's second quadrennium as bishop). More specifically, these pages focus on his rise to the episcopacy during the 1868–1872 period, his first missionary sojourn as bishop during the 1872–1876 years, and the 1876 General Conference and election of T. H. Lomax as bishop. Examining these topics underscores Hood's major leadership role in the development of black institutional Christianity during this era by providing an understanding of Hood as an episcopal candidate, the ecclesiastical climate in which he was chosen, the episcopal style of the new bishop, and his active role in ecclesiastical politics from the early years of his episcopacy. Furthermore, Hood's rise to the episcopacy reflects the growing influence of southern black Christians in the once northern-based black churches, Methodist and Baptist. Southern religious people, laity and clergy, native born southerners and northern transplants, were demanding a greater share in the decision making apparatus of the African American churches.

HOOD'S RISE TO THE EPISCOPACY, 1868–1872

The year 1872 was a momentous one for the young missionary leader: his eighty-year-old father, Levi Hood, died; he abandoned political office holding and some overt political activities in North Carolina; and at the age of forty, he became a bishop in the AMEZ Church.[1] What were the events leading up to Hood's ascendancy to the episcopacy? Throughout his career Hood emphasized, often in the context of debates, that both his political and ecclesiastical positions, including the bishopric, were attained through the efforts of others on his behalf, and not at all through self-promotion. There is, of course, much truth in this statement regarding Hood's selection for the episcopacy. By all accounts he had done magnificent missionary and pastoral work in spreading Zion Methodism in North Carolina and portions of South Carolina and Virginia. No doubt his political activities as a leader in the black state convention in 1865, his participation in the 1867–1868 State Reconstruction Convention, and his role in the state department of education gave him a prominence that spoke well of his abilities and his influence, qualities that the Zion denomination would have valued in an episcopal leader as they struggled to establish the group in an atmosphere of vigorous competition with the AMEs and other Methodist groups.

According to Hood, the subject of his election as bishop did not arise more than twice between the 1868 and the 1872 general conferences. The first time was during the annual conference of 1868–1869 under Bishop Moore, and the second took place at the 1870 and 1871 annual conferences headed by Bishop Brooks.[2] According to Hood, the AMEZ was involved in a serious struggle to hold on to its churches in the eastern portion of the state, where two disgruntled former ministers of the Zion church—Ellis Lavender, whom Hood appeared to admire deeply, and G. W. Price, for whom Hood held little regard—were working actively to siphon off members to other churches.

One point of tension in the eastern section centered on the leadership style of Bishop John Delaware Brooks (1803–1874). Around 1870 Brooks "offended" Ellis Lavender, a highly regarded local, southern Zion minister. Lavender left the Zion denomination and cast his allegiance with the newly organized and southern-based Colored (later Christian) Methodist Episcopal Church (CME), which was organized with about eighty thousand former members of the Methodist Episcopal Church, South in 1870.[3] Hood provides little detail regarding the specific manner in which Bishop Brooks offended Lavender. Apparently, Brooks's personality and style of supervision left something to be desired. The modern historian, the late Zion bishop Walls, provides us with a much clearer portrait of Brooks, who became bishop in 1864, and the difficulties surrounding his episcopacy.[4] Walls describes him as a bishop of unusual seriousness. A solid minister of the gospel with an irreproachable character, Brooks was also fiercely dedicated to the rules and regulations of Methodism. He was long on discipline but short on offering patience and constructive help to those under his charge.[5]

The Zion Church retired Brooks as active bishop in 1872; that is, they did not reelect him as bishop. (The AMEZ did not begin electing bishops for life until 1880.) In 1874 Brooks served as an associate of Bishop Moore's at the Philadelphia and Baltimore Conference. Though he was retired as active bishop, Brooks was still regarded as a bishop for life and, according to the policies of Zion Methodism, could be employed when his services were needed. Later he was elected manager of the Book Concern, the publishing arm of the denomination. Thus it appears that Hood's election resulted in the replacement of an active bishop. It seems, furthermore, that the trouble with Lavender was more the result of Brooks's stern policies than of Lavender's own shortcomings or character flaws. This incompatibility between a minister and the one under whom he worked appears often in various denominations of the time, including the AME Church. For example, Theophilus G. Steward felt so suppressed and restricted by his ministerial supervisor, the future bishop Richard Harvey Cain, that he successfully sought transfer to Georgia from South Carolina in 1867.[6] In addition, this episode might reflect the tensions that often erupted between northern-based denominational leaders, white and black, and the local southern ministers, many of whom were former "slave preachers" and often lacked the educational backgrounds that their northern counterparts possessed. Again, we witness a tension, this time explicitly sectional, that transcended Zion, as the conflict between AME Bishop William F. Dickerson and W. E. Johnson in South Carolina reveals. Johnson, a local minister, believed that Dickerson, identified with the northern party, exercised domination over him and the local churches. As a result Johnson and others established in 1885 a separate, southern-based black Methodist church, the Reformed Methodist Union Episcopal Church.[7]

Hood's comments about the Reverend G. W. Price, the other minister who was causing problems for the connection in the eastern portion of the state, are more precise and derogatory.[8] According to Hood, Price was "envious" of the close relationship between Hood and Bishop Clinton. Perhaps Price saw Hood as a possible rival for leadership and influence in the church. At any rate, Price attached himself to Bishop J. J. Moore, becoming his advisor. If we accept Hood's account, Price succeeded in establishing sufficient influence with Moore so that the bishop, at his request, removed Hood from his station in Fayetteville, turned it over to Price, and transferred Hood to Charlotte. Perhaps overconfident of his influence with the bishop, Price embarked on a course of action for which Moore had to check him. Price had illegally, i.e., contrary to Zion's rules and regulations, tried a conference minister. Bishop Moore set aside the action, and the minister, when legally examined, was found innocent. This action must have enraged and embarrassed Price. When the annual conference convened, Price, supported by only one ally, unexpectedly took the floor at the appropriate time and brought a charge against the bishop's character, charging him with maladministration. Price, according to Hood, had convinced Moore that Hood had sided against the bishop. Then Hood came to the bishop's defense by taking issue with Price's attempt to bring charges against a presiding bishop, a parliamentary move on Hood's part that allowed the shocked prelate opportunity to collect himself.[9] Upon his defeat, the disgruntled Price seceded to the Methodist Episcopal Church (the predominantly white group based principally in the North), "and did all he could to break up Zion."[10]

While we have only Hood's account of the Moore-Price conflict, there are a number of observations that can be made about this situation. First, this was a period in which Zion ministers felt freer to challenge the decisions and judgments of bishops. Zion originated as a church that placed great emphasis on the rights of the laity and the limitations of the superintendency or episcopacy. Second, whatever their origins, there were tensions or conflicts between Hood and Price. Perhaps each recognized in the other an episcopal or ministerial ambition detrimental to his own. Third, until Price publicly challenged Moore's administrative decision, he was favored by Moore, just as Hood was favored by Bishop J. J. Clinton. Though *Bishop* Hood would in future years often attempt to discourage younger ministers from having overt ambitions for higher office within the church, Zion, like other religious denominations, had its share of internal political maneuverings, and Hood's elevation to the episcopacy, at the very least, was a direct result of such.

By the time of the General Conference, the stage seemed set for Hood's election. The 1872 Annual Conference of North Carolina decided that, given the fact that the General Conference of the connection was to convene in Charlotte during the year, it would be best to retain Hood as pastor in that city. This final pastoral charge to Hood was the only instance in which he retained a post over three years.[11] It appears that not only eastern Carolina Zionites, but the consensus of the whole annual conference, supported Hood for the episcopacy that year. It is understandable that Zionites in eastern North Carolina saw Hood as their hope and wanted to make him bishop. He had led the fight against Price in the past, and now his help was needed to fight the battle to retain churches being sought by Price and Lavender. In addition, Hood's original church work in the South had been in Craven County, the Wilmington area, and around Fayetteville, all in the eastern portion of the state, prior to his Charlotte appointment. Hood had founded churches, ordained many ministers, and retained a great deal of influence in that region. It was also in eastern North Carolina that he had been politically active. Furthermore, one would suppose that Hood's defense of Moore brought him the goodwill of the current episcopal office holders and their supporters. Hood had probably gained Moore's personal gratitude and perhaps his active or de facto support for Hood's episcopal candidacy.

Of course there was also Hood's close relationship with a current bishop, J. J. Clinton. As previously outlined, Clinton had originally assigned Hood to work in the South during 1863. Both Clinton and Hood were born in Pennsylvania, a fact that might have affected the relationship between the two men. Clinton entered Zion history as one of its greatest bishops in terms of expanding the boundaries of the church, and Hood's similar contributions no doubt delighted the prelate. Clinton must have felt a tremendous gratitude and pride toward Hood, a man of many talents, an affable and agreeable personality, and a hard, dedicated worker for Zion and the uplift of African Americans. Price was probably not totally wrong. Hood perhaps was in some great sense a favorite of Clinton's.

It should also be noted that the 1872 General Conference was held in Charlotte, Hood's current city of residence, and the sessions took place in Clinton Chapel, Hood's pastoral charge. Furthermore, a considerable number of Zion delegates actually stayed in Hood's home during the sessions.[12] There is clear evidence of developing sectional tensions between the North and South in Zion, as in other independent black denominations, conventions, and associations, during this period. A conference site in Charlotte would have augmented the strength of the southern Zion majority in the connection and contributed to Hood's election. On July 1, 1872, James Walker Hood was elected and, on July 3, consecrated as the seventeenth bishop of the AME Zion Church. Though all sitting bishops were up for reelection each quadrennium, Hood was the only newly elected bishop at the 1872 General Conference. Ending on July 3, the General Conference had lasted for thirteen days. Because of prior speaking engagements on behalf of the Republican party, the new bishop did not embark on his new duties in earnest until September.[13]

HOOD'S COMMENCEMENT OF EPISCOPAL DUTIES IN THE SOUTH, 1872–1880

Hood's account of his episcopal sojourns reveals much about his personal character, his approach to ministry, and the nature of the AMEZ Church and evangelical Christianity during the 1870s and 1880s. Early in September 1872 Hood began his episcopal journey in South Carolina and then shifted to Virginia, since his more extensive ministerial efforts in North Carolina had made him thoroughly familiar with church work in that state. He first traveled to Bushy Fork, South Carolina. The Bushy Fork church held that name because it did not meet in a conventional church building but in a structure of forks of wood overlaid with bushes, a characteristic of many churches in the region at the time. Hood's account also reveals the deep poverty of the people. For example, the bishop stayed with one family of a mother and eight daughters, all occupying a one-room home. The family's desperate straits, however, did not diminish the warmth and hospitality they extended to Hood. On Sunday morning Hood collected two dollars from the church, the required annual contribution to the connection, but the sum did not include his traveling expenses. The bishop, however, was pleased that they had contributed to the best of their knowledge.[14] Hood's account reveals a preacher not merely expounding the gospel but identifying with the people and feeling comfortable under adverse conditions.

After sojourning in South Carolina, Hood spent a short time in Charlotte and then journeyed to Virginia for a more extensive visit. In Petersburg, Virginia, Hood confronted a church crisis, the like of which he apparently never afterward encountered. The congregation contained three major factions. One faction, offended by the episcopal style of J. D. Brooks, had elected to secede from Zion for the CME and sought to carry church properties with them. They awaited a court's final resolution of the matter. The other two factions consisted of those who believed that the local pastor was guilty of immorality and those who supported the pastor. Hood could do nothing about the dispute over church property except, like everyone else, wait for the final ruling of the courts. On the matter of ministerial immorality, Hood persuaded the people to avoid making formal charges against the pastor prior to the meeting of the annual conference set for October 16, at which time, the bishop promised, he would remove the minister from the parish. After a diligent and difficult search, Hood succeeded in placing a pastor acceptable to the people and promised to return later to check on the church's progress. Hood clearly adopted a more conciliatory, respectful, and less rigid modus operandi than that of his episcopal predecessor. This approach was perhaps based on Hood's greater sensitivity to the feelings and opinions of the local church people and perhaps occasioned in part by the stark reality that, during a period of heavy competition for church members and properties from AME, CME, and the ME churches, circumstances demanded that the people's interests be kept in high regard.[15]

Zion lost the Petersburg's court case. Hood listed it and a church in Spartanburg, South Carolina, as the only two church properties ever lost from his episcopal jurisdiction. But the loss of church property in Petersburg did not doom the growth and vitality of Zion's mission in the area. The minister whom Hood had appointed to take the station in 1872 died before the next annual conference in 1873. Hood had, in his opinion, the providential pleasure of appointing an old acquaintance, the Reverend James Jones, to succeed the deceased pastor who had chaired the committee that examined Hood for ordination to elder. Having been elected in 1872 by the General Conference as general secretary, Jones had signed Hood's episcopal credentials. The bishop had extremely high praise for Jones. More to the point, Jones's pastorate had been so effective with the people that when the state supreme court ruled against Zion, only sixteen of the Petersburg members remained with the old church. The remainder followed Jones. Having used a hall for worship services for a while, they eventually constructed a very attractive brick building.[16]

After the Virginia Annual Conference in 1872, Hood attended the North Carolina Annual Conference in Fayetteville. Things were much improved for Zion in North Carolina. People were happy over Hood's selection as bishop; defections from Zion because of G. W. Price's activities had ceased; and churches in Wilmington, Charlotte, and New Bern, along with Fayetteville, were all experiencing great increases in membership. When Hood arrived in Union, South Carolina, for the Annual Conference scheduled there, he found that the church where the conference was to convene had been turned over to the AME Church because the owner who held the deed for the land of the church site had joined the AME and carried the property with him. Sympathetic white and black people, however, helped the connection to locate a comfortable meeting place. After a couple of years, the Union church became a strong point in Zion. When the South Carolina Conference adjourned in December 1872, Hood was unable to return home because he suffered from rheumatism, an ailment that would afflict Hood periodically throughout this period. During Hood's absence, his daughter Maggie was born.[17]

In his description of this first episcopal journey, Hood also detailed the camp meetings that were usually held during the summer months of July, August, and September. These activities were part of an evangelical Christian tradition in the United States that dated back to the eighteenth century. People came from many miles and in great numbers, many seeking to experience a new birth from God that would free them from all sins. This experience often manifested itself in shouting and other overt spiritual behavior. Hood commented that camp meetings played a strong role in increasing membership in Zion, particularly in South Carolina. Furthermore, they provided the new bishop with the opportunity, which he had sought since the 1850s, to experience the mighty works of God about which older Methodist ministers had talked.

Hood provided an account of a camp meeting in South Carolina that was extended by the church people beyond the original closing time. God's power was greatly manifested, and 105 sinners found salvation, including some who had traveled from distant places and then returned to establish new churches in their communities. Indeed, on the last day of service Hood had to wait until approaching sunset in order to give the benediction. Hood eagerly embraced the opportunity to be part of such events. While he did not claim to be a great singer, Hood cherished singing "the plantation [melodies] and old ballads." The bishop permitted the lead singer to play his or her role in the meeting, but when that person had reached his or her limit, Hood would then take charge of the singing, like a wise military general who holds himself in reserve until needed.[18]

These religious services reveal a number of significant points relevant to this study. First, they illustrate that there were yet persons and groups in the North and the South during the post–Civil War period who maintained the revivalist tradition of earlier evangelistic Christianity. Second, camp meetings and revivals provide a look at "slave religion" and, more broadly, the southern evangelistic religion that survived into this era. Third, a study of these meetings reveals their often interracial character, with many whites having the opportunity to experience first hand black worship and preaching. Finally, Hood's account demonstrates that unlike some ministers who came from the North, this new bishop felt comfortable with southern black religion.[19] While strongly emphasizing the acquisition of knowledge, proper training, church discipline, and order, Hood, unlike Daniel Alexander Payne, a contemporary bishop in the AME Church, loved "plantation melodies"; furthermore, there is no evidence that Hood ever refused to sleep in a room with no heater, or to lay hands of ordination upon a minister because his hair was not combed to the bishop's satisfaction, rumors associated with Payne.[20] One can easily understand why Hood was held in such high esteem and affection by many Zionites.

On September 13, 1875, and prior to the end of the first quadrennium of Hood's episcopacy, the bishop was severely pained by the loss of his second wife, of seventeen years, Sophia Jane Nugent Hood.[21] Circumstances surrounding her demise compounded the pain felt by Hood and perhaps left a deep feeling of guilt in the young bishop. Hood had left his ill wife to begin an evangelistic journey, having no idea that her sickness might be fatal. They had made arrangements to meet in Carthage, North Carolina. For a number of days Hood was in a wilderness area isolated from telegraph or other communications. Six days after her death, Hood received the news from a minister who was to meet with him in Carthage. Hood found some comfort in the fact that he learned about Sophia Hood's death prior to arriving in Carthage, where he expected to see her. Still days away from home, Hood busied himself with church matters and found solace in that Sunday morning church service. Returning home Monday morning, Hood made financial arrangements with the recently widowed woman next door, apparently the future Keziah P. Hood, to care for his children and home. The bishop then began anew his episcopal work, striving feverishly to keep his mind off his sorrow, returning home only shortly before Christmas. In Hood's first episcopal journey we have a glimpse of the physical and emotional strains on bishops who traveled extensively, adjudicated trying church controversies, endured legal contests over properties, experienced the grinding poverty of their parishioners, suffered illnesses far from home, and sometimes were at great distances when children were born and relatives died.

Despite the loss of his wife and other adversities, Hood's first quadrennium was largely successful. During his first year Hood was able to gather his full salary of $1,500 and traveling expenses, no mean accomplishment in Zion during this era. Of the other bishops, only J. J. Clinton, a man much loved by various societies in the church, accomplished this goal. Hood could also happily report that there had been a significant expansion of membership in his appointed Third Episcopal District. The 1872 General Conference had based representation in the subsequent Conference on a formula that would have meant that approximately twenty delegates would have come from the Third District. But church expansion had been such that fifty-eight delegates attended the 1876 General Conference from that district.[22] Here one sees the tremendous impact that Hood's ongoing organizing efforts and his dedicated episcopal leadership had on the numerical expansion of Zion and the independent black church.

HOOD, THE FOURTEENTH QUADRENNIAL CONFERENCE, AND THE ELECTION OF THOMAS H. LOMAX, 1876–1880

The Fourteenth Quadrennial Session of the General Conference of Zion convened in Louisville, Kentucky, on June 1, 1876, at the Fifteenth Street AMEZ Church.[23] The country was in an economic depression, which largely accounts for the fact that only two-thirds, or about 150, of the designated delegates attended the conference. Also, death had dealt heavy blows to Zion during the quadrennium, claiming Bishop Jermain Loguen in 1872 shortly after his reelection; Bishop J. D. Brooks in 1874; Superintendent William H. Bishop, who had served during the trying days of Zion's schism in the 1850s, in June 1873; Superintendent James Simmons in February 1874; and the newly elected secretary of the General Conference, the Reverend James A. Jones. Then there was the death in July 1873 of the highly respected Christopher Rush (b. 1777). More than any of the others, and perhaps more than any person in Zion, he represented the contemporary church's connection to the days of "the fathers." He had been ordained deacon and elder in July 1822 and had assumed the superintendency from the first elected officer, James Varick, in 1828. As early as 1843 Rush provided a historical sketch on the rise of the AMEZ Church. And having been born in the New Bern, North Carolina area in revolutionary times, Father Rush symbolized the unity of the church across the lines of North and South, and the pre– and post–Civil War years.

Lasting thirteen days, this General Conference had many vacancies to fill and had the challenge of making or modifying rules of the church, among other responsibilities. William Howard Day, a professor from Pennsylvania, was chosen to replace Jones as the conference secretary, though he did not follow through with his responsibility to print the minutes of the 1872 General Conference, thus depriving the connection and historians of vital primary data. Hood, S. T. Jones, J. J. Clinton, and J. J. Moore were reelected as bishops. J. P. Thompson, W H. Hillery, and T. H. Lomax were the newly consecrated bishops, bringing the episcopal force to seven.

There were other significant developments in the church, particularly concerning the connectional discipline. Now penitents, like probationers, could attend the Love Feasts services, though it was emphasized that one still "must have a positive faith in the saving grace of Jesus Christ," that is, give testimony of conversion prior to becoming a full church member.[24] Deacons no longer had to be accompanied by church elders to perform marriages or baptisms. One must now have been a traveling minister for four years as a requisite for representing an annual conference at the General Conference. Zionites came even closer to establishing a denominational newspaper, a movement aided by Hood that would eventually result in the founding of the *Star of Zion*. The connection took specific steps to purchase property for a school in Fayetteville, since its attempt at establishing Rush Academy in Pennsylvania was failing. As a result of these moves, within two years Bishop Hood would serve as the first Board of Trustees chair for Zion's major college, eventually named Livingstone College after relocation to Salisbury, North Carolina, where it still stands. These and other events reflect the dynamic institutionalization of Zion in particular, and black Christianity in general, that transpired during the post–Civil War years. The connection, like the AME, was becoming less informal, more stratified, and more precise regarding many of its laws and practices. As Zion ventured into new enterprises or revived older ones, Hood stood forth as a major player, increasingly representing the ties between more recently affiliated members of Zion, particularly in the South, and the church's previous northern-based, pre–Civil War leaders and founders.

Hood's support of Thomas H. Lomax (1832–1908) is very revealing in regard to Hood's sense of personal loyalty, internal Zion politics, and the conflicts between many southerners and northerners in the church.[25] The blending of northern and southern elements within Zion transpired with relative ease, particularly in comparison with the AME, the black Baptists, and the mainline, mostly white, denominations that had split over slavery before and during the Civil War and, with the exception of the Episcopalians, had yet to reconcile across sectional lines. This is not to say, however, that there was not significant sectional tension or rivalry within the connection. As early as the 1870s there was a deliberate effort to elect southern—and often North Carolinian—Zionites to episcopal office. I suspect that the issue of Hood's candidacy, even if it was promoted by persons other than Hood, figured significantly in the insistence on holding the 1872 conference in Charlotte, North Carolina, where Hood pastored, rather than in the mother conference of New York.

According to Hood, fifty-six of the fifty-eight delegates from the Third Episcopal District of South Carolina, North Carolina, and Virginia traveled from Richmond, Virginia, to Louisville, Kentucky, the site of the conference. The delegates decided to cast a bloc vote for Thomas Lomax, which guaranteed his election. It was clear that a number of northern Zionites did not take kindly to this action by the Third District. Though Lomax was elected, the committee in charge of assigning the episcopal districts, chosen from each of the annual conferences of the connection, placed him in a mission district where he would receive a meager salary. Hood claimed that this was a tactic used to force Lomax from the episcopacy, a technique that Hood claimed had been used at least twice before with some success.

But Hood came to the assistance of his North Carolinian colleague by permitting Lomax to retain the pastorate of Clinton Chapel in Charlotte, one of the most prosperous Zion churches, and arranging for pastoral care when the bishop was away on episcopal business. He also bought Lomax's property in Fayetteville, paying him twice the sum he could possibly get from another buyer, a deal that lost Hood an estimated thousand dollars. A grateful Lomax continued to prosper in his business enterprises, and, spiritually, Clinton Chapel continued to succeed. But in later years Hood still lamented that Zion had tossed away the chance to exceed the membership of the AME in certain southern states because it had not assigned a truly great preacher to an area where he could have brought a greater number of members into Zion. It appears that the tension between Lomax and many in Zion continued until his death. Perhaps many northerners continued to resent the manner of Lomax's election and the fact that the southern Zionites were now taking over an originally northern church. At any rate, this whole episode demonstrates that Hood was adept at playing ecclesiastical politics, although he insisted that he promoted others rather than himself, and that he identified with southern Zionites during these early years. Although he would always hold North Carolina dear, the bishop in subsequent years would make a point of being a bishop in the entire connection, transcending any annual conference or geographical section.

This sectional tension in Zion reflected a wider reality in African American independent Christianity in the post–Civil War decades of the nineteenth century. The southerners Richard H. Cain and Henry M. Turner's challenge to northern domination in the AME Church mirrors greatly the Hood and Lomas 1872–1876 contests in Zion. In 1880 Turner and Cain, with the enthusiastic support of southern AME delegates at the General Conference, succeeded in securing two of the three available episcopal posts. In 1888 the AME General Conference went even farther and selected two bishops, W. J. Gaines and Abraham Grant, who not only were southerners, but had actually experienced slavery. James Washington's brilliant account of African American Baptists during this era demonstrates clearly that sectional tensions contributed immensely to black Baptists' failure to achieve nationwide, enduring denominational union until the 1895 formation of the National Baptist Convention. Even thereafter the emergence in 1897 of the Lott Carey Baptist Convention, fueled largely by the displeasure of Virginians and North Carolinians with the operations of the new national convention relating to matters of foreign missions, illustrates the lingering impact of sectional conflict, though this division was not always a clear separation of North and South.[26]

CONCLUSION

This chapter examined Hood's leadership in the Zion connection by focusing on his election to the episcopacy in 1872, his first episcopal sojourn in North Carolina and portions of South Carolina and Virginia, and his role in the election of Lomax at the 1876 General Conference. It reveals that while Hood might not have promoted himself for the office of bishop, he was aware of the workings of church politics. The preceding pages show a compassionate, diplomatic, and sensitive prelate who moved among his parishioners with ease. We have also observed the tremendous emotional and physical costs that the episcopacy levied on its holders, exemplified perhaps most dramatically by the fact that Hood was away on church business at the time of the birth of his daughter Maggie and the death of his second wife, Sophia. Finally, a look at the 1876 General Conference reveals that the denomination was moving into a new era with the deaths of many Zion leaders and the adoption of new rules of discipline. Lomax's election to the episcopacy and Hood's role in supporting him point to sectional tensions within the AMEZ. In sum, the AMEZ, like other black denominations, was engaging in internal politics, dealing with tensions between northerners and southerners, and making a transition from a smaller, more informal, northern-based group toward greater formality and a southern-based membership and southern-based denominational operations. From his initial elevation to the episcopacy, Hood provided impressive leadership among the bishops of Zion during this era of change and crisis.

Chapter Five

Hood's Early Episcopal Leadership, Part II

The Hillery Episode and the Western Sojourn, 1880–1885

A bishop then must be blameless, the husband of one wife, vigilant, sober, of good behavior, given to hospitality, apt to teach; Not given to wine, no striker, not greedy of filthy lucre; but patient, not a brawler, not covetous.
—1 Timothy 3:2–3, Holy Bible, King James Version

As previously stated, this work is the first critical effort to recover for scholarly appropriation Hood's entire public career as a major religious and political (especially regarding racial matters) leader during the nineteenth and early twentieth centuries. The abundance of available material pertinent to the study of such a dynamic individual combined with limited space necessitates the selection of representative aspects of his career. The preceding chapter examined Hood's ascent to the bishopric, a case study of Hood's first episcopal sojourn, and Hood's participation in the election of T. H. Lomax as bishop in 1876. This chapter focuses upon two additional and highly significant events during Hood's first years as bishop: the disrobing of Bishop W. H. Hillery in 1884 and Hood's episcopal journey to the far west in 1885, one year after Hillery's forced retirement from the episcopacy. These events provide us with vital insights into the character of both Hood and the AMEZ Church during this era. They demonstrate that African American Methodists, as most American evangelicals during this period, held very high and stringent standards regarding the behavior of both laity and ministers. Though Zion leadership was no longer formally evaluating the character of its bishops quadrennially, it did not disregard the standards of the church regarding the use of alcoholic beverages and immorality. The episcopal trip to the far west among other things demonstrated that Zionists, like black Baptists and other Methodists, had significant presence in western territories and states. Significant for the thesis of this study, Hood's place at the forefront of church expansion and maintenance of strict codes of morality demonstrates the powerful leadership role that he exerted in the AMEZ Church, even during the earlier years of his episcopacy. Indeed, his involvements in these matters not only equaled but appear to have excelled those Zion bishops of more senior rank. Both of these examples demonstrate that Hood's active episcopal leadership encompassed a strong commitment to Christian temperance and the Wesleyan doctrine of holiness.

The Hillery Episode, 1880–1884

On May 12, 1884, Bishop William H. Hillery (1839–1893) became the first of only two Zion episcopal officers to be disrobed. Hillery, a native of Virginia, migrated to Pennsylvania at an early age and began his ministerial career at eighteen. Later he did missionary service in parts of Tennessee and West Virginia, where he successfully organized a number of congregations. In 1868 Hillery moved to the Far West, where he received an appointment as presiding elder. After eight years of service in a number of annual conferences, Hillery ascended to the episcopacy in 1876. Interestingly, William J. Walls, author of the most comprehensive history of Zion, touched on the Hillery affair only briefly. According to Walls, Hillery succumbed to a failure that resulted in his removal from the episcopacy in 1884 on charges of intemperance and immorality, with the Genesee Conference in Western New York, his home district, making final disposition of his case.[1] This account is, of course, correct but does not convey the profound impact, both immediately and over the long term, that the episode had on the Zion Church, and its significance for understanding the actions and convictions of major leaders of the time. David H. Bradley, another Zion historian, provides a more in-depth look at the controversy and offers some personal, critical comments.[2]

Hillery, as previously noted, was elected and consecrated the nineteenth bishop of the AMEZ Church in 1876. Within two years of his reelection in 1880, rumors had begun to surface of Hillery's intemperance. As these persisted, the Board of Bishops decided to conduct a more formal investigation to determine the truth of these reports. A charge of simony, or sale of ministerial appointments, that arose in the Kentucky Conference was subsequently investigated, but not sustained. Other charges, of drunkenness and immorality, originated in California, and eventually doomed Hillery's episcopal service to the church. Hood traveled to the state in 1883, perhaps in part to investigate these charges, and consulted with George F. Norton, a member of the then-named Starr King AMEZ Church in San Francisco. Norton accused the bishop of "drinking whiskey at a public grocery bar" and of "owing a bill of groceries at the same place." Indeed, the owner of the establishment, Catherine Hinds, had publicly posted Hillery's debt and made a notarized statement to that effect. Upon his return to Kentucky, Hood, according to his account, offered help to Hillery if he would refrain from the use of alcohol. For a while it seemed as if Hillery was abandoning drink, but he subsequently fell back into the habit and actually spoke to Hood on an occasion when he was drunk!

Hillery's case went to trial before the Kentucky Annual Conference. He was apparently not convicted on the charge of simony, or sale of ministerial appointments, but a special judicial committee of the Kentucky Conference proceeded to try him on the charges contained in the affidavit submitted by Hinds in California, that is, buying alcohol, publicly drinking it, and being in debt for alcohol and groceries. Another affidavit presented by a number of other individuals sustained the accusations brought by Hinds. The Judicial Committee, however, found that the evidence was insufficient to find the bishop guilty. The Annual Conference as a whole convened the following day and "evidently took no action."[3]

At this point the whole affair took a controversial turn, with Hood at the center of events. Hood believed that as presiding officer of the Kentucky Annual Conference he had the right and responsibility to appeal the matter to the General Conference, given the fact that the Annual Conference had taken no action. When the General Conference convened in New York City at Mother Zion AMEZ Church, the Mother Church of the denomination, on May 7, 1884, two charges were brought against Hillery—immorality and rape. Bradley provides no further information on the basis for either of these charges. Hood's appeal to the General Conference caused quite a stir within the denomination. Many felt that Hillery was being subjected to double jeopardy. He had been duly tried in the Kentucky Conference and found not guilty. It was one thing for the accused to appeal a guilty verdict; it was something else for the denominational counsel to appeal a not-guilty verdict. Indeed, two members of the Kentucky Conference,

J. E. Price and A. J. Warner, took this position, noting that the Kentucky Conference had voted and found Hillery not guilty.[4]

But the discussion continued. The General Conference finally went into executive session and agreed that the matter had not come before them in the proper order; that is, it had come by means of the presiding officer, meaning Hood, rather than the Annual Conference of Kentucky. Also, the General Conference and the Board of Bishops reached the conclusion that the General Conference did not have the power to try Bishop Hillery beyond deciding his fitness for episcopal service. The General Conference could circumscribe his episcopal duties, but it could not try him on the charges. Hillery, upon hearing the pronouncement of the Board, decided to tender his resignation. But the conference, led by C. R. Harris (who was elected twenty-second AMEZ Bishop at the 1888 Conference and, like Hood, a firm supporter of temperance) successfully blocked Hillery's attempt, claiming that the accused should have resigned before the start of the proceedings against him.[5] A motion to accept Hillery's resignation was set aside. In the final analysis, the conference disrobed Hillery and sent the question of his character to the Genesee Annual Conference, the place of his residence, for resolution. An unfavorable motion in the General Conference passed overwhelmingly, 120 to 5, but Bradley notes that a significant number of delegates abstained from voting.

The fallout from this episode lingered beyond 1884. The *Star of Zion,* in a March 5, 1886, account taken from the *Newburgh Daily News,* discussed subsequent conflicts between Bishop J. P. Thompson of the Genesee Conference and Hillery. Thompson noted that Hillery had been expelled from the Genesee Annual Conference after he failed to show up for his trial. Now the conference was considering whether he should be retained in the ministry. Thompson also noted in the article that Hillery at one point had filed a lawsuit against both Thompson and Hood. In the lawsuit, which Hillery later dropped, he sued Thompson for twenty-five thousand dollars for slander in stating that the former bishop had been expelled. Hillery was of the opinion that the Genesee Annual Conference had no authority to put him on trial.[6]

In April 1885 Bishop Hood made his own assessment of the affair and his conduct when he addressed the Philadelphia and Baltimore Annual Conference in Washington, D.C.[7] There were Zionites who strongly criticized Hood's actions in the Hillery matter. Hood first defended himself by claiming that the General Conference had validated his decisions. The General Conference had unanimously, he claimed, sustained his right to appeal the matter to the conference because the Kentucky Annual Conference's failure to deal with the committee's report had left the matter unresolved. In addition, the conference had agreed that sufficient evidence existed to warrant a "charge of drunkenness"; upheld Hood's right to silence Hillery "while the case was pending"; and agreed that Hood correctly permitted the California Conference to turn the matter over to its Kentucky counterpart.[8] Besides the actions that he had taken in defense of episcopal and ecclesiastical powers, Hood had also made a number of decisions, supported by the General Conference, that rendered the trial of Hillery fair and impartial by having ruled that California Zionites had no right to put Hillery on trial since they had not asked him to attend; decided that no new charges could be added to the current ones unless the accused had the opportunity to review them; and ruled that a second group of charges could not be employed to fortify the first set until the first group had been resolved.[9] The General Conference, Hood correctly pointed out, had decided that the extent of its powers over Hillery was to render the decision of his unsuitability for the episcopacy. For administering discipline beyond that General Conference action, the Genesee Annual Conference retained authority. Reflecting that many individuals still felt uncomfortable with the proceedings, Hood said that they erred in thinking that a special committee must examine the case prior to its presentation at the General Conference.[10]

Second, Hood attacked the behavior of his former episcopal colleague. Hood's account, like Thompson's discussed above, indicates that Hillery did not simply resign himself to the decision of the Zion Conference. Even after the ruling of the General Conference, Hillery fought back. It seems that Hillery leveled a number of attacks against his episcopal colleagues, accusing them of conspiring to eliminate him from the bishopric. At that point, the bishops felt compelled to publish "the facts and rumors" brought against Hillery. Hood also mentioned Hillery's alleged "attempt to usurp the chair of the Virginia Conference," but he does not elaborate. Yet it is clear that Hillery, according to Hood, had succeeded in fomenting "discord and confusion throughout that district." After Hood's decision to appeal his case from the Kentucky Conference, Hillery, Hood claimed, proceeded to slander Hood by publishing "a false circular which he . . . sent all over the country."[11] Apparently, Hillery was also suing Hood, charging him with conspiracy in the whole affair. Hood, however, believed that the entire case against Thompson and himself was utterly without foundation and saw little hope of legal victory for Hillery, although it may have brought a certain amount of personal satisfaction to the defrocked bishop. As for Hood, he was absolutely comfortable with his decisions and conduct in the matter.[12]

ASSESSING THE HILLERY EPISODE

How do we assess this affair? On one hand the General Conference and the Board of Bishops agreed that in a sense Hood was not correct in attempting to try Hillery before the General Conference, that such constituted a case of double jeopardy for the defendant, and that the General Conference had no jurisdiction in the case other than deciding on Hillery's fitness as an episcopal officer. The Reverend R. H. Simmons's comments four years after Hillery's trial emerged in the heat of a nasty debate between Simmons and Hood. But while they might have been self-serving for Simmons, these statements indicate the ambivalence that many members of the connection felt about the whole episode and Hood's role in it. Simmons still believed that Hood had actually done Hillery an injustice by appealing the case to the Zion Conference. The minister claimed that he offered the motion to uphold Hood's action because he believed that Hood was "the least guilty of the two." "But our action against Bishop Hillery has caused the connection to spend dollars,"[13] presumably in court costs.

Hood, still feeling the sting of strong dissenters who remained dissatisfied with the proceedings, put the best light on his "appeal" to the conference. Hood was not *wholly* sustained by the conference, as his account would leave one to believe. On the other hand, both Hood and the Board of Bishops attempted to work with Hillery after learning of his weakness. This was not a case where a person guilty of one transgression was immediately and unceremoniously brought before the Annual or General Conference and disrobed with no attempt to help him with his problem. In addition, Hood portrayed himself as having exercised a great deal impartiality in the execution of the trial. Though Hood, like most people, might have occasionally put his own actions in the best light, there is no reason to believe that he was lying about his efforts to be impartial in the process. Such a portrait of deception would not fit the overall character of the man, however one-sided his presentation of the matter.

We must also understand this whole drama in the context of evangelical and Methodist history. Discipline in the church during this era was tight. Christian men and women, especially leaders, were expected to live pure, holy lives unspoiled by the sinfulness of the world, to be shining exemplars of Christian conduct. One of the worst offenses that even a layperson could commit was imbibing alcohol, particularly in public. The Bishops' Address before the 1884 General Conference clearly put forth their conviction, and most likely that of an overwhelming majority of Zionites, that such conduct by a bishop, one who held an "honored and fearful trust" and "awful responsibility," stymied the growth and influence of the Zion Church.[14]

This was the age of temperance in most evangelical and Christian circles, a time when individuals and groups were pressuring the states and the federal government to outlaw the manufacture, sale, and use of alcoholic beverages. Indeed, as recently as 1881 Hood and the Zion connection in North Carolina supported a state prohibition amendment. Many black leaders were especially concerned about the toll that alcohol consumption took on the African American community. Hood had been brought up in a religious atmosphere of strict temperance. There were few things more repugnant to Hood than a fellow leader of a temperance church imbibing alcohol and, even more seriously, making a public spectacle of himself. Furthermore, charges of drunkenness and immorality leveled against blacks by the enemies of racial equality could easily be sustained in the minds of many whites by pointing to consumption of alcohol by some African Americans. Hence, leaders of various black churches feared the charge that African Americans, a people barely a generation removed from chattel slavery, were unfit for freedom and unqualified for equal citizenship rights because of alcohol abuse. It mattered not that the overwhelming majority of blacks were lawabiding and responsible; the destructive and irresponsible behavior of a few could hinder the advancement of the entire race. Thus, Hood and the Zion leadership stood in the larger company of black religious and secular leaders in emphasizing that Christian bishops and other leaders must set living examples by which all blacks would be judged. They had the weighty obligation of living free from any hint of scandal and absolutely beyond acts of public immorality and drunkenness. Against this general background, we can understand, perhaps even sympathize with, the position of both Hood and the AMEZ.

On the other hand, some critics, while fully appreciating Hood's clear and forceful leadership and understanding his strong commitment to Christian temperance, might lament that his historical era and operative theology hindered the bishop's ability to demonstrate greater care and sympathy toward a fellow Zionite and bishop. Influenced by a less absolutist stance against alcoholic beverages and understanding alcoholism more as a disease than a moral failure, many American Christians around the turn of the twenty-first century might call for more compassion toward Hillery. In addition, the refusal to accept Hillery's res-

ignation prior to a church trial and the issue of double jeopardy in trying him before both the Kentucky Annual and the General Conferences raise serious questions about procedural fairness. One commentator, the Zion historian David
Bradley, indicated his misgivings regarding the church's handling of Hillery's
case. Bradley insisted that the church of Christ should always include "grace" in
its mission, though grace was too often missing in the midst of controversies.[15]

HOOD'S EPISCOPAL SOJOURN TO THE WEST COAST, 1885

Blacks, like other Americans, had been steadily taking up residence in the
states and territories west of the Mississippi River since the pre–Civil War days.
In addition, the close of the Reconstruction period in the South, the rise of acts
of racial terrorism directed against blacks, and worsening economic conditions
spurred an increased movement of African Americans to western states in the
1880s. For a number of decades, black independent denominations, conventions,
and associations had ministered to the religious needs of these settlers. Hood's
episcopal journey west, like those of other Zion and AME prelates, illustrates the
presence of blacks in the west and black churches' efforts to serve them.[16] During the 1880s the AMEZ rotated its episcopal districts so that each bishop would
traverse the entire country during the term of his episcopacy. During the mid-
1880s part of Hood's episcopal district included the West Coast. He traveled to
the area as part of his official duties as well as to evaluate the condition of the Zion
Church there after the removal of Bishop Hillery. Because of considerations of
space, this chapter focuses on Hood's visit in Portland, Oregon, and San Francisco, California.

In the pages of the Zion news organ, *Star of Zion,* at that time published in Petersburg, Virginia, Hood provides a firsthand, often city-by-city, journal account
of his episcopal trip. The railroad journey from Fayetteville, North Carolina, the
bishop's resident city, began in May and ended August 1885, and included visits
to Salisbury and Statesville, North Carolina; Knoxville, Tennessee; Louisville,
Kentucky; Wamega, Kansas; Cheyenne, Wyoming; Portland, Oregon; San Francisco and San Jose, California; Idaho; Ogden and Denver, Colorado; and St.
Louis, Missouri. Along the way Hood, with the help of a literary guide, informed
his readers about various aspect of geography, topography, economics, population, and various types of plant and animal life. Various encounters on Hood's
journey provoked discussion of the African American presence in the West, race
relations, black farming and other examples of black enterprise, church lawsuits,

the presence of AME and AMEZ congregations, and, of course, the spiritual state of the laity and clergy. For people in a pre-television age who had never visited the West, Hood's letters proved to be immensely informative and entertaining.

In his writings Hood highlighted the accomplishments and sacrifices of a number of "stars in Zion." The bishop delivered words of high praise for an individual of long acquaintance, the Reverend W. H. Goler, pastor of an AMEZ congregation in Salisbury who had left the predominantly white Methodist Episcopal Church for greater religious freedom.[17] Calvin C. Pettey in Knoxville, Tennessee, struggled to maintain the Zion mission there amid serious "confusion" and fierce competition from other denominations. Indeed, Pettey, who would become bishop at the next General Conference (1888), had sacrificed his health establishing Zion in the City.[18] Hood himself was ill when he left Louisville, Kentucky—hardly able to walk and having suffered weight loss.[19] Both Hood's and Pettey's circumstances indicate the huge sacrifices that many clergy and religious leaders, including Methodist bishops of all independent black churches, made as they spread the gospel and worked to build up their denominations during the era. Undoubtedly, many of these individuals' recurring health problems were tied to the physical and psychological strains of traveling long distances, adjudicating difficult church matters, and getting insufficient sleep and rest. It was in St. Louis, Missouri, according to Hood, that his wife, Keziah P. Hood, honored her first request to make a public speech. With Mrs. Hood and the children remaining in Wamega, Kansas, Hood and his episcopal party journeyed to the West Coast.[20]

Hood's visits to Portland, Oregon, and California are of special interest. In ecclesiastical matters things had been less than sanguine for the Zion denomination in Portland.[21] Most of the ministers assigned to the work had been "adventurers," more concerned about selfish interests than building up Zion or commitment to God. Hood attributed the wondrous survival of the congregation to the strength of the denomination and the Divine decree that a Zion church would be established in the city. A "Bro. Mitchell," apparently an unordained lay minister, was the key person guiding the church out of troubled circumstances. Having found the church with few members and in debt, Mitchell turned things around and improved the physical condition of the church. People returned to the church with some promising to remain, provided Mitchell was allowed to remain as its leader. Hood noted the unorthodox nature of this situation (that is, leaving an unordained layperson in charge of a congregation), but he asked readers to note the many negative experiences that the people had endured with previous pastors. Here we observe a very significant ingredient of Hood's leadership success and his ability to garner both the love and admiration of the Zion membership. Hood, though at times quite opinionated and obstinate, had the ability to be flexible in the application of denominational rules. Consistent with the tradition of John Wesley and early Methodism, he gladly utilized the services of lay ministers in certain circumstances.

Hood found his stay in Portland quite delightful, notwithstanding its history of church problems. The vast majority of prominent blacks "of all denominations" entertained him and his episcopal party lavishly. The country itself was incredibly wonderful for an individual who had suffered health problems for years. "Though I have preached nine times in eight days and lectured twice, I feel fresher than when I came." Hood also believed that the presence of a bishop in the city not accustomed to hosting black prelates was advantageous to both the church and the area's wider black community. "Our people in the East who see bishops frequently, cannot realize how greatly the visit of a bishop is appreciated here."[22] Hood was impressed with the economic well-being of African Americans in Portland. "The colored people of this city are nearly all doing well and live in their own houses. The value of their possessions range from $5,000 to $25,000."[23]

From Oregon Hood and his party traveled to San Francisco, California.[24] Hood noted in his fifth letter to the *Star of Zion* that he had visited San Francisco previously, probably in 1883 to investigate charges against Hillery. Since then the spiritual condition of the church had markedly improved, and the possibility of "a mortgage foreclosure" that would "have swept away the last hope for Zion on the coast" had disappeared.[25] Hood laid the previous sorry spiritual state of affairs squarely at the feet of the now defrocked William H. Hillery, who had worked in the area for thirteen years as elder and later bishop. According to Hood, he had nearly destroyed his predecessor's fine work for Zion. He sharply criticized the former bishop for causing serious harm to the church by excluding numbers of people from the church. Some of the victims of Hillery's maladministration continued to feel the hurt; "it is feared that they have been wounded unto death."[26] Hood, besides giving what he believed was an accurate assessment of Hillery's tenure, was also validating the correctness of his own actions in having led the charge for Hillery's disrobing.

In marked contrast to the immorality and the arbitrariness of Hillery, his predecessor at Stockton Street (First) AME Zion Church, elder Alexander Walters (1858–1917), who assumed the post in 1883 with high recommendations, had brought new vitality, respect, and strength to the work. Indeed, Walters's religious and political career would make an indelible mark on Zion and general African American history. A native of Kentucky, Walters was partially educated in San Francisco. In 1879 and 1882 he was ordained a deacon and elder, respectively. During his ministerial career, Walters pastored churches in California and in the South, as well as the famous mother congregation of Zionism, Mother Zion in New York City. As a subsequent chapter will note, Walters became a leader in the civil rights and pan-African movements in the late 1800s and early 1900s. Only several months shy of his thirty-fourth birthday, Walters, when consecrated bishop on May 18, 1892, would become the second-youngest individual elevated to episcopal office in the Zion connection. J. J. Clinton, who commissioned Hood for southern work in the 1860s, holds the record as the youngest, with his June 30, 1856, ordination occurring several months before his thirty-third birthday.[27] Though he differed with the bishop on some denominational and political issues, Walters's Christian sincerity and zealous support of the doctrine of sanctification (or Christian perfection or holiness, the idea that Christians should strive to be free of all known sin) won Hood's heart, and much of the younger Zionite's ascendancy in the connection can be attributed to Hood's support.

Unlike his predecessor, Hillery, Walters clearly exuded piety and responsible Christian behavior. Given the bad experiences that the people had had with previous pastors, it was understandable that Walters's original acceptance by the people was probationary. Blacks of economic and social prominence regarded him with either "indifference" or "contempt" upon his entry into the city. Things were different now. Walters had impressed church people with his earnest piety, and others in the community, white and black, now regarded him with respect.[28] In such a "land of the free" as California, ministers emulating Walters would make the church a primary influence there. Hood's belief in the ability of blacks to rise above racially imposed limitations in California was strong.[29] Although Hood's account of race relations in the West was rather sanguine, many western blacks enjoyed greater freedom than their counterparts in the South and even in the northern states east of the Mississippi River.

Hood also had high praise for the Reverend Julia A. Foote. At this point she had not been ordained elder in the church, so Hood referred to her as "Sister." During this period of American history, women were not generally accepted as ministers of the gospel. Those women who preached did so without official certification by their respective denominational bodies. This applies to Foote, who did not receive ordination in Zion until the turn of the century. It is true, how-

ever, that Methodism was more liberal than many other denominations in granting a role for women as lay preachers or exhorters. Foote, by the time of Hood's
visit to California in 1885, had been engaging in lay preaching for thirty years.
But usually women exercising public ministry, such as pastors, missionaries, and
preachers (ordained or lay), faced ridicule and stern opposition.[30] Walters and
Hood had shown support for women's equality in the church. Though she initially met opposition in California from many because of her gender, Foote had
been one of the major instruments in successfully establishing Zionism on a firmer
basis and had succeeded in winning the people's favor. The bishop also had high
words of praise for Foote's published book, *A Brand Plucked from the Burning.*
Having read the book, Hood connected its substance with that of early Methodist
women writers and encouraged the readers of Zion to purchase a copy of it.[31]

Sister Foote was not the only woman Hood praised in his letters to the *Star of
Zion.* "There are some good sisters like those who helped Paul, but a pen better
fitted will most likely record their good deeds ere long."[32] In a subsequent letter
from San Jose, Hood praises a "Sister Davis," who had worked tirelessly to promote temperance. And perhaps reflecting a more typical role for women in
church circles, the bishop commends a number of women for providing or hosting "private entertainment" for the episcopal entourage.[33]

In early August 1885 Hood began his long journey back to North Carolina.
Along the way he lamented the recent death of former president and Union general Ulysses S. Grant, regarding him as a great military hero who had, prior to
his death, abandoned the use of alcohol and tobacco and embraced Christ. Returning to Kansas, where his family awaited him, Hood called for the immigration of 500,000 southern blacks to the Midwest and West, where they might enjoy
greater economic and political opportunities. With the demise of Reconstruction,
accompanied by diminishing political and economic opportunities for southern
blacks, many secular and religious leaders during the late 1870s and thereafter
counseled blacks to exit the states of the former Confederacy, though Hood's emigration call did not reflect as pessimistic state of affairs in the South (certainly
not North Carolina) nor did he counsel emigration for as many persons as other
emigration proponents. While in St. Louis, Missouri, both Hood and Mrs. Hood
suffered serious illnesses. Hood suffered malaria that had been preceded by chills
and a persistent bout of rheumatism. He had not suffered such high fever in
twenty years. Soon the Hoods recovered sufficiently for their return to North
Carolina.[34] The episcopal sojourn to the West Coast in 1885 highlights many of
Hood's leadership qualities: physical stamina, sacrificial commitment to service,

a major emphasis on temperance and holiness, flexibility in dealing with local situations, and an amazing openness to women's equality in church leadership. No wonder Hood was deeply loved by Zion parishioners and greatly admired by even some of his most steadfast religious and political critics.

CONCLUSION

Hood played a major role in denominational affairs, in terms of church governance and expansion. The Hillery episode illustrates that Hood and Zion, like other black denominations, placed a premium on moral conduct for its membership, including their leading church officers. The episcopal sojourn to the West Coast points out the increasingly national scope of African American churches, including the Zion denomination, as their leading men and women, exemplified by Hood, worked to solidify and expand the boundaries of their organizations. African Americans, continuing the trend set in pre–Civil War years, were settling throughout the nation and its territories, taking their religious organizations with them.

Despite what many might regard as Hood's questionable role in the Hillery affair, the last two chapters contribute immensely to our understanding of his positive traits of leadership, including a fierce desire to build up the Zion connection. Hood's greatest success and admirable traits presented themselves most lucidly when he labored among ordinary, lay Zionites or when the prelate was admonishing leaders to tend their flocks with care and attention. Controversies and contests, religious or secular, however, often reveal shortcomings and negative side of leaders, including Hood. Subsequent chapters will reveal that Hood's involvements in such controversies with church leaders took their toll on his reputation in the minds of some people. Still, Hood by and large retained the admiration of Zionites and the wider community, playing a key leadership role in religion and politics.

PART IV

SINGING ZION'S SONG IN A STRANGE LAND

The Political Philosophy and Leadership of Hood, 1872–1916

Chapter Six

Hood and Black America during the Post-Reconstruction Years

An Overview of the Political Philosophy of a Black Leader, 1872–1916

> We remember him in our boyhood as he frequently visited our section of
> the country in his triple capacity as Minister, Educator and Political adviser
> of his people. . . . [M]en of all political phases regarded him not a politician,
> but a statesman.
> —The Reverend J. W. McDonald, *The Star of Zion*

This chapter and the next examine Hood's political leadership from the time of
his assumption of the episcopacy and resignation from public political life in 1872
to the final year of his active episcopacy in 1916. While 1876–1877, when Rutherford B. Hayes was elected president, is normally cited as the year of the demise
of Reconstruction, it effectively ended as early as 1872 in North Carolina. Although his assumption of episcopal duties in 1872 severed his personal involvement with political office holding, James W. Hood continued to exert strong
political leadership, especially regarding matters of racial justice and equity. The
following chapter focuses upon Hood's support of the Republican party. This
chapter places emphasis upon Hood's overall political philosophy, particularly as
it relates to racial matters, and his active response to the issues of jim crow segregation and disfranchisement of black voters. This chapter, more specifically,
lays out the bishop's general prescriptions for racial advancement; examines

Hood's positions on domestic issues of the labor movement, immigration, segregation, and disfranchisement; and looks at Hood's views of American foreign policy, in particular the Spanish-American War and how it related to African Americans' concern for racial progress. There are three significant, noteworthy points about Hood's political philosophy. One, Hood saw his primary vocational responsibility as a minister and bishop of the AMEZ Church, leaving specific political involvement to laypeople. Two, the Zion prelate adopted a moderate, conciliatory approach to political matters, predicated in large part on cooperation with the "better class" of whites. Three, neither of the first two points should be interpreted to mean that Hood did not persistently struggle for full racial equality both under the law and in actual practice.

Hood's Prescriptions for Racial Advancement

Hood saw his role fundamentally as a Christian bishop and minister, one whose primary task was guiding the people of God. On the other hand, he insisted that the Christian minister should be a watchperson for the temporal as well as the spiritual dimensions of life. Overall, Hood's political philosophy fell between the views of Bishop Alexander Walters and Tuskegee president Booker T. Washington. He advocated a more politically active role than Washington for African Americans in their quest for racial justice. While advocating interracial cooperation and reasoned moderation, the bishop was not an accommodationist. On the other hand, the senior bishop found some of the views of his episcopal colleague Walters to be too "radical" and ill-considered.

We might describe Hood as a proponent of moderate political activism, a concerned and realistic optimist who supported consistent, but "gentlemanly," agitation for civil rights and advocated working assiduously to cultivate cooperation with the "better class of white people" in order to secure liberties for blacks. The term "conservative" as it applied to Hood does not signify inaction or obsequiousness in the quest for black justice and equity, as it might be interpreted in the closing decade of the twentieth century.[1] The more precise description would be "moderate." Hood believed that the worsening political and economic conditions of his people would be reversed. He believed that God's working through history would someday restore the liberties of African Americans as God had secured the freedom of the Hebrews from Egyptian bondage. Humanity, of course, has to cooperate with God. African Americans must assist God's work on their behalf by being vigilant for their rights in a "gentlemanly" fashion, using their political rights and economic resources wisely, adopting Christian lifestyles, and continuing to see the positive side of even the most distressing situation.

HOOD AND COMPENSATION FOR FORMER SLAVEHOLDERS

Hood was hailed almost universally within Zion and the general black community as a defender and promoter of the civic and economic opportunities of the race. On occasion, however, his wish to be conciliatory in the hope of building consensus across racial lines for progressive social change or reform caused him to adopt positions that placed him outside the mainstream thought of black leaders and, as far as can be determined, beyond the collective wisdom of the black church and community. An excellent example of such a faux pas, and perhaps his most outlandish, was the post–Civil War speculation that African Americans' quest for justice would have been easier after Emancipation had former slaveholders received compensation for losing the labor of the formerly enslaved. On a Wednesday, April 18, 1888, Hood, knowing beforehand that he would face severe criticism, shared this belief with the New York Annual Conference.

His declaration came across not as "off the cuff" remarks, but as a detailed, carefully reasoned philosophy. To be sure, Hood had a strong antislavery perspective that predated the Civil War. Furthermore, Hood thoroughly identified with the formerly enslaved and clearly denied that he regarded them as former "property." Yet, he contended, the federal government had certainly regarded them as such since during the early phase of the Civil War, all branches of the federal government—the presidency, Congress, and the Supreme Court—and the army had accepted and defended slavery. Northern cities, like southern cities, had profited immensely from the slave traffic. Thus, beyond the price paid in human lives on the battlefield and funds to execute the war, the federal government should have paid its financial share to remove the evil blight from the nation. Hood believed that white southerners continued to oppress and cheat the formerly enslaved because they felt that the federal government had cheated them by taking away their "property." In other words, because former slaveholders could not exact satisfaction from their financial investment in the enslaved through compensation from the federal government, they turned to oppression to do so. Furthermore, a former slaveholder "transmits his claim with compound interest to his posterity, and the idea that the freedom of the race was procured by theft goes down to future generations unless obviated by a suitable ransom."[2]

Reactions to such a shocking viewpoint coming from a distinguished African

American leader were quick and sharp. The 1888 AMEZ General Conference assembled May 2 in the same place where Hood had begun his work in the South twenty-four years earlier, at Saint Peter's AMEZ Church (formerly Andrews Chapel) in New Bern, North Carolina.[3] Thirty-year-old elder Alexander Walters, whom Hood had highly praised and promoted, submitted to the Board of Bishops a series of resolutions that called on Bishop Hood to provide a copy of the address in which the bishop had allegedly made such a proposal. Walters's resolutions, furthermore, called on a committee representative of the church's annual conference to examine the matter after Bishop Hood had explained the document and to set forth resolutions "expressing the sentiments of this body." Interestingly, the Board of Bishops considered Walters's resolutions, and, having *no objections,* submitted them to the conference. An intense, lively discussion ensued in the assembly, with Professor J. C. Price of Livingstone College, John C. Dancy, and an Elder Chambers from Louisiana making "very strong speeches" advising "conservative action," apparently in defense of Hood.

As the discussion progressed, the consensus emerged that whatever the bishop may have said, it was clear that he was a person of Christian character and devoted to the African American community. As outraged as they were by Hood's alleged comments, the conference delegates could not forget the hard work and sacrifice that the bishop had expended not only for the expansion of Zion but for the liberation of his race. They could not bring themselves to condemn or publicly humiliate Hood. Perhaps some, aware of his splendid record for racial advancement, could not even entertain the possibility that Hood made such comments. Thus, amendment after amendment was affixed to the Walters's resolutions "in deference to the respect for Bishop Hood" so that in the final analysis they became ineffectual and rather meaningless. Whereupon Dancy provided a substitute resolution that received unanimous support. Dancy's substitute resolution expressed confidence in Hood's Christian integrity and made it very clear that the General Conference, whether Hood actually made the statements or not, dissented from the substance of the newspaper reports concerning the payment to slaveholders for the emancipation of the enslaved.[4] It seems that the conference decided that subjecting the bishop to submitting a copy of the address, having it read, and then defending it might not have been the most respectful posture to take toward a beloved leader, particularly since they had clearly stated the position of the denomination.

This event is revealing on a number of fronts. First, it demonstrates that clergy felt free to challenge bishops in the General Conference. Second, it points to the developing debate between the "conservatives" and the "radicals" within the denomination around issues relating to church and politics, with "radicals" such as Walters the most critical of Hood's compensation idea. Third, it reflects that Hood's "conservative" or "moderate" course sometimes offended even some of his moderate followers. Fourth, the General Conference explicitly rejected the notion of compensated payment for slaveholders, regarding such to be a legitimation of a system they abhorred on racial, humane, and moral grounds. It is interesting that delegates repeatedly expressed confidence in Hood's Christian character, as if making such a proposal for compensating slaveholders (even when theoretical and after-the-fact) by definition constituted a mortal sin. The issue also surfaced in a very acrimonious debate between Hood and the Reverend R. H. Simmons during the fall of 1888, but in that exchange Hood refused to respond to the specific issue of compensating former slaveholders. Surely, he was aware that such a viewpoint was clearly unacceptable in Zion and in the larger black community.[5]

As outrageous as Hood's compensation idea was, it should not obscure the fact of the bishop's lifelong and fierce opposition to the institution of slavery or his awareness of its lingering, detrimental effects on efforts to achieve racial justice. Addressing the Central North Carolina Annual Conference in 1900, Hood stated that slavery had poisoned the minds of many whites toward blacks, causing resentment toward blacks that had resulted in efforts to disfranchise blacks. Even whites who did not overtly hate blacks still were affected by the general climate of prejudice. Hood blamed this climate on the legacy of slavery. It would take time to root out prejudice.[6] Thus, Hood in part advocated a more moderate course because the overthrow of racism was not going to occur overnight or even within one generation. It was necessary for leaders to be progressive and assertive but also careful that they were not so advanced that they left the masses of people behind them and henceforth accomplished little.

HOOD AND BLACK EMIGRATION

A more permanent aspect of Hood's prescription for racial advancement, and one more in tune with mainstream black thought, was his endorsement of limited emigration to the American West and to rural areas. As racial antagonism intensified in the 1870s and the 1880s in certain parts of the American South, many blacks resorted to emigration in response to their depressed situations. Some black spokespersons, such as AME Bishop Henry M. Turner, advocated the return of blacks to Africa or called for the emigration of a select number of African Americans. Usually those who favored leaving the South looked to other areas in the United States: the North, Midwest, or West. Hood, like most black religious and secular leaders, consistently rejected the idea that blacks should relinquish their citizenship in the United States, but he did favor limited migration within the United States. As the movement to eliminate black voting by means of inconsistently applied literacy tests and grandfather clauses grew in North Carolina and achieved legal sanction in the early 1900s, some African American leaders advised blacks to leave the state. Hood continued to insist that North Carolina was one of the best places in the country to live; but he also was open to blacks' migrating to improve their condition. In some instances, Hood pointed out, emigration was not a feasible option. For those blacks Hood advocated the ownership of homes and farms. Some blacks could easily purchase farms with the money they were paying in rent. A taxpaying landowner had greater respect, regardless of color or race, and such a person would have a greater inducement to take good care of property.[7]

Yet on occasion, Hood encouraged blacks to emigrate to more hospitable surroundings. A previous chapter discussed Hood's episcopal sojourn during the summer and early fall of 1885 (a journey that took him from North Carolina, through the border state of Kentucky, through the midwest, to the Far West and Southwest) and continuous correspondence to the *Star of Zion* documenting his travel activities and experiences. On his return trip, Hood wrote a letter recommending that a half million blacks, facing increasing racial proscription and low wages in the South, should consider settling in the West. Hood noted that there was little social interaction between whites and blacks now living in these areas, but did not find that to be an obstacle to black settlement and the enjoyment of life.[8] Of course, some observers might have pointed out that had half a million blacks inundated certain areas the easy relationship between the races that Hood described might have been upset somewhat, much as happened in the northern cities when blacks began to settle in them during the Great Migration.

Hood also recommended that blacks leave the cities and take up residence in rural areas, a position consistent with his advocacy of home and farm ownership and migration to the West with its vast open areas. The senior bishop idealized rural life as one that guaranteed physical, social, economic, and spiritual enhancements.[9] Of course the competition with European immigrants for jobs and the pervasive racial discrimination of labor unions also served as inducements for many leaders such as Hood to embrace urban-to-rural migration as a significant tool for blacks to advance themselves, though in North Carolina the competition of immigrants did not factor into the equation as much as it would in the larger cities of the North and Midwest. Hood's genuine conviction, perhaps reinforced by memories of his own rural upbringing in Pennsylvania, was that rural living represented a more wholesome and prosperous lifestyle than that in urban areas, which he believed provided too many opportunities for sinful living.

In an address by Hood, "The Black [Man's] Opportunity,"[10] Hood claimed that both wealthy planters and some less than wealthy individuals, particularly whites, were journeying to the cities and suburbs to make their fortunes. This created an opportunity for blacks to fill the void created by their absence, to take over farm care and employment. Black people, the cleric pointed out, were particularly suited for living in the South. They found the climate comfortable and knew the soil and the types of crops that could be grown and in what manner. With great numbers of people migrating to the cities, they would require farm produce for survival. African Americans could take advantage of this golden opportunity in these ways: buying small farms, renting farms, or doing farm work until one could afford one of the other options.[11] If farm workers would give their best effort to the farm owners, demonstrating that they were working for the interest of their employers, they then, Hood was confident, would soon be able to accumulate sufficient financial resources to rent or purchase farms of their own.[12]

A critic, however, could accurately point out that the efforts to disfranchise, lynch, and segregate blacks were all efforts motivated by a common purpose: to render blacks politically and economically impotent, to remove them from any measurable influence and power. What Hood and many other black leaders of the South at times failed to realize or overlooked was that most of lynchings of blacks were racially motivated responses to the economic and political empowerment of black people, rather than retaliation for actual sexual crimes or even the belief that blacks had committed them. People like the renowned antilynching crusader Ida B. Wells-Barnett persuasively demonstrated this fact with statistical data. In other words, blacks who owned property constituted a significant threat to many whites fearful of the prospect of black domination. It is also clear from history that most southern blacks who rented and worked on farms were greatly exploited. The system was set up so that blacks, far from amassing economic resources, were continually reduced to greater and greater levels of indebtedness. Many "equitable" or "just" contracts were only as good as the farm owner or employer, supported by an increasingly white supremacist array of judicial officials, would permit them to be. Many blacks who did not know beforehand later learned a painful lesson: the acquisition and maintenance of economic security and prosperity depended in large part on the possession and exercise of political power to safeguard those economic benefits. Hood did not downplay the significance of black political activity. Nor is it fair to overlook those blacks who were able to achieve economic advantages under adverse conditions. But Hood's positive interactions with the "better class of whites" may have blinded him to the greater number of instances where the apparatus of white supremacy curtailed the ambitions of even the most frugal of African Americans. One might argue that North Carolina witnessed less exploitation of African Americans than did states farther South. Still, the heavy hand of racial injustice fell hard on this state as well.

The Role of Education

For Bishop Hood another lever for racial uplift was the acquisition of education. Hood understood appropriate education, however, as encompassing both the industrial and liberal arts and directed toward both the clergy and laity. Consistent with other secular and religious leaders, Hood extolled education as a means of opening up opportunities previously closed to blacks, a way to uplift the race by developing the intellect, and a means of demonstrating to the larger society that African Americans were as capable of progress and citizenship as any other people.[13] Speaking to the North Carolina Annual Conference in 1899, Hood insisted on making available to blacks all types of education: "[r]eligious, moral, industrial and literary education," making it clear that African Americans required more than the industrial or manual type of education advocated so strongly by Booker T. Washington. With many southern states now in the hands of conservative whites who had curtailed support for black public education, Hood said that the church must take up the slack by offering all aspects of education, along with the religious, since this latter training contributed to the well-being of society as a whole by fostering strong moral character.[14]

Hood's endorsement of education is consistent with his belief in the importance of black institutions and his conviction regarding the providential role played by the black church in helping black people advance both spiritually and temporally. For example, in his address to the New York Annual Conference in 1904, Hood extolled the value of black- and Zion-supported Livingstone College in Salisbury, North Carolina, claiming that it was better able to prepare students for racial uplift than white-supported schools with black student bodies such as

Saint Augustine in Raleigh, Tuskegee Institute, and Hampton Institute in Virginia.[15] Such an emphasis on racial independence is hardly a capitulation to white supremacy.

The commitment to education on the part of Hood, the AMEZ Church, and other black leaders and organizations during this period might also be tied to the fact that southern states were quickly adopting literacy requirements for voting. Almost all black leaders saw voting as a fundamental right that must be preserved; thus, they urged upon the masses the necessity to be properly educated to meet these standards. Unfortunately, black leaders often gave legitimacy to these educational requirements for voting—to the detriment of black suffrage. Not only Hood but more "radical"-leaning individuals in Zion, for example, condemned the unequal application of these literary tests to blacks compared to whites, rather than opposing them in principle as the devices they were: tools to eliminate black voters from the rolls.[16] One might argue that these individuals were simply attempting to make a political fait accompli as racially equitable as possible. Still, it appears that too many black leaders accepted, in fact if not theory, the questionable notion that only the "intelligent" or educated black or white person should vote.

THE ROLE OF MORALITY AND TEMPERANCE IN RACIAL PROGRESS

Almost all black leaders of the period, both secular and religious, advocated strong moral and spiritual codes of conduct as necessary for individual and racial self-improvement. Late-twentieth-century scholars of this era often label such admonitions as "middle class," "bourgeois," or "Victorian" morality. Such terminology is unfortunate because it does not reflect the strong motivation of *Christian* morality, not *cultural* values, for those pursuing social reform. In part this emphasis on Christian morality was based on the idea that God exalts a people or a nation that adheres to the Divine will. Few, if any, black leaders of note failed to link the moral advantages of religion vis-à-vis political and economic development, however much they might criticize the actual behavior or failures of certain church leaders or question orthodox teachings of the church. Both Booker T. Washington and W. E. B. Du Bois, clearly unorthodox in their religious beliefs and differing considerably with each other regarding strategies for racial advancement, found themselves in full agreement on the importance of developing moral character. Second, black Christians undoubtedly wished to demonstrate that their spirituality and morality were second to none (in contradiction to the stereotypes that many whites then held about blacks) and, thus, they were acceptable for inclusion within the larger body politic. In addition, and perhaps more important, these leaders and the laity saw the practical significance of developing and maintaining a strong system of values. They understood the importance of morality for the internal strengthening of individual, family, and communal life. Hood, as religious leader and spokesman for his race, joined others in linking racial progress with the development and maintenance of a strong system of Christian values.

In addition to emphasizing virtues like frugality, sexual purity and proper conduct, generosity, kindness, hard work, avoidance of criminal behavior, and respect for others, black leaders strongly condemned the use of tobacco and alcohol, an attitude reflected in the lifelong teachings of Hood, the AMEZ, and most Protestant religious leaders. In the bishop's November 1882 address to the Central North Carolina Conference held in Statesville, Hood strongly denounced alcohol. According to the Zion leader, God had made a promise to deliver the entire world to the Lordship of Jesus Christ, but the realization of that promise depended on the elimination of all traffic in alcohol. Hood, urging the assembly to avoid all compromise on the issue, compared the traffic in alcoholic beverages with the system of slavery. Indeed, in 1908 two Zion bishops actually supported the Prohibition Party presidential candidate.[17]

This stringent stance on temperance mirrored the position of most white and black evangelicals of the latter part of the nineteenth century. Earlier in the nineteenth century many churches defined intemperance as the excessive use of alcohol. By the 1840s many had arrived at the conclusion that the best and most conclusive means to avoid drunkenness was to abstain totally from the use of liquor, a position that in turn led to the belief that the use of alcoholic beverages in any quantity was evil. More specifically, the Methodist tradition had a record of opposition to the use of alcohol traceable to the eighteenth century and its founder John Wesley. We must bear in mind the terrible impact that the excessive use and abuse of alcohol was having on society at the time: broken families, unemployment, crime, and in general preventing persons from taking full advantage of their potential. Not surprisingly, then, Hood and other black Christians saw the affliction of these often alcohol-related ills upon a people who were already politically and economically disadvantaged as a form of slavery with willing victims.

Furthermore, Hood and others viewed tobacco use in a light comparable to alcohol consumption. The bishop found tobacco use to be disgusting in appearance, and, perhaps more significantly, it made its user a slave of habit. How could a Christian follow Christ's command to be self-denying if he or she had made himself a slave of habit to tobacco?[18] In his 1884 episcopal address to the Kentucky Annual Conference, Hood called the use of tobacco in any form—"chewing, sniffing or smoking"—to be "useless, filthy, obnoxious, hateful, undignified, unreasonable, unnatural and ungodly."[19] Tobacco, he conceded was less of an evil than drinking, but "scarcely" so. Indeed, it serves the purpose of leading people to alcohol intoxication![20] It is little wonder, therefore, that candidates for the Zion ministry often faced closed scrutiny concerning the use of alcohol or tobacco and that during the mid-1880s a bishop of the Zion Church, W. H. Hillery, experienced expulsion from the episcopacy because of charges that included the use of alcohol.[21] As the 1891 New England Conference minutes reveal, however, Zion ministers and laity more readily supported Hood's views concerning alcohol than those regarding tobacco.[22]

CRIME, LYNCHING, AND HOOD

Hood, like other Zion and black religious leaders of the era, exhorted African Americans to avoid criminal behavior. Theft, robbery, murder, and other crimes were not only against the law but they contradicted proper religious conduct. Often these exhortations to steer clear of criminal behavior seemed oblivious to sociological context. At other times black Christians, including Zionites, recognized underlying causes and influences, such as ignorance or unemployment, but they refused to allow these circumstances to exonerate the criminal of moral or legal culpability. Black Christians understood that charges of criminal behavior on the part of any black person cast a negative light on the entire race, a position exemplified in the Report of the State of the Country by John C. Dancy and other Zionites at the 1899 Central North Carolina Conference.[23] The condemnation of crime by Hood and others, especially alleged rape and sexual assaults, may have unwittingly legitimized racist propaganda relative to lynching. As stated earlier in this chapter, these black leaders often accepted the idea that lynchings of blacks were white responses to alleged sexual crimes, when in fact they were usually perpetrated against politically and economically assertive blacks, especially black males, who threatened the system of white dominance and supremacy.[24] Gilmore concludes that these black leaders were acting as the "Best Black Men" of the race, exercising responsibility for the oversight of the less enlightened members of the race.[25]

As such, we must place Hood's approach to criminal activity in the context of the thought of other black religious leaders of the time. Baptist leaders like E. C. Morris, president of the National Baptist Convention, rushed to condemn sexual assaults and rapes while concomitantly maintaining that the alleged perpetrators of these cruel offenses should be duly tried and convicted in a court of law rather than being subjected to vigilantism.[26] Obviously, Hood, his fellow Zionites, and other black Christians wanted to calm any fears on the part of whites that they condoned the alleged attacks of black men on white women. They feared that a refusal to make the strongest possible denunciation of these alleged crimes would bring down the wrath of whites even more intensely and that the whole situation could result in racial warfare. Also, there was often a subtle attempt in the denunciation of these sexual crimes to provide legal protection and remedy for African American women against such brutalities and an obvious plea that punishment should adhere to the rule of law, guaranteeing the rights of all, including those who may have been wrongly accused.

Those Zionites and other black leaders who resided in the northern states appear to have offered much harsher denunciations of lynching, recommending more "radical" responses than those of Hood and most blacks living in the South. W. D. Clinton, M.D., of Pittsburgh, Pennsylvania, despite the strong objections of some, called upon blacks as early as September 1897 to prepare to defend themselves from murderous mobs who not only lynched men but also women.[27] In 1906 Bishop Alexander Walters, in an episcopal address to the New England Annual Conference, denounced lynchings much more strongly than I have observed in addresses and pronouncements by Hood. Walters called attention to the fact that recently two persons, one in Missouri and another in Tennessee, had been lynched, only to have subsequent investigations reveal that both were innocent of the charges against them.[28] When Bishop C. R. Harris, at the 1896 General Conference held in Mobile, Alabama, stated that intelligent and morally upright black ministers working in the South should have no fear about lynchings and other acts of brutality, a minister, a bishop, and a prominent layman rose to dispute the belief that these acts were things of the past and confined to lower-class white perpetrators and immoral black victims.[29]

Zion ministers did not escape these acts of barbarity. In 1902, in one confirmation of Harris's critics, the pastor of what is now Johnson Chapel AMEZ

Church in Courtland, Mississippi, experienced a savage beating arising from his disagreement with a white store owner concerning the minister's account at the business. W. R. Payne, described as college-trained, humble, unpretentious, and gentlemanly, barely escaped alive, fleeing to Memphis, Tennessee, about sixty miles north.[30] It is not surprising, therefore, that Bishop Walters in 1906 and the collective episcopal board in 1912 harshly condemned lynchings and called for federal legislation to protect African Americans.[31] I see no evidence that Hood dissented from the 1912 declaration and in fact apparently adopted a more aggressive stand regarding acts of racial terrorism when the rights of blacks continued to decline with the passage of time. Nonetheless, Dr. Clinton's, Walters's, and the General Conference's approaches contrasted markedly in tone with some of Hood's earlier pronouncements on the issue of racial violence.

Hood's response to the Wilmington Massacre of 1898 is further evidence of his belief in caution and calm even in the face of overwhelming brutality and his concern that the races in the South avoid a full scale violent conflict. In 1898 a group of reactionary whites literally overthrew the duly elected mayor and other officials in the North Carolina coastal city, killing many blacks and chasing others into exile. Shock waves went through the local African American community. Even months after the massacre, blacks continued to leave the city. The ire of the murderers fell particularly hard on the African American middle class and property holders. It was clear that the ringleaders of the mob sought to eradicate black and racially moderate influence and restore white supremacy.[32] Hood, speaking to the 1899 North Carolina Annual Conference, touched briefly on the events of a year earlier. He blamed the event on demagogues and overwrought passions "on both sides" and put the best face on the unhappy turn of events. According to the Zion leader, the two contending forces had reached an understanding, that there were sincere "apologies" and "regrets" on both sides, and Hood was confident that such a tragedy would not occur again.[33] Hood was not alone in his temperate analysis of the massacre. John C. Dancy, a prominent Zion layperson, federal office holder, and resident of Wilmington, blamed the incident on immoderate and irresponsible comments regarding liaisons between white males and black females by a local black newspaper editor.[34] Some Zionites were not as forgiving and sanguine about the situation in 1898 or 1899. There appear to have been calls for armed retaliation against the white reactionary forces or at least preparations for armed self-defense if such became necessary. The senior bishop, however, counseled peace on two grounds: the command of Christ and the practical consequences of destruction.[35]

Hood's more "moderate" approach to such cruel behavior did not go unchallenged in the African American community. The editor of the Philadelphia *Tribune,* a writer for the *Odd Fellows' Journal,* and Dr. N. F. Mossell of Philadelphia harshly attacked Hood for his moderation, his alleged attempt to appease southern whites, his poor judgment, and his refusal to condemn specifically the Wilmington Massacre, since the bishop had condemned only lawlessness in general.[36] The senior bishop of Zion did not waver. Hood defended his moderate approach, crediting it to the Quaker influence of his childhood environment in Pennsylvania. Pointing to his decades of work in the South, the bishop invited those who thought they could do a better job of advancing the cause of the race to come down and try their hands at it.[37] Hood and others reasoned that taking radical stands far removed from the perils of a situation showed little courage and an abundance of recklessness. It must also be noted that Hood expressed the sentiments of a number of moderates, including the *Star* editor, John W. Smith, who on occasion had serious and public differences of opinion with Hood.[38]

While the bishop never became a "radical" in his denunciation of lynching and acts of violence directed at blacks, he appeared to strengthen his criticism of such lawlessness in subsequent years, perhaps as a result of the reactions to his 1899 responses to the Wilmington Massacre and the ever-worsening conditions of African Americans in the South, including black disfranchisement in North Carolina. In his episcopal address to the Central North Carolina Conference in November 1901, Hood provided a carefully worded, moderate, but clear critique of the nation for allowing the atrocities of violence against blacks to continue. Noting with sadness the recent assassination of President William McKinley, the senior prelate took the occasion to remind the nation that those who sow violence would reap it.[39] This was a common theme propounded by black Christians, especially those of a more moderate bent: unlawful violence toward the black accused would contribute to general lawlessness in the nation transcending the boundaries of race. "Lynch law," said Hood, "never has, nor never will improve the condition of mankind."[40] Apparently, Hood realized that while his basic approach to issues would remain moderate, there reigned a passion for white supremacy in the land that heeded neither radical nor moderate appeals.

Hood and Booker T. Washington

An examination of Hood's philosophy thus far reveals some striking affinities with that of accommodationist Booker T. Washington, the head of Tuskegee Institute and the most powerful African American leader of the day, a man who had the ear of a number of U.S. presidents and wealthy philanthropic, white leaders. Washington has been described as the Great Compromiser on matters relating to racial justice during the 1895–1915 period.[41] Essentially, he counseled blacks to be wary of constant agitation for political rights and focus instead on economic self-help, emphasized industrial skills over the acquisition of literary and liberal arts education, stressed self-help and racial solidarity over efforts to achieve "social" integration with whites, and strongly advocated a view of southern whites as friends rather than adversaries (as he advised whites to regard blacks in the same fashion). Between approximately 1895 and 1905 the Tuskegee giant wielded considerable power. Black people who sought political appointments, as well as individuals, groups, and institutions, including churches, who sought financial support from charitable agencies and philanthropic individuals, had to meet with Washington's approval, since these white benefactors tended to seek Washington's advice on such matters involving blacks. With such power it is no wonder that many black leaders, secular and religious, spoke highly of him and attempted to steer clear of any direct attack against him, even when they held sharply different philosophical positions. With the rise in 1909 of the National Association for the Advancement of Colored People (NAACP), a coalition of "radical" black leaders and more liberal wealthy whites, Washington's influence began to decline.

It would be unfair and incorrect, however, to place the credit for all of Washington's influence on his connections with powerful whites or their promotion of him over other leaders. In many ways Washington reflected the sentiments of the masses of blacks. As exemplified by the words of Hood, African American leaders agreed with the Tuskegean in extolling the advantages of good moral character, economic self-help and empowerment, an approach to education that presented tangible results for advancement, a lukewarm approach toward the idea of mingling socially with whites, and an endorsement of racial pride, among other ideas that Washington promoted. Indeed, an analysis of pre– and post–Civil War speeches, addresses, and writings of religious and secular black leaders reveals that these ideas clearly preceded Washington's ascent to a position of influence. Thus, leaders such as Hood and even the "radical" Walters would continually pay homage to Washington not only because of his practical power and influence, but because he was voicing some ideas that transcended secular-religious and conservative-radical divisions.

There were, however, at least two crucial areas in which Hood and other black leaders differed from Washington. First, they placed greater emphasis on protecting the political and civil rights of blacks: for example, publicly defending black suffrage and political participation, clearer denunciations of Jim Crow segregation, and a greater willingness to condemn lynching publicly and unambiguously, whether moderately expressed in the words of Hood or fiercely denounced by Walters. Second, they laid greater stress on African Americans having access not only to "industrial education" but also the liberal arts. In other words, most leaders, including Hood, philosophically and strategically fit somewhere between William E. B. Du Bois—the civil rights activist, college professor, and sociologist who became Washington's greatest critic—and Washington, with some leaning more toward one than the other, but almost all of them embraced some aspects of both platforms. Thus, we should be wary of drawing sharp lines of demarcation between Washingtonian conservatives and Du Boisian progressives or radicals. Furthermore, both conservatives and progressives generally coexisted peacefully in the AMEZ and other independent black denominations, as exemplified by the mutually warm, courteous, and supportive relationship between the moderate or "conservative" Hood and the progressive or radical" Walters.

Hood often expressed high praise and respect for Washington, noting on one occasion that Baptists and Methodists, who represented the vast majority of African American Christians, always welcomed in a spirit of deep honor and respect Washington's presence at their conventions and conferences. "There was no other visitor to [the 1908 AMEZ] General Conference who received anything like the ovation that was given Dr. Washington." But Hood, like most other black spokespersons, clearly signaled that he did not accept without question all of Washington's strategies. Even while defending Washington against his critics, the "noisy pessimists" and the "radicals," Hood offered a soft rebuke of Washington by emphasizing the necessity of all types of educational opportunities for blacks. Hood's insistence on the availability of all types of education pointed to agreement with the "radicals" and the majority of black leaders that African Americans should strive for all their rights and reject relegation to any particular socioeconomic station in life.[42]

Hood and Zion leaders also more forcefully fought the disfranchisement of African American voters in the South than did Booker T. Washington. The state of Mississippi began this assault on black suffrage in 1890. Usually southern reactionaries attempted to camouflage their white supremacist motivations by requiring dubious procedures like poll taxes and literacy examinations applied in a discriminatory fashion to blacks who met these requirements and to those attempting to vote in courageous defiance of the reign of economic and physical terror against them. Throughout his life Hood recognized the immense importance of suffrage for African Americans, claiming that the deprivation of that right relegated one to the status of a slave.

In the late 1890s and early 1900s, when reactionaries struggled successfully to disfranchise most North Carolina blacks, the bishop forcefully fought back. He was disappointed that North Carolina, where in his opinion there had been amicable race relations, would now imperil such harmony and regretted that the U.S. Congress had not used its power to discourage such unconstitutional schemes by reducing Mississippi's congressional representation after its disfranchisement of black voters, a constitutional right the Congress clearly possessed. Like some other Zionites, Hood believed it legitimate that the state should seek to demand an educated electorate. (As a matter of fact, Hood would have imposed morality as an additional prerequisite, though he knew that the majority of the people would never accept this criterion.) Yet Hood believed that such educational requirements should not take effect until all classes of people truly had educational opportunities. The bishop strongly asserted, furthermore, that it would be a gross injustice to apply these literacy requirements in such a manner as to take the suffrage from those who currently enjoyed it; such would be sheer robbery.

As we have observed, Hood had served in the North Carolina State Reconstruction Convention in 1867–1868, had participated in other state Reconstruction activities, and had lived in the state since 1864. The bishop, thus, could speak with authority based on historical experience concerning postwar North Carolina and the black franchise. White North Carolinians should bear in mind, said Hood, that they too had benefited from the progress brought to the state largely because of the black vote, through measures such as greater educational opportunities, homestead exemption provisions, enlargement of women's rights, and other public benefits. It was obvious that African Americans had never used their right to vote in a selfish, racially prejudiced fashion but to serve the needs of all North Carolinians. The elimination of the black vote, thus, would adversely affect the entire state, not simply blacks. Despite the success of the disfranchisement movement in most areas, Hood remained optimistic about the future reinstatement of the black vote and the ultimate success of blacks' quest for freedom and equity. For a time many North Carolina blacks and some whites entertained strong hopes that the U.S. Supreme Court would invalidate the state's disfranchisement amendment. In the face of such discouragement Hood continued his attempts to build and maintain bridges of cooperation between the black community and the "better class of white people."[43]

Hood and Zionites equally opposed the jim crow segregationist measures that intensified during this era. Whereas whites' general rejection of "social equality" was predicated on the desire not to be equal with blacks in social or other terms, Hood, like most blacks, saw the issue more as "social intermingling." He did not accept the notion that blacks were socially *inferior* to whites, but he saw no need for blacks' pressing themselves into relationships and circumstances that were purely social in nature. Thus, while disclaiming any attempt to force "social equality," Hood steadfastly opposed jim crow segregation in situations such as public or rail transportation, correctly recognizing such as systematic attempts to rob blacks of their dignity and to force them to live according to the white supremacist declaration of their supposed inferiority to whites. Furthermore, despite the "separate but equal" propaganda, facilities reserved for blacks were almost always inferior.

Hood's episcopal address to the West Central North Carolina Conference in 1913 amply demonstrated Hood's rejection of both segregation and disfranchisement. Noting that the people were gravely disturbed over segregation measures that were seen as efforts to "degrade" and "dispossess them of their hard-earned possessions," Hood stated, "We are told that it [segregation] will be a benefit to the Negro. That is what they told us about disfranchisement, but we have learned by sad experience that the opposite to this has been the result."[44] Though he was moderate and conciliatory, Hood's forthright stands for African American access to all forms of education, his opposition to jim crow segregation, and his fervent denunciation of disfranchisement clearly distinguish him and most black leaders, secular and religious, from the correspondingly tepid and sometimes publicly ambivalent stands of Booker T. Washington.

OTHER ISSUES AND CONCERNS

Hood's positions on several other race-related issues can be briefly outlined here. Regarding the U.S. Supreme Court and the quest for racial justice, Hood, like other Zion leaders, realized that the Supreme Court had generally opposed civil rights for African Americans by declaring that blacks had no civil rights in 1857, invalidating post–Civil War civil rights measures during the 1880s, and upholding Jim Crow segregation in 1896. In 1912 Zionites recalled the courageous and meritorious dissent of John Marshall Harlan in the 1896 *Plessy* v. *Ferguson* decision upholding segregation, and they expressed deep sorrow and loss over his death. Otherwise, in reference to the Supreme Court, Zionites noted, and Hood agreed, "That August body has never been a conservator of our interests."[45] By 1916 the Court had issued a ruling outlawing so-called grandfather clauses used by many states to disfranchise black voters. Zionites hailed the decision and noted with glee that the unanimous decision had been authored by a southerner from Louisiana. But given the damage that the executive, legislative, and judicial branches of state and federal governments had inflicted on blacks for decades, it would be a half century before that last-cited decision, buttressed by other civil rights measures, would benefit most African Americans, particularly in the South.[46]

On issues not clearly understood as civil rights concerns, the Zionites, including Hood, largely reflected the opinions of the majority of Americans, though there was often a racial twist or consideration involved. Also, where Hood's views are known, no fundamental contradictions between his opinions and most other black religious leaders are apparent. Hood and the Zionites, like most American Christians, were rather ambivalent concerning the growth of the American labor movement. On one hand, there was sympathy for the workers' plight. On the other hand, the traditional Christian viewpoint looked rather askance at the notion of workers organizing for collective bargaining with their employees and resorting to strikes that often resulted in violence, though the disturbances were often instigated by the employers or their sympathizers. Nor was the relationship between employee and employer to be disturbed by governmental intervention, in the minds of most American Christians during this era. To be sure, there were Christian socialists, like the black Baptist minister George W. Woodbey and social gospel advocates like Reverdy Ransom of the AME and the white Baptist Walter Rauschenbusch, the most systematic and forceful proponent of the social gospel. But generally Hood, Zionites, and other denominational leaders (Methodist or Baptist), though sensitive to human suffering, did not explicitly advocate the *systematic* approaches characteristic of Christian socialism or the social gospel.

Hood, like other Zionites, was not comfortable with the numerous strikes and acts of violence connected with the labor movement. Furthermore, organized labor's discrimination against African Americans in membership and hiring alienated many African Americans. In 1886 Hood saw the breaking of work stoppages by employers' hiring blacks, who were ordinarily denied employment, as providential and asserted that labor woes would continue until the sin of racial prejudice was obliterated in the union movement.[47]

In addition to sharing Hood's labor views, other Zionites agreed with the bishop on a related issue, foreign immigration. African Americans saw foreign immigrants, most of whom were white, as displacing potential black employees. Furthermore, black Christians, as well as most American Christians, looked on the United States as a Christian nation now imperiled by the huge influx of foreigners alien to true Christianity. Even some resident Catholics and Jews found the immigrants repulsive because these newcomers threatened the status and respectability of these older Americans by customs that were often in sharp contrast to the accepted way of life in the United States. The participants in the AMEZ Philadelphia and Baltimore Annual Conference of 1891 clearly represented the sentiments of most black and white Christians regarding immigration when they stated, "We regard the unrestricted immigration of foreigners of the criminal and illiterate classes as a threatening menace to our Christian civilization." These Zionites advocated policies that restricted immigration "to the better class of foreigners" and insisted that potential citizens should first speak English and comprehend the principles of American democracy prior to naturalization. Such sentiments represented the consensus of Zion leaders, and I have found no evidence that Hood fundamentally disagreed with them.[48]

In matters of foreign policy neither Hood nor Zionites as a body differed profoundly with the general American consensus, though, again, the issue of race often entered into their discussions. This lack of strong dissent on the part of the denomination as a whole probably reflects the reality that black Christians, like their white counterparts, understood the United States to be a Christian nation whose obligation was to spread Christianity and democracy throughout the world, even though black Christians differed occasionally on the precise methods to accomplish this end. Black Christians, in many instances, saw war as an opportunity to demonstrate their patriotism and loyalty as faithful citizens who loved their country and, given their success on the battlefields, were quite deserving of all the rights accorded other Americans.

Undoubtedly there was dissent within the ranks of Zion concerning the United States' role in the Spanish-American War of 1898. But as early as April 20, 1898, the Board of Bishops approved a resolution introduced by Hood that gave ringing endorsement to President William McKinley in his pursuit of the war.[49] Those favoring the war saw it as a case of the United States's acting to free the inhabitants of Cuba, the Philippines, and other countries from the oppression of the Spaniards. Whatever misgivings some Zionites held, there was a clear consensus that the outcome of the war presented the churches with a golden opportunity to expand Christian missions (since they, like most American Protestants, did not regard the Roman Catholicism of the inhabitants of these foreign countries as a true form of Christianity) and the principles of American civilization. And, more immediately, the war offered African American soldiers the chance to demonstrate their bravery and loyalty, a service viewed by most black Christians as boosting black Americans' pursuit of equal justice in the eyes of whites.[50]

Hood echoed these views but went further in his interpretation of the meaning and purpose of the Spanish-American War. He saw the conflict as a fulfillment of biblical prophecy since the war had finally crippled the naval might of Roman Catholicism's major sponsor, Spain. The Reformation, though highly significant, was not the complete fulfillment of biblical prophecy that the power of Papal Rome would be broken. (Strangely, Hood was *not* as anti-Catholic as many Protestant leaders during this era.) Though Hood was cognizant of opposition, because of racial prejudice, the bishop, nonetheless, advocated that full rights of American citizenship be granted to all the inhabitants of these lands, predicting that such would come to pass. Furthermore, discussing the conflict and its resolution, Hood spoke of a coming millennial period of justice, peace, racial brotherhood, and righteousness over all the earth prior to the Second Coming of Jesus Christ.[51] These are fascinating ideas, and I have discovered no evidence that the great body of Zionites disagreed with Hood's pronouncements and predictions.

Zionites as a body sided with the British in the Boer War against the Afrikaners. Hood asserted that the Afrikaners had more right to the land than the British, but he, too, deeply appreciated Britain's perceived great democratic tradition.[52] Most blacks recalled Britain's role in ending the Atlantic Slave Trade, for abolishing slavery in its domain during the 1830s, and serving as a refuge and in many quarters a source of financial support for black and white American antislavery supporters prior to the Civil War. Interestingly, Hood did not speak of the needs and rights of the greater numbers of indigenous Africans and their many ethnic groups, though other Zionites suggested that the Afrikaners should offer indigenous Africans the same justice and equity for which they themselves strove. The preponderance of Hood's political views and his legacy of defending the oppressed suggest that he agreed with that exhortation. Nor did Zionites, in their praise of British democracy, note Britain's support of the African Slave Trade down to the nineteenth century, the support of some in England for the Confederacy during the Civil War, and the imperialistic adventures of Britain in Africa and other places in the world.

With regard to the First World War, neither Hood nor other Zionites offered any critique of the European colonialism and imperialism that lay as root causes of the conflict. These black Christians tended to focus more specifically on the discrimination faced by African Americans in their attempts to join in combat roles.

CONCLUSION

Although Hood retired from political office in 1872, he continued to exercise leadership as a political adviser for Zion and African Americans in general. Politically, Hood might be categorized as a moderate in that he pursued a strategy of moderation and conciliation in the quest for social justice for African Americans. Hood firmly believed that blacks would eventually attain the full exercise of all their constitutional rights, that the United States and the world, through the work of righteous men and women, were approaching a millennial period of full justice, righteousness, and equality for all humanity. Sometimes Hood's moderate approach brought disdain from those termed "radical" or progressives and who generally resided in the North. Such criticisms probably helped Hood to recognize the necessity of becoming more forceful, though never "radical." Yet Hood, significantly, was in the mainstream of black leadership, generally speaking. His recipe for racial progress included the development of strong moral values, conciliation with liberal or moderately minded whites, the acquisition of education, opposition to racial segregation, the responsible exercise of the ballot, and an insistence that African Americans should work to attain and retain their full citizenship rights.

After 1872 Hood continued to cultivate ties with black and white politicians and officeholders, both giving them support and being wooed by them, although he insisted that a minister's first duty should be to the church, leaving little if any time for political office seeking. Hood's support of the national Republican party, as shown in the following chapter, demonstrates, however, that while the bishop might have rejected the appellation of "politician," he was undeniably both philosophically and pragmatically *political*.

Chapter Seven

THE LOYAL REPUBLICAN

Hood's Political Leadership and
the Presidential Elections of 1908 and 1912

A wise son *heareth* his father's instruction . . .
    —Proverbs 13:1, Holy Bible, King James Version

[M]en of all political phases regarded him not a politician, but a statesman.
    —The Reverend J. W. McDonald, *The Star of Zion*

This chapter continues the treatment of Hood's role as a political leader after his retirement from active officeholding in 1872. The previous chapter outlined Hood's political philosophy, especially as it related to issues of racial advancement. In the following pages, we shall observe that Hood's leadership in the political arena during the 1872–1916 period transcended the mere enunciation of positions on various issues, but included active efforts on his behalf to support the national Republican party and its presidential candidates. Rather than attempt to cover the entirety of Hood's political activities, this chapter adopts a case study approach. In describing Hood's support of Republican presidential candidates in 1908 and 1912, we are able to observe that Hood's retirement from political office holding did not reflect a lack of interest in politics, particularly regarding civil rights for African Americans. With the presidency of the Democratic Woodrow Wilson, blacks, even those who had staunchly supported him, realized the wisdom of Hood and mainstream black leaders who had consistently counseled loyalty to the Republican party.

As noted in the previous chapter, no matter how strongly the bishop insisted that his calling as a minister precluded a political role, he, nonetheless, continued to provide crucial leadership. Relatedly, this chapter demonstrates that Hood was a part of the larger denominational leadership of Zion that, regardless of political party preferences, was fervently committed to racial progress. These connectional leaders envisioned religious leadership as encompassing the responsibility to guard the secular or temporal interests of church members as well as the spiritual. The years 1908 and 1912 are targeted because during this period, more than any during the entire life of Hood or prior life of the party, loyalty to the national Republican Party met its greatest contest within Zion and the general black community.

REPUBLICANS, DEMOCRATS, AND BLACK RELIGIOUS LEADERSHIP

The two major parties of the late nineteenth and early twentieth centuries were the Democratic and Republican. The Republican party, the party of Abraham Lincoln, guided the country through the turbulent years of the Civil War, demonstrated the most support for abolition of slavery, and helped to extend the legal and constitutional rights of African Americans throughout the nation, particularly in the South, after the War. Most blacks, understandably, looked on the Republicans as their political saviors or at least as more sympathetic than their Democratic rivals, and heavily supported them both nationally and at the local and state levels. When Grover Cleveland, the Democrat, won the presidency in 1884, he broke the twenty-four-year hold that the Republicans had had on the presidency since the election of Abraham Lincoln and caused concern among most African Americans. From that point to 1916 the presidency alternated between the parties, with most elections very close, at least in terms of the popular vote.

In many ways, this was an era of worsening conditions for African Americans, politically and economically. The Democrats, historically aligned with slavery and antiblack positions on constitutional rights, were gaining power throughout the South by means of ingenious "legal" and outright brutal methods of disfranchising black voters, and the Republicans nationally were gradually losing interest in the concerns of African Americans. In addition, as the 1890s drew to a close and the momentum for black voter disfranchisement increased, there were strong Republican elements in the southern states who sought to purge black participation and fashion a "lily-white" party. Clearly, the general white populace, both North and South, had grown weary of issues connected with black freedom. Even some of the most racially enlightened whites decided to leave matters of racial politics to the (white) South, with all the social, economic, and political ramifications for blacks of such a move. The Reconstruction era's legacy of black empowerment and equal justice had largely come to an end, and reactionism on racial matters was on the rise.

On the other hand, there were elements of the Democratic party that made overtures to African American citizens during this period. Given these overtures and the dissatisfaction that many African Americans felt with the Republican party, not surprisingly, there were African American leaders who believed that racial self-interest lay in steering a politically independent course between the two parties. Blacks should support acceptable Democrats so that the Republican party would not take their votes for granted. Of course there were a minority of blacks who aligned themselves with the Democratic party because they saw it as more representative of their socioeconomic interests. By and large, however, most blacks, including Hood, remained committed to the Republican party while occasionally supporting more progressive-minded Democrats, particularly on the state and local levels.

The "independents," such as AMEZ Bishop Alexander Walters, AME Bishop Henry McNeal Turner, and the civil rights advocate and educator Dr. W. E. B. Du Bois, correctly perceived that Republican presidents mouthed platitudes about racial equality and justice and even made token federal appointments but refused to move aggressively to enforce the Thirteenth, Fourteenth, and Fifteenth Amendments to the Constitution (amendments that guaranteed physical freedom, citizenship, and suffrage for blacks) in the face of relentless and often calculated attacks on these rights by means of disfranchisement, voter intimidation, lynching, unfair labor practices in the South, and Jim Crow legislation. More moderate blacks like Hood, while willing to support progressive-minded Democrats on state and local levels, countered that the *national* Democratic party had a proven track record of suppressing blacks, that that party was not advancing proposals equal to or superior to the rival party, and that, therefore, it was dangerously premature to vote Democratic in national presidential elections. Blacks, they argued, owed a debt to the party of Thaddeus Stevens and Abraham Lincoln. Additionally, although the Republicans may have been doing less than possible in the interest of African Americans, the Democrats would do more *against* the interests of the race. For the most part, in supporting the Republican party, Hood was clearly within the mainstream of black leadership, religious and secular, as well as the mainstream of the African American population. Even independents, in the final analysis, would grow disillusioned with the Democratic party.[1]

This struggle between the Republican loyalists and the independents or independent Democrats was reflected in the AMEZ denomination. The Democrat Grover Cleveland's election to the presidency in 1884 ended a twenty-four-year monopoly of that office by the Republicans. Undoubtedly, his election also raised quite a bit of concern among African Americans since he represented what was for them the proslavery party. While he may not have supported Cleveland, Bishop Hood dissented from the pessimistic outlook of many African Americans regarding the Democratic president. The bishop believed that racial progress was not dependent on any particular person holding the presidency. Rather, blacks must take advantage of whatever opportunities were at their disposal and work to eliminate "poverty, ignorance and vice" from the community.[2] Generally, Zion leaders were not particularly satisfied with Cleveland's performance, but they at least did not witness the realization of their worst fears.[3] While most Zionites were greatly dissatisfied with a number of Republican administrations between Cleveland and William H. Taft, the strong push for an independent or pro-Democratic course in national politics did not really capture the attention of the denomination until the 1908 presidential election. The controversy that embroiled elements within AMEZ mirrored the conflict that transpired in the entire black community during these decades. With the disfranchisement of most blacks in the southern states by the early 1900s, one might be inclined to consider this debate largely academic. On the other hand, some African Americans in the South, a small percentage, continued to vote, undeterred or unaffected by violence and threats and undaunted by poll taxes and literacy tests. With this background, let us examine Hood's steadfast support of the Republican party in the presidential elections of 1908 and 1912.

THE 1908 PRESIDENTIAL ELECTION AND ZION METHODISM

Within the Zion membership the first, effective effort to deliver a sizable portion of the AMEZ vote to the Democratic candidate, in 1908, was led by Bishop Walters and supported vigorously by George C. Clements, the editor of the denominational paper, the *Star of Zion*. Alexander Walters (1858–1917) was a remarkable personality, church leader, civil rights advocate, and scholar.[4] One of the youngest individuals ever consecrated bishop in the Zion church, Walters was highly esteemed and a major influence in church and community life. He was born in Bardstown, Kentucky, and died in New York City. During his ministerial career he pastored two of the most prestigious churches in the AMEZ connection: the First AMEZ Church on Stockton Street in San Francisco and Mother Zion AMEZ Church in New York City. He held numerous posts within the connection, traveled extensively overseas, including Africa, and was actively involved in Methodist ecumenical activities. He was a founder and president of the Afro-American Council, a forerunner to the National Association for the Advancement of Colored People (NAACP). He also figured prominently in the early growth of the NAACP, serving at one time as a member of its executive board. Though perhaps not as politically outstanding or renowned as Walters, George C. Clements[5] (1871–1934) also played a very influential role in Zion circles. A North Carolina native, Clements attended Livingstone College, the denominational school in Salisbury, and taught public school for a number of years. In 1904 he was elected editor of the *Star of Zion,* a post from which he ascended to the episcopacy (1916), like others before and after him. According to Walls, Clements was a well-informed, productive editor who expanded the circulation of the *Star* into many new arenas.[6] Clements and his wife, Emma Clarissa, also hold the distinction of having parented a number of successful children, including one who served as the president of Atlanta University in Georgia.

In 1908 the American voter was faced with several interesting choices for the presidency: the Republican William H. Taft, the Democrat William Jennings Bryan, the Socialist Eugene V. Debs, and a Prohibition Party candidate. Walters, Clements, and some other Zionites came out strongly for Bryan, the Democrat, for a number of reasons: it was consistent with the political strategy of diversifying the black vote; they represented a new group of leaders advocating a more "radical" approach to civil rights compared with the more moderate Hood camp; and they were reacting to President Theodore Roosevelt's response to the Brownsville Incident. From the perspective of the Republican Zionites, the formation of the pro-Democratic faction was stimulated in great part by jealousy directed at Booker T. Washington (a black leader who exercised a great deal of influence with Roosevelt and Taft) and at those blacks appointed by Theodore Roosevelt. Jealousy and envy are perhaps too strong and biased terms to apply to Zionites such as Walters and other black leaders like Du Bois and Bishop Turner. But it is easy to understand the pro-Democratic group's opposition to what they considered a too-conservative, status quo black leadership, represented by pro-Republican blacks.[7]

The Brownsville, Texas, Incident crystallized the pro-Democratic opposition, and it easily became the focal point of their campaign against the Republican party and what they saw as its lukewarm, and even antagonistic, attitude toward black voters. The Brownsville episode incensed not only the Walters group but almost all blacks in the United States. In 1906 black soldiers stationed near Brownsville, Texas, came under allegations of having rioted. President Theodore Roosevelt, who had an ambiguous record of support and opposition to black freedom, on this occasion responded abysmally by discharging from service three companies of black soldiers in the Twenty-fifth Regiment without having the charges substantiated. According to Meier, this presidential action angered blacks above all others.[8] Furthermore, Roosevelt delivered a message to Congress in the same year that repeated the misconception that black men had suffered lynching in the South because of sexual assaults on white women. There were major questions about Taft's possible involvement in the injustice done black soldiers, because he was serving at the time as secretary of war. Furthermore, Taft had advocated industrial education with a fervor that left little room for liberal arts education for blacks, and he had endorsed restricting the ballot by a strict reading of the Fifteenth Amendment to the Constitution that many blacks and liberal whites felt compromised the spirit of the law. Not surprisingly, Walters and others attempted to elicit clarifications and stronger statements of support for black freedom from the Republican Taft, but to no avail. They then led the charge within the Zion membership to deliver over a half million votes to Bryan, an effort that they believed would tip the scales in a closely contested race and open a door of opportunity for blacks in the Democratic party.[9]

John C. Dancy rose to the defense of the Republican party, strongly backed by Bishop Hood. A prominent layman, Dancy had served as the editor of the *Star of Zion,* customs collector at the port in Wilmington, North Carolina, and was the current editor of the *AMEZ Quarterly Review.* In terms of secular and church politics, Dancy was somewhere between Hood and Walters. Had he been an ordained clergy, his drive, forcefulness, brilliance, and dedication to church and race might very well have earned him the episcopal chair. In response to actions taken by Walters and Clements, current editor of the *Star of Zion,* Dancy contacted all of the bishops of the AMEZ Church to secure their support in holding Zion support and the black vote within the Republican column and committed a considerable portion of the July–September 1908 issue of the *Quarterly Review* to publishing their responses.[10]

One of the first and most vigorous responses to the efforts of Dancy was from the senior bishop himself. In an article entitled "No Open Door in the Democratic Party," Hood gave a comprehensive apologia for continued black support for the Republican ticket. In this same issue of the *Quarterly Review,* four other Zion bishops—George W. Clinton, J. W. Smith, J. S. Caldwell, and A. J. Warner—wrote articles supporting the Republican ticket.[11] Hood's article pointed out the historical position of the national Democratic party toward African Americans. Making allowances for southern state Democrats in some instances, Hood vigorously asserted that nationally the party had always been dominated by those who favored slavery and sought to block the constitutional and legal advancement of blacks. More pointedly, he saw the candidacy of William Jennings Bryan, the Democratic nominee, as an economic threat to the whole country. Voting for Bryan would bring down on blacks a great expression of vengeance from the white voters of the country should the votes of the former succeed in helping to elect the Democratic ticket. Black voters, Hood urged, must focus on the real Bryan, whose economic policies would vastly reduce the earning power of most Americans. Even some Democrats were frightened of him, the bishop argued. Bryan's only hope for victory was to seduce a sufficient number of blacks from supporting the Republican ticket so that he might defeat Taft. Hood warned the people not to be misled. Furthermore, in an obvious reference to the Brownsville Incident, Hood rejected the strategy of voting against Taft to spite Roosevelt, of allowing one episode to supersede all other important issues.[12]

Hood saw the election as a great test of the wisdom of the black electorate, a test that could have tremendous ramifications for how white Americans viewed their black counterparts. The senior bishop praised past glories of the black soldiers on the battlefields. Now he called for the community to respond with equal valor and sound judgment at the ballot box. It seems that Hood still hoped and expected that, despite the continuing adverse political and economic fortunes of American blacks, full inclusion of his people into the mainstream of American life might be achieved as blacks proved themselves worthy of the standards of solid citizenship.[13] Dancy, the editor of the *Review,* for his part reinforced the comments of Hood and other bishops supporting the Republican Taft, speaking specifically of the good fortune of the church in having someone of balance, training, and wisdom to guide it through rocky and turbulent times.[14] The lay leader called attention to the fact that the great majority of the bishops had come out in favor of the Republican party. In other comments he made it clear that such comments by Hood represented the clear position of the Zion membership and went so far as to say actions by those like Walters in support of the Democrats were in obvious conflict with "the teachings, history and polity" of Zion Methodism.[15]

William H. Taft won the 1908 presidential election rather handily with 51.6 percent of the popular vote.[16] Only three other candidates in the nine presidential elections held since the reelection of Ulysses S. Grant in 1872 polled more than 50 percent of the popular vote: McKinley in 1896 (50.8) and 1900 (51.7) and Roosevelt in 1904 (56.4). Taft's percentage was noteworthy in that 1908 was his *first* election to the presidency. McKinley in the 1900 and Roosevelt in the 1904 campaigns both won reelection as incumbents, with Roosevelt having taken the presidency in 1901 upon McKinley's death and soon after his reelection. Bishop Walters' Democratic candidate, William Jennings Bryan, in his third run for the office, registered only 43.1 percent of the overall popular vote, down from his totals in the 1896 (46.7) and 1900 (45.5) races. Discounting Eugene V. Debs's 2.8 percent and that of the other minor candidates, Taft's victory over Bryan was a clear landslide in both popular and electoral votes, a fact consistent with Hood's earlier appraisal of the American electorate. Dancy estimated that 90 percent of Zionites had voted the Republican ticket, a clear repudiation of the politics of the independents.[17] Seven bishops (including Franklin and Blackwell) had supported the Republicans, two had supported the Prohibition party (C. R. Harris and John W. Alstork), and only one, Walters, had supported the Democrats.[18]

As early as one year after the election, Hood remained the eternal optimist and loyal Republican. He praised the administration of Roosevelt and expected great things from Taft's presidency.[19] There were many blacks, and not all in the pro-independent camp, who did not so optimistically assess the legacy of Roosevelt. Furthermore, Hood's belief in Taft's progressivism in racial matters proved equally flawed with the passage of his administration. The fortunes of blacks did not materially improve with his election and might even have declined. Theodore Roosevelt had made fewer black appointments to federal office than McKinley, and Taft reduced the number even more. The new president made it clear in word and deed that he would not appoint blacks to offices in localities where whites opposed them. Those whites dedicated to ridding black people from the Republican party and divorcing it from the issues of racial progress, the "lily white" contingent, had even greater success under Taft than his predecessor. While racial segregation of federal government offices came to fruition under his successor, the Democrat Woodrow Wilson, Taft set a precedent by segregating a few offices. By the end of his first and only presidential term, Taft had politically alienated African Americans.[20]

Woodrow Wilson, the 1912 Election, and Zion Leadership

Black voters had a poor selection of candidates in the 1912 election: Woodrow Wilson, the Democrat and native of the South who promised little to the black community; Taft, who had completely alienated many voters; Theodore Roosevelt, running under the Progressive party label, who had at best a mixed record; and Eugene V. Debs, the Socialist party candidate whose stance was as alien to the black community as it was to most whites. Blacks split their vote, with most supporting Roosevelt as the least of the evils: Roosevelt, 60 percent; Taft, 20 percent; and Wilson, 20 percent.[21] Bishop Walters once again launched within the black community a vigorous campaign to vote Democratic. The 1912 election, however, was probably devoid of the same urgency as the 1908 race. In 1912, Roosevelt's challenge caused a split of votes among those who were progressive on racial matters, however lopsided that split might be. Besides, Wilson did not run as the rabid segregationist he would prove to be, but rather as a learned scholar and statesperson who was in sympathy with much of Roosevelt's progressivism. With the bad experience of Taft, the sorry record of Roosevelt, and the unacceptable program of the Socialists, it would not be surprising if matters were too confused and complex to occasion the all-out anti-Democrat activities of 1908. Roosevelt and Taft split the "Progressive-Republican" vote and ensured Wilson's election. Wilson scored 41.8 percent of the popular vote, less than Bryan in the previous election but more than enough to win, given the splitting of votes by Roosevelt (27.4 percent) and Taft (23.2 percent). Eugene V. Debs, the Socialist, gained a greater percentage than he had in any of his four serious runs for the presidency, 6 percent.[22]

To be sure, the Zionite and non-Zionite supporters of Wilson were not naive. These black leaders understood that Wilson was a native southerner, had served as president of a university that barred black students, and had taken no forthright positions on racial matters. Yet they were "taken in" by the "Christian gentleman" whom they deemed too learned and cultivated to act with the meanness and shortsightedness of white supremacists like South Carolina politician Benjamin Tillman and Mississippi Governor James Vardaman. They expected Wilson to refrain from eliminating blacks from appointive office, engaging in hypocrisy, and furthering segregation. The pro-Democrat faction also believed that Wilson and the Democrats would be more supportive of black concerns if African Americans, by demonstrating that the Republican party held no monopoly on their votes, gave Wilson the support needed to win in a close race.[23]

Bishop Hood stood by the Republican candidate, William H. Taft, in the 1912 election. It would have been surprising if Hood, committed as he was to the Republicans and as cautious as he was about the Democrats, had departed from the Republican Taft or the Progressive and former Republican Roosevelt for the less than forthright Democrat Wilson. Even had his opinion of Taft diminished, Hood's high estimation of Roosevelt, even after the president left office in 1909, suggests that he would more likely have supported him than the Democratic Wilson.[24] For those inclined to support Roosevelt or torn between him and Taft, the senior bishop noted that the incumbent president was the legitimate Republican nominee who had properly and fairly secured the nomination. Hood was firmly convinced that Taft completely embraced Republican principles, including support of the gold standard, endorsing civil and political freedoms guaranteed by the Constitution and extended to all without regard to race or color, and tariffs that would protect American industries and secure good wages for labor.

While the majority of blacks concluded that Taft had been a poor president from the standpoint of protecting the civil and constitutional liberties of African Americans, Hood portrayed Taft as the great defender of the Fifteenth Amendment, which guaranteed blacks the right to vote.[25] Indeed, in Hood's opinion, support for this amendment was eminently more important than Taft's record of making so few black political appointments, since voting was the foundation of black political progress.[26] Critics of Taft could easily point out that by 1912 most blacks in the South, where the overwhelming majority of African Americans still lived, had already suffered disfranchisement, and the president had done little to reverse such actions already taken.

But Hood dealt forthrightly with criticism that Taft had failed to appoint more blacks to the South and that he had been unduly sensitive to the objections of white southerners to the appointment of blacks to positions there. The bishop claimed that part of the problem lay in the fact that the president had raised standards for appointments to federal posts. This course of action had disadvantaged prospective black appointees, but many more white ones had been negatively affected than blacks. Besides, Hood pleaded, one could not reasonably expect a person not to make mistakes; all that could be expected of a virtuous person is that he or she act fairly based on knowledge at that person's disposal.[27] Hood's critics could reply that though more white individuals than blacks might have been adversely affected by these new "standards," more whites than blacks also had benefited from them. One might also be justly alarmed that worthy office holders had been replaced with some unworthy ones and that this had occurred in an administration that was supposedly raising standards. Despite Hood's appeal, the majority of blacks did not cast their votes for Taft.

Though he had supported Taft, the post-election Hood, a strong temperance partisan and advocate of prohibition, was unduly impressed with the professed Christian character of Wilson, particularly his decision to ban all alcoholic beverages from the inaugural celebration.[28] Hood also found himself easily agreeing with Wilson's statements discouraging individuals' self-promotion for political office. In both church and state affairs, Hood had found that this type of ambition runs counter to the best interests of constituents. The senior bishop also advised all Methodists to follow the directives of the Bible and the Zion *discipline* and "show proper respect as a matter of duty to all those in authority." When the people have the good fortune of governance by a "righteous ruler," meaning Wilson, they should render respect as more than a duty "but as a pleasure."[29] The committee that reported on "The State of Country" for the New York Conference echoed much of the bishop's sentiment.[30]

Before long, Wilson's distaste for black people became obvious to even his black supporters. He made fewer appointments than Taft, even refusing to place blacks in traditionally black-held positions such as minister to Haiti and recorder of deeds. He blatantly reneged on some campaign promises and expanded considerably the scope of racial segregation in the government. When a group of blacks met with Wilson in 1914, he boldly dismissed the leader, Monroe Trotter, from the meeting because in Wilson's prejudiced opinion Trotter had been insulting by his candid reporting of the complaints of the black community. Because Wilson's election had been assured even without the support of pro-Democrat blacks, the new president felt no particular obligation to his African American supporters. Furthermore, the national political climate was such that the presidency was likely to follow the trend that had prevailed since the election of Rutherford B. Hayes in 1876 and become less and less sensitive to the needs of African Americans, regardless of which party was victorious.[31]

Many Zionites openly expressed their anger and dismay at the current state of affairs. The New York Conference of the AMEZ in 1915 revealed a much greater sense of desperation for American blacks than it had two years earlier. They complained about the racially motivated exclusion of approximately two million males from military service in the First World War; the showing of the explicitly racist motion picture the *Birth of a Nation* (commending the NAACP for opposing it and other wrongs inflicted upon the race); and the gerrymandering and outright disfranchisement of black voters so that not a single black person now held a seat in Congress.[32] Bishop Walters's relationship with Wilson continued to sour to the point of a clear break between the two. Bishop Hood, the aged church leader and loyal Republican, did not have influence with the Democrat Wilson and, perhaps aware of his advanced age, seemed to turn his attention increasingly to emphasizing connectional history.

The General Conference of 1916 also sounded negative notes about the political legacy of Wilson's presidency vis-à-vis African Americans. It contrasted its elation at the recent Supreme Court's decision that outlawed "grandfather clauses" in some state constitutions with Wilson's sorry record on racial matters. The conference also approved a report roundly condemning Wilson's stated intention not to include black candidates on possible presidential appointment lists because of opposition from a number of southern senators, members of the legislative body that would have to ratify these presidential appointments. Wilson's position on this matter seemed objectionable, incomprehensible, and unjust in light of the fact that the president had made Native American and Jewish appointments, persons "who appeared equally objectionable" in certain prejudiced sectors. Not only was Wilson making fewer appointments of blacks than former presidents, even the traditionally "black" positions were going unfilled by African Americans. The Conference registered its chagrin and humiliation at Wilson's policies.[33] But pained or not, blacks would have to endure Wilson's continued antiblack policies. Unfortunately, things would get worse in the United States for blacks before they got better. It would be the actions of another Democrat, Franklin Delano Roosevelt, and his economic policies during the Depression and World War II that would finally attract significant numbers of black voters to the Democratic party.

CONCLUSION AND ANALYSIS

Hood's leadership during the presidential elections of 1908 and 1912 clearly shows his keen interest in political matters and illustrates his ability to act quickly and decisively when he felt that certain courses of action jeopardized the best interests of the black community. The Zion leader was not hypocritical or ambivalent regarding his stance that Christian ministers should not seek public office or play the role of politicians. Hood emphasized that all of his forays into the world of politics as an office holder were on behalf of the black community, rather than for personal aggrandizement or to fulfill personal ambitions. He believed that minister-activists during the Reconstruction era had to take political leadership roles because of the paucity of qualified black laypeople. According to the Zion prelate, it was a matter of record that, on a national level, Republicans had been friends and Democrats had been enemies of the civil rights of African Americans. Although Christian ministers must focus on ecclesiastical matters as a first calling, they also had an obligation to warn people of disasters, inform them of opportunities, and to encourage them to take responsibility for both their temporal and spiritual well-being. Hood exemplifies black leaders of this time who saw no discontinuity between helping the race and spreading the gospel. Indeed, the two were linked indissolubly, regardless of how individual religious leaders might differ in their political analyses and recommendations.

Of course one might express concern that Hood's conception of the Christian ministry, while broad enough to encompass the political and other temporal needs of people, failed to consider the need for "ministers of community action." Much can be said for an approach that recognizes varied forms of ministry, including those not primarily associated with the pulpit and altar. Even in Hood's lifetime church people recognized that some persons were called to the pastorate, while others were called to evangelism, for example. During the second half of the twentieth century many Christian churches in the United States officially sanctioned ministerial roles focusing on community involvement as opposed to the traditional vocations of the pastorate and evangelism.

Nonetheless, in Hood, we have witnessed the actions of a person passionately dedicated to racial uplift, even at the risk of his own personal safety. It would be unfair and incorrect to dismiss him as a "conservative" as that term is used in the second half of the twentieth century. Conservatism for Hood might be better termed "moderation." The Zion bishop did not favor accommodation to racial proscription or put forth dubious proposals of self-improvement at the expense of governmental obligations to safeguard the rights of the oppressed. "Radical" leaders did not represent the majority sentiments of black leaders. As much as they might question the wisdom or practicality of Hood's moderation in given situations, they could never deny his track record of service and commitment for racial uplift. Indeed, Hood's views, for the most part, represented mainstream black thinking of the era.

PART V

TROUBLE IN ZION

Hood's Leadership in Controversies Involving
the AMEZ Church, 1872–1918

Chapter Eight

Hood as Leader in Religious Controversies, 1872–1916

For it hath been declared unto me . . . that there are contentions among
you.
  —1 Corinthians 1:11, Holy Bible, King James Version

Hood was distinguished for his coolness and deliberation in excitement.
He was a great projector of measures in council; a conciliator, a deep rea-
soner, . . . an invulnerable spirit, very discerning, genial and affable in his
personal bearing, and kind to friend and foe, aged and young.
  —John J. Moore, *History of the AME Zion Church in America,*
    quoted in Walls, *Zion*

Turning from Hood's political leadership and philosophy, this and the following
two chapters examine Hood's religious leadership as demonstrated by his involvement in some of the major controversies and disputes affecting not only
Zion but the black church in general during the period of his active bishopric,
1872–1916. There were numerous debates, contentions, and disputes involving
Hood during his episcopacy, but because of limitation of space, this study treats
a selected and representative number. This chapter focuses in particular on two
significant controversies: Hood's response to Booker T. Washington's 1890 critique of southern black clergy; and the attempts during the 1880s and 1890s to
achieve institutional union or merger with Zion's chief Methodist rival, the
African Methodist Episcopal Church, highlighting the exchanges between Hood

and AME Bishop Henry M. Turner. The vigorous debate in the late 1890s over the ordination of women elders in the AMEZ and the contentions within Zion regarding the episcopacy will each unfold in the next two chapters respectively.

Both debates illustrate a significant element of African American religion during this era. The Booker T. Washington controversy reveals the response of the black church to criticism leveled against it from outside, as Washington's criticism of black ministers derived not so much from his role as a church member as from his position as a racial and educational leader. The controversies surrounding attempts to unify the two major strands of black American Methodism demonstrate the commitment of blacks to unify their denominational forces to achieve spiritual and temporal, and specifically racial, ends. Like the Washington controversy, the ecumenical disputes reflected external challenges and pressures on specific black denominations, in this case, Zion. In addition to their relevance for Hood and the AMEZ Church, these controversies reflect issues faced by all the major independent black denominations and in a sense the entire African American populace during this era. Washington directed his criticism at the masses of black clergy, not simply the Zionites, and all the major black Methodists and Baptist groups struggled to achieve organizational and programmatic unity of some sort with their respective African American institutional counterparts.

BOOKER T. WASHINGTON'S CRITIQUE
OF BLACK CLERGY, 1890

During the summer of 1890, five years before he received national attention as a spokesman for accommodationism, Booker T. Washington ignited a storm of controversy involving both religious and secular leaders in the African American community with a powerful, stinging critique of the black ministry, particularly in the South. In August 1890, the *Christian Union* published a version of a commencement speech first given in June of that year at Fisk University in Nashville, Tennessee.[1] Apparently the publication of Washington's critique, rather than the address itself, created the greatest outburst of disagreement and calls for retraction on part of the ecclesiastical and general black community. Washington, mincing no words, was direct and pointed in his analysis of black religious leadership. Washington opined that black ministers in the Episcopal, Congregational, and Presbyterian churches were generally fine professionals, but their denominational commitments rendered them inaccessible to the great majority of

African Americans. The overwhelming majority of blacks belonged to the Baptist and Methodist churches,[2] but both the intellectual and spiritual conditions of the leaders of these latter churches were deplorable, he argued. His eight years of close experience with a wide range of African American clergy in the South had convinced the Tuskegee leader that two out of every three Methodist and three out of every four Baptist ministers were morally and intellectually incompetent to preach or pastor.[3] Washington asserted that many of these individuals entered the ministerial profession, not out of earnest and sincere commitment to the gospel, but in search of a more comfortable line of work. Most black southern ministers, in his estimation, were too emotional in their discourses, overly concerned with money, and had little respect from the general populace regarding either morality or business savvy. Most black religious leadership, therefore, was ignorant and poorly trained, especially in the poorer rural areas.[4] Moving beyond analysis and criticisms, Washington proposed the establishment of a southern seminary or training school, operated nondenominationally, to provide one or two years of study covering the areas of biblical studies, sermon preparation, hymn reading, methods of study, and ministerial and outreach training.[5]

Washington found his share of influential supporters within the confines of the black denominations, including the renowned Presbyterian minister Francis J. Grimke and, more important, Daniel Alexander Payne, education advocate, president of Wilberforce University and current senior bishop of the AME Church. As a matter of fact, Payne thought that Washington's critiques should have been a bit stronger.[6] Payne's standing certainly gave some legitimacy to Washington's remarks and occasioned the need for many other black leaders to respond in support of African American ministers. These defenders of the black clergy included Theophilus Gould Steward, a prominent AME minister; John C. Dancy, editor of the *Star of Zion* and later the *AME Zion Quarterly Review;* and, of course, Bishop Hood.[7] Actually, Hood and these spokespersons were not only defending black clergy but strongly opposing the view, implicit in Washington's argument, that black people, led by incompetent leaders, reflected the same degree of ignorance and moral failings.

In his response in early 1891, Hood first insisted on the necessity of all statements being grounded in facts and inquired about the data that Washington had employed. Second, he used his thirty years of experience with the AMEZ Church as minister and bishop to lay the foundation for his own defense of black ministers. He pointed out that the time span during which he had dealt specifically with black churches and their ministers in the South was three times that of

Washington's work at Tuskegee. Third, Hood responded in detail to the accusations of immorality and ignorance leveled against black preachers by Washington and seconded by Bishop Payne of the AME. Fourth, he, like others called on Washington, in the absence of corroborating data, to withdraw his damaging statements, which he considered a grave slander against black clergy.

Hood, who was himself mostly self-taught, responded specifically to Washington's charge that the black clergy was largely too ignorant to do an effective job of leading the churches by noting that there were very few highly trained, formally educated ministers in any denomination. Yet lacking a high degree of formal education does not automatically render one ineffectual. Critics could easily find faults in the grammar of ministers, or, moreover, in the discourse of members of Congress—or even college professors (like Booker T. Washington?). Hood, nonetheless, could authoritatively posit that Zion had an amazing number of effective and great leaders, and he suspected the same applied to the other churches. The Zion bishop had always emphasized the need for intelligence and training in ministers of the gospel. He, however, did not automatically equate the absence of formal education, credentials, or the inability to master the fine points of grammar with ignorance and general leadership incompetence. Nor did he believe that the average Christian did so. Reflecting his evangelical background and intimacy with the common people, Hood responded to Washington's and Payne's finding fault with the discourses of the average black preacher. Most congregants, according to Hood, were "not critics" but persons earnestly desirous of "simple, common sense statement of truth." Those ministers who lived up to that noble standard, regardless of the level of education, succeeded.[8] As a bishop in Zion, Hood attested forcefully to the stern code of morality imposed upon all ministers. If Washington would pay greater attention to the facts, the slanderous nature of his charges would be fully evident to him.[9] On the other hand, should Washington persist in his charges after examining all the evidence, then Hood would have to admit that he had overestimated the character of the man.[10]

Apparently, the controversy receded somewhat during the winter of 1891.[11] As time passed, the critics somewhat moderated their positions. According to Dancy in a March 17, 1892, editorial, Payne had retreated from his earlier position of staunchly defending Washington by clarifying that he meant that only one-third of the ministers were actual leaders and not, presumably, that the rest were morally and intellectually unfit to perform their ministerial obligations, a clarification that Dancy did not find satisfactory.[12] In subsequent years Booker T. Washington demonstrated that, aside from any specific critiques of black

churches and their ministers, he had great appreciation for the power and influence of the black church. He often attended gatherings of Baptists and Methodists
and in various contexts pointed to the contributions of African American
churches to the elevation of the race and the accomplishments of the black church
as models and success stories for black people.[13] As for Bishop Hood, he continued to emphasize the spiritual and mental improvement of black clergy and laity,
but never wavered in his conviction that Zion ministers were overall very successful in the execution of their responsibilities. As late as February 1904, the
bishop still maintained that Washington's assessment thirteen years earlier "even
then, was entirely too sweeping" and that Zion ministers were still "doing a very
praiseworthy work, and are doing it well."[14] By that date the 1895 Atlanta Exposition Address had catapulted Washington to national fame and leadership,
but even during the first decade of the 1900s Hood stood by his earlier refutation
of Washington's critique of ministers even at the zenith of the latter's political
power and influence.

This controversy reveals some significant facts about the black church and its
relationship to the larger black community during this era. First, the black church
and its ministry were significant elements of the community, a fact that both religious as well as secular black leaders recognized. It is not surprising, therefore,
that secular as well as religious black leaders responded with outrage to Washington's sweeping indictment of southern ministers. This controversy over the
moral and intellectual qualifications of black clergy, particularly in the South, to
be effective leaders originated outside denominational walls, involving individuals and newspapers whose leadership roles were not directly tied to the African
American churches. Washington, reared a Baptist but rumored to have Unitar-
ian sympathies, advocated "pragmatic religion," with less emphasis on meta-
physical or supernatural concerns, less emotion, and greater emphasis on
developing people's reason, talents, resources, personal morality, and the acquisition of property and wealth, essential ingredients for the elevation of any people.[15] Other contemporaries, such as Orishatukeh Faduma and W. E. B. Du Bois,
voiced similar criticisms of the black church and its ministry.[16]

A second significant point emerging from this controversy is the insistence on
the part of most black denominational leaders that black ministers had been unfairly attacked and vilified. Angell's biography of Henry M. Turner points out,
for example, that Payne's support of Washington's position caused such a furor
within the AME Church that the bishops had to take decisive action distancing
themselves from the senior bishop's comments in order to prevent a secession on

the part of some South Carolina Methodist churches.[17] Third, Washington's critique, however exaggerated or unfair, reveals a tension within evangelical and southern religion during this period. Evangelicalism incorporates the essential principles that the individual is blessed with the glorious opportunity to make direct contact and maintain a personal relationship with God and that true ministerial leadership is based on God's calling, not on ordination ceremonies or formal training at the hands of others. Thus, there has at times developed a strong strand of anti-intellectualism, often accompanied by an emphasis on individual, as opposed to social, ethics. Some scholars have theorized that post–Civil War white southerners took a more nostalgic, traditional, and individualistic approach to Christianity in response to their defeat and "isolation" from the rest of the nation.[18] It would not be surprising that black southerners somehow shared in that religious approach, especially given the fact that during this era they were increasingly "isolated" from the region and the nation by lynchings and other forms of racial terrorism, Jim Crow segregation, and disfranchisement. Finally, this controversy reveals that though Hood was modest about his ability to speak for other denominations, his response, nonetheless, conveyed an understanding, respect, and defense of the entire black independent church tradition. In other words, Hood's reply to Washington demonstrated an exercise of leadership not only on behalf of Zion but all independent black Christianity.

AME-AMEZ Merger Controversies, 1880s and 1890s

Predating and extending beyond controversies between Booker T. Washington and black ministers were debates surrounding the proposed merger of the AME and the AMEZ denominations. For some time there had been considerable interest in merging the various black Methodist bodies into one pan-black Methodist body.[19] Some black Methodists disliked the idea of schism or disunity in the Body of Christ, and others saw advantages in combining resources in their efforts to evangelize the race, do humanitarian work, and strive for racial uplift. Both Zionites and AMEs regarded the creation of the Christian Methodist Episcopal Church in 1870 from the remaining membership in the Methodist Episcopal Church, South, as a serious, but not insurmountable, setback for black Methodist unity. Ever since the founding of the CME in 1870, there had been efforts to merge all three, or a combination of two, of these black Methodist groups. Circumstances seemed particularly ripe for such a union during the 1860s when the AMEZ and the AME, both comparably small bodies, extended the ministerial reach of their organizations to their racial siblings in the South. Indeed, each of the two bodies had agreed to a union plan in 1864, but by 1868 merger attempts had collapsed. Hood suggested three main reasons for the failure: Zion's greater support for lay rights, difficulties surrounding the exact title or name for the new denomination, and concerns about the validity of Zion's episcopacy.[20] Angell suggests that from the AME perspective, the June 1864 merger talks in Philadelphia resulted in bad feelings that dampened enthusiasm for union and that the AMEs were somewhat divided as to whether to pursue a distinctly pan-black, racial Methodist unity or, as leaders such as James Lynch argued, a union of black and white Methodist bodies.[21] There was also a party within Zion that sought merger across racial lines.[22] During the 1880s the AME and the AMEZ denominations were once again discussing merger, and once again representatives of those groups were engaging in denominational debates surrounding the proposal. These debates included a number of personalities from both denominations, but this section will focus on Hood's exchanges with representatives of the AME, especially Henry M. Turner. Although there were attempts at merger with the Christian Methodist Episcopal or CME Church, the following discussion focuses on the two largest black Methodist bodies, the AME and the AMEZ.

During the 1885–1886 years an "Elder Blackson" and the esteemed Bishop Jabez Pitt Campbell, both of the AME, engaged Hood in debate.[23] These exchanges revolved around the validity of Zion's episcopacy, the proper mode of consecrating episcopal officers, the educational qualifications of Zion ministers, and the question of which church originated first. Hood vigorously defended the validity of Zion's episcopacy by claiming that the denomination did in fact have a third ordination (to the bishopric), that while Zion had used the term "superintendent" in the past, it always carried the connotation of "bishop," that Zion's quadrennial election or reelection of episcopal officers prior to 1880 did not mean that Zion considered the episcopacy polity (or system of church organization) optional, that he had absolute confidence in the intellectual capabilities of Zion ministers and their more important qualifications of character and commitment, and insisted that Zion preceded Bethel or the AME in establishment. Hood's strongest point regarding the episcopacy was that the AME Church panel on merger had already accepted the validity of Zion's episcopacy, thus the mode of consecrating officers did not constitute a barrier to merger plans. The Zion bishop indicated his awareness of how the history and custom of Zionites might lead to misunderstanding about the episcopal nature of the connection: the quadrennial election of bishops, the means of installing earlier selected episcopal leaders, and the "nonsensical" description of Zion by some of its followers as "a republican form of government."[24]

Of course this last observation of Hood's points to a fact that Hood at that point in history was not willing to accept. The Zionites had set out to have a church government that was more "republican" and democratic than either the AME or the ME. Why else would they have always placed great emphasis on the rights of the laity and the quadrennial election of its "bishops"? Yes, Hood was correct in saying Zion was following the example of John Wesley, the Methodist founder, in using the title "superintendent." Wesley clearly was not ready to designate the leaders of the Methodist bodies in the United States as bishops. What is obvious is the decisive movement of Zion from a church with a "looser" form of episcopacy prior to the Civil War to a bolder episcopacy more closely resembling the main American Methodist bodies as it competed for new converts in the South and sought to merge with other Methodists during and after the War. On the one hand, then, the above exchanges were superfluous, wrestling with moot issues. On the other hand, they gave many in Zion the opportunity to argue for a stronger episcopacy and to review their discipline.[25] They also probably point out why this union proposal met ultimate defeat. There was still tension in Zion over the republican-strong episcopacy issue, and there were those in Bethel who still regarded Zionites as less than equal to their church. Fortunately, these exchanges did no permanent damage to the relationships of the persons involved.[26] Though an avid debater, the Zion bishop admirably separated the points of contention in the controversy from his personal feelings toward his opponents.

THE HOOD-TURNER DEBATE, 1886

Perhaps the most fascinating exchange between Zion and Bethel partisans took place during the summer of 1886 between the episcopal giants, Hood and Turner, two strong leaders of their respective denominations who possessed markedly different temperaments. While Hood was more of a conciliator, Turner was a firebrand. Turner despaired of African Americans' achieving equality in the United States and advocated emigration; Hood held opposite views. Turner was a stronger advocate of African missions and spoke in explicit pan-African tones; Hood strongly supported missions but with apparently less fervor than Turner and generally did not emphasize a pan-African approach, though he was interested in advancement for all persons of African descent. There were many similarities. Besides being close in age, both were key builders of their denominations in the South, active in Reconstruction state governments, supportive of gender equity in the church, and learned and skilled in debate.

The AME and the AMEZ boards of bishops met during that summer of 1886 as a combined body, approved the plan of an earlier joint commission on unity, and agreed to submit the matter to their respective denominations for final ratification. One issue, however, pushed strongly by Bishop Turner, caused many to have second thoughts about the advisability of the merger: the title for the new denomination. (Another issue raised by Turner, regarding the consecration of Zion's bishops, was quickly dropped by him with his assertion that he might have received incorrect information and, in any case, it was a matter that could be easily corrected.) While Hood was primarily concerned about the equality of Zion in any proposed merger of the two groups, AME Bishop Turner slowed any rush to union with his concern regarding the "African" identity of the proposed body.[27] Turner insisted on the retention of the word "African" but the elimination of the term "Zion" from the proposed title of the future church: "The United African Methodist Episcopal Zion Church." Hood would gladly support "The United African Methodist Episcopal Zion Church" or "The United Methodist Episcopal Church" but not "The United African Methodist Episcopal Church." Turner, of course, disapproved of the first two appellations and had explicitly risen at the joint board meeting to amend an earlier title, "The United Methodist Episcopal Church," to include "African." Hood then insisted that should "African" be affixed to the title, "Zion" should likewise be added. Thus, the assembly had agreed to the title including both "African" and "Zion." Turner claimed that legally it was necessary to retain "African" because of the property holding of the AME. Hood replied that if such was the case with "African," the same concern applied to "Zion" regarding the AMEZ Church. Hood lamented Turner's efforts to wreck the chances for union "[a]ll for a name," as he quoted Senior AME Bishop Daniel Payne, who had long favored deleting "African" from the title of his church. Turner's view was that since "African" was a part of the titles of both denominations, the Zion Church should have no difficulty deleting "Zion" and retaining "African" in the title. "Zion," Hood pointed out, had become as essential a part of his denominational title as had "African" for Turner's, whereas the Zionites had never employed "African" with the same relish as the Bethelites.[28]

Since the AME had worked assiduously to identify "African" as denoting that organization, it was understandable that the AMEZ had dedicated itself equally to employing "Zion" to denote that church. Yet Zionites, by their many years of insistence that they were "African Methodists" and their acceptance of the title

"The United African Methodist Episcopal Church" for a proposed Bethel-Zion merger twenty years prior, had now placed their denomination in an awkward if not apparently inconsistent position regarding the matter, an inconsistency that Turner would partially take advantage of in his response to Hood.

Likewise, Turner's argument for retaining "African" while deleting "Zion" also showed an inconsistency in logic.[29] The AME bishop demonstrated no sympathy for the significance that "Zion" held for the AMEZ, calling it a "nickname," unlike the legal appellation of "African." Turner neglected to give weight to Hood's reasonable argument that "Zion" had specifically designated the AMEZ, while "African" had been used most vigorously by AME to designate that denomination.[30] It is obvious that Turner was being less forthright than Hood along these lines. Hood, understandably, read Turner's title as designating a united *AME* Church that had absorbed the Zionites. Turner's opposition to the longer title would be more defensible had he admitted that the addition of the term "Zion" conveyed the converse impression regarding the absorption of the Bethelites into the Zion Church.

Despite Turner's inconsistencies, the AME bishop made an insightful and brilliant defense of the term "African" and made no concessions concerning its retention. He admitted that he would resolutely defend the term as part of the title of the AME, the AMEZ, or any union of the two bodies. Insightfully, Turner observed that many persons wished to rid themselves of any association with blackness. They had identified themselves so thoroughly with a white frame of thought that they automatically identified all things black as evil and degrading and all things white as good, and this attitude prevented African Americans from achieving true power.[31] Turner also responded to those who regarded the term "African" as racially restrictive, denoting the exclusion of persons not black. The AME bishop pointed out the inconsistency of asking black American church people to drop "African" from their titles but not requesting Greek Orthodox, Roman Catholics, and Anglicans (or Church of England) to eliminate those prefixes from theirs. If these three bodies, bearing names reflecting specific geographical areas, were free to use these prefixes without these names bringing the accusation of ethnocentrism or racial exclusion, why should etymological derivatives of *Africa,* the name of the second-largest land mass in the world behind Asia, be regarded as exclusive and unacceptable by people of African descent?[32] This defense of the term *African,* whatever the possible ulterior motives, ring consistent with Turner's biography and overall philosophy. The AME bishop, more than any other participant in this debate, including Hood, dealt with the issue of racial self-love and its psychological connection with temporal advancement. Turner would not permit anyone, not even Daniel A. Payne, the senior bishop of the AME Church, to dissociate the black church from racial self-acceptance and self-love. This, I believe, is his most vital and long-lasting contribution to the black church and racial justice. Hood and others in both denominations would have done well to heed the philosophical significance of Turner's call for black identity and self-love.

Later the title for the proposed merger was changed to "African and Zion Methodist Episcopal Church," an appellation accepted by all sides. By May 2, 1889, however, it appeared that once again the two bodies had failed to realize union. John Dancy, the editor of the *Star,* contended that consuming ambition and feelings of superiority had doomed the work of the joint committee. It appeared now, according to Dancy, that a union would be effected between the CME and Zion churches. He rated progress in talks between the two groups at that point as proceeding "with far more promising results."[33] But history witnessed the failure of this union attempt as well. Again in 1892 hopes rose that union would occur between AME and Zion.[34] But by the spring of 1893 Hood publicly stated in the presence of AME Bishop B. T. Tanner that while he expected an eventual union of the two black Methodist bodies, the experience of the failed 1860s merger had taught him to be cautiously optimistic about any current prospects.[35] With his publication of *One Hundred Years* in 1895 Hood was much more blunt. The Zion bishop wrote that only a few persons in Bethel had been truly committed to a merger of the two groups on equal footing. What the majority of the Bethelites had always wanted, according to the AMEZ historian, was the absorption of his church into theirs.[36]

The black Baptists in 1895 would have the distinction of being the first major black denominational grouping to forge an enduring unity of various regional and national bodies, resulting in the formation of the National Baptist Convention, though it has suffered divisions and secessions since that time. The predominantly white Methodist groups made successful moves toward unity in 1939 and again in 1968. As recently as 1997, the union of black Methodist bodies had not materialized.

CONCLUSION AND ANALYSIS

This chapter demonstrated Hood's leadership in black ecclesiastical circles during the 1880s and 1890s by focusing on two significant controversies. Hood's response to Booker T. Washington's harsh critique of southern black Baptist and Methodist leaders showed the bishop's concern not only for the reputation of Zion but his respect for black leadership, both religious and secular. Of course Hood correctly maintained that Washington's critique, so sweeping and devoid of input by more reliable observers, was simply untrue. The bishop, like many others, clearly understood that an attack on black leadership ill-served the fortunes of those on whose behalf those leaders worked. Hood's response highlights the appreciation that even his major critics had for him and for his clear, deliberate debating style, generally free of the reckless rhetoric that did little in the long run to win over opponents or those in the middle ground of an issue.

In his debates with AME Bishop Turner and others regarding elements of the proposed AME-AMEZ merger, Hood exerted more of a distinctly denominational leadership role. Though we might initially find aspects of these debates amusing and esoteric, they are crucial for comprehending the developing identity of the Zion Church and independent black Christianity in general. First, by the 1880s most black Christians in independent denominations, Methodists and Baptists, had come to the realization that any interracial merger or consolidation was beyond reach. Black churches could not forgo their racial identity and the significance it held for their sense of a providential charge to uplift the black race. Predominantly northern and southern white denominations meanwhile concerned themselves more with reunification with one another across geographical lines than creating interracially merged churches in which the color line played no role. Second, these controversies reflect the partial triumph of a "high church" tradition in Zion, with Hood as one of its major advocates. In its early history the AMEZ had emphasized the rights of the laity, eschewed the title of "bishop" in favor of "superintendent," and elected or reelected its chief officers quadrennially. In the 1860s "bishop" became an official designation, and these officers were elected for life beginning in 1880. While the rights of the laity were safeguarded, many Zionites, as a result of ecumenical dialogues and cooperation, interdenominational debates, and proposed mergers, began to emphasize the idea that episcopacy carried the same connotations for their denomination as it did for other major Methodist bodies. Hood's leadership in the defense of Zion's episcopacy, thus, placed him at the forefront of significant changes in the ecclesiastical character of the AMEZ.

Chapter Nine

THE WOMEN'S ORDINATION CONTROVERSY, THE AMEZ CHURCH, AND HOOD'S LEADERSHIP, 1898–1900

But I suffer not a woman to teach, nor to usurp authority over the man, but to be in silence.
 —1 Timothy 2:12, Holy Bible, King James Version

There is neither Jew nor Greek, there is neither bond nor free, there is neither male nor female; for ye are all one in Christ Jesus.
 —Galatians 3:28, Holy Bible, King James Version

I as much doubt a woman's call to the ministry as I do my ability to fly.
 —The Reverend S. A. Chambers, *The Star of Zion*

There are those who attempt to crush others with the word of God—and the way some men talk of women, we are sorry for their mothers, and pity their wives.
 —Bishop John Bryan Small, *The Star of Zion*

The controversy in the AMEZ Church surrounding the ordination of women as elders, the highest ministerial order, engulfed that body in a deep, divisive debate during the 1898–1900 period, and especially during the summer and fall of 1898. It would be an exaggeration to credit Bishop Hood with single-handedly managing the crisis. He, however, provided valuable leadership, walking a precarious line between maintaining unity and a reasonable degree of harmony within the connection and forcefully advocating full gender equity in church life, a position ratified by the Zion General Conference in 1900. Though Hood and others might normally be labeled "conservatives" on certain denominational matters, on this issue Hood was clearly "progressive," another indication that we should take care when employing labels.

This highly significant controversy erupted with the ordination of the Reverend Mrs. Mary J. Small to the order of elder by Bishop Calvin C. Pettey, upon recommendation of the Philadelphia and Baltimore Annual Conference in 1898. Ordaining a woman to the highest level of ministry was a new step for Zion, as it was for most other Christian denominations during this era. Indeed, it challenged much of the standard interpretation of Scripture and church tradition regarding this issue, interpretation and tradition that extended back to the earliest centuries of Christian history.[1] The specific and central question in the debate was not Reverend Small's character or education but the legitimacy of ordaining women to the ministry. The broader issue was the complete equality of women in all spheres of church life. The entire chapter is devoted to the ordination controversy for at least two reasons. First, the Zion's ordination of woman elders for quite some time remained a revolutionary and rather novel action among most mainline American churches. The 1940s and the 1950s witnessed some significant progress in the ordination of women as pastors, but it was not until the 1970s and the 1980s that women's ordination became widely accepted among American Protestants. Even after the decade of the 1980s the Roman Catholic Church and the Orthodox Church remain opposed to women's leadership in this regard and the Southern Baptist Convention (SBC), the largest Protestant body in the United States, stands officially opposed though there are a number of women pastors in the SBC. Second, even as late as the 1990s some Christian groups that ordain women still struggled over gender-related matters, with women and men in many churches still reporting in the 1990s (when this is being written) issues of mistreatment and inequity confronting women pastors.[2]

BACKGROUND TO THE CONTROVERSY

As early as 1876 the General Conference of Zion voted to abolish the word "male" from the church discipline. This change allowed women to serve as delegates to the General Conference and in other capacities as well. Many conservative Zionites argued then that such a broad modification of the discipline would effectively allow women to receive ordination to the orders of deacon, elder, and even bishop.[3] Most likely some proponents of this change heartily welcomed those possibilities, but they apparently did not then openly register this sentiment. The decade of the 1890s, however, witnessed even greater steps toward full ministerial equality for women. Bishop Hood took a monumental step when he ordained Mrs. Julia A. J. Foote as deacon at the New York Annual Conference in May 1894. The Reverend Mrs. Foote, as her autobiography indicates and as other portions of this study reveal, had served as an active minister and evangelist for decades. When Hood ordained her in Poughkeepsie, New York, he did so with the approval of that annual conference, ordaining one who had served as a "conference missionary." (The Reverend Mrs. Foote received ordination to elder in November 1900 just prior to her death from Bishop Alexander Walters of the New Jersey Annual Conference.)

In May 1895, the Reverend Mary J. Small, who had previously received her preaching license from John E. Price, presiding elder of the Philadelphia and Baltimore Conference, received her ordination to the diaconate from Bishop Alexander Walters at the same conference. Neither of these actions, the granting of a preaching license and the diaconate ordination, appears to have aroused much controversy in Zion. Most likely the more conservative ministers understood these ordinations as granting women the opportunity to continue their missionary and evangelistic work. The authority, however, that came with eldership—to pastor a local congregation, perform the sacraments, and become a candidate for bishop—was another matter entirely. Unsurprisingly, a storm of controversy, involving laity, ministers, and bishops, erupted in the summer of 1898 after Bishop Pettey ordained Mrs. Small as elder. It is important to note that Foote, Small, and other women, such as Florence Randolph, were *active* ministers. Whether Small became the first of these women to be ordained elder because of her position as a bishop's wife is unknown. Quite possibly, the bishops reasoned that a bishop's wife might escape heavy criticism and thus pave the way for other women to receive elder's orders. Nevertheless, neither her spousal relationship nor possible church politics should obscure the reality that Small was in fact a bona fide minister.

Mary Julia Blair Small (1850–1945) was a native of Murfreesboro, Tennessee, who converted to the faith on October 26, 1873, at the age of twenty-three, three years after she had wedded Elder (later Bishop) Small. From her childhood Mrs. Small had envisioned herself as a foreign missionary, a dream that was partly realized when her husband became bishop with jurisdiction over the Zion churches in Africa. Mrs. Small had not always approved of women preachers and did not surrender to the call to preach until January 21, 1892, the year she received her preaching license. A vigorous evangelist, Small was a modest woman of sterling character. By 1898 she had held many evangelistic gatherings in northeastern places such as Rochester, Brooklyn, and various cities and towns in Pennsylvania. In 1912 she defeated Keziah P. Hood, Bishop Hood's wife, to become the third president of the Woman's Home and Foreign Mission Society, an office she held until 1916, apparently the last wife of a bishop to preside over this body. She died in 1945, one month shy of ninety-five years of age.[4]

Responses to the Ordination

The ordination of the Reverend Small by Bishop Pettey, a close associate of Hood's, and the annual conference elicited three major responses from the Zion clergy and laypeople. The traditionalists on gender questions registered complete opposition and a demand that the General Conference, the highest judicatory in the connection, rescind the ordination at its next meeting in 1900, a position exemplified by S. A. Chambers, a Rock Hill, South Carolina, minister. Second, the progressives on gender equity voiced full support of women's equality in all aspects of church life, including eldership. This position was expounded by Bishop John B. Small, who was also the husband of the Reverend Small. Though Bishop Small offered the most systematic, sustained theological arguments for women's ordination, he was by no means her sole supporter. Third, there was the moderate opposition, made up of those who strongly denied the religious basis for ordination of women or were undecided on the matter but recognized that denominational law as currently written gave Small the right to seek ordination.[5] This group did not push for nullification of *her* ordination by the General Conference, but some, such as Elder John W. Smith, current editor of the *Star of Zion,* argued that no more women should receive ordination. Others, such as layperson B. F. Grant, did not voice a public position on the ordination of other women but appeared to relish the fact that many ministers who had supported and mandated equality of the genders as it applied to laypeople, for example, in representation to denominational conferences, were getting a taste of their own medicine with the ordination of women as elders—and these male clergy did not like the flavor of women's equality after all!

In addition to these three positions, there were a variety of responses from women in support of the Reverend Mrs. Small, as expressed by Mrs. Sarah Pettey and others. Based upon materials available to me, women took little direct part in the debate. It was perhaps thought appropriate by supporters of women's ordination that the Reverend Mrs. Small refrain from active, public controversy, particularly since it was the action of the annual conference in accordance with church law that was the issue, not she. Besides, Bishop Small appeared to delight in his role as a husband duty-bound to defend the honor of his wife from all slights and insults. Perhaps also this paucity of women's input revolves round the ministerial context of the debate. Finally, I would imagine that many women were also firm adherents of the traditionalist camp, some of whom perhaps held to the conviction that women should not participate in such openly controversial and even acrimonious displays.

Both sides in the controversy, the traditionalists and the progressives, hailed the Bible as the sole authority for faith and practice and appealed to it to support their respective positions. It was the interpretive principle around which they differed. The progressives focused on those passages that supported gender equity; the conservatives or traditionalists appealed to those passages that justified or argued the subordination of women to men. The progressives defended their position of support for women's ordination along a number of lines.[6] First, they emphasized biblical passages pointing to gender equity in principle and concrete instances of women's leadership in the Old and New Testaments. Second, they downplayed those biblical passages that counseled the subordination of women by claiming that they addressed specific situations that no longer applied or that the proscriptions had been subsequently invalidated in Scripture. Third, they used the argument of "historical progressivism," that history, inspired by the principles of the Bible and the Christian faith, has progressively unfolded greater truths and freedoms. Thus, what might have been unthinkable, even to Christ's first-century disciples, were much clearer to his followers in later epochs. Fourth, from a practical point of view, the current church required the labor of women ministers to offset the dereliction of duty by so many male ministers.

The opponents to women's ordination, the traditionalists, countered these arguments.[7] First, yes, the Bible strongly endorses the principle of spiritual equality for women, and there are instances of women's displaying strong leadership roles in the Bible. Nonetheless, these truths and instances did not, and were not intended to, contradict the other principle that women were to be in subjection to men, exercising no spiritual authority over them. Second, the traditionalists, contradicting the progressives, insisted that the passages restricting women to subordinate roles were not simply instructions for particular occasions and circumstances but were general principles to be followed by all the churches in all ages. Third, historical progressivism must not be employed to abrogate the expressed, clear commands of Scripture against ordaining women. Fourth, traditionalists claimed that female ministers were not needed to fill the so-called vacuum in leadership by male ministers. Besides, if male ministers had proven unworthy, why compound the problem with the addition of females seeking church appointments? Occasionally, a traditionalist would put forth the argument that women were not physically capable of enduring the physical strain associated with the job of pastors, or that a wife's ordination might cause disharmony in the marital relationship, or that women parishioners would not submit to the pastoral authority of females as they would to that of males. These latter arguments, however, were clearly secondary to the insistence that the Bible and church tradition unambiguously opposed ordination of women in roles where they would exercise authority over men.

HOOD'S RESPONSE TO THE CONTROVERSY

Hood clearly stood on the side of the progressives, though as senior bishop he moved cautiously to maintain a sense of harmony and consensus within the general Zion body. Also, he could have been acting in deference to his episcopal colleague, John Bryan Small, and he was already involved in other controversies regarding the episcopacy. First, Hood and the other bishops took action to safeguard the Reverend Small's denominational rights. In the July 14, 1898 issue of the *Star of Zion,* Hood denounced Presiding Elder W. H. Snowden's actions, which had effectively excommunicated Mrs. Small from the local church, an act subsequently and unanimously overturned by the Board of Bishops in accordance with an 1872 denominational law. According to the senior bishop, Snowden had made a ruling that was religiously and procedurally wrong according to the laws of the connection, and there was no legitimate defense for his actions.[8] Hood seemed to have been particularly concerned that neither presiding elders nor local pastors mistreat the people under their charges. In part, there was the practical consideration that persons or even entire congregations could secede and join other Methodist bodies. Yet there is also a strong indication that Hood was genuinely and gravely concerned about the abridgment of lay liberties. Thus, paradoxically, Hood maintained the traditional principle in Zion Methodism of lay rights while working concomitantly to increase the power of the episcopacy.

The intensity of the controversy subsided by late October 1898. In a letter to the *Star* that month, Hood acknowledged "that the discussion on the ordination of women has closed," though he did not bow to the inevitable without taking shots at his theological opponents. He fumed that a suggestion not to ordain any more women prior to the General Conference meeting in 1900 was, in addition to being "presumptuous," devoid of "wisdom." Hood explained that to the best of his knowledge there would be no further ordination of women elders simply because no women at this point had completed the necessary requirements for ordination. Nor was it likely, predicted Hood, that "the ground of necessity" could be invoked to ordain a woman elder because it was unlikely that there would be such a necessity prior to the General Conference. What if a qualified woman presented herself as a candidate for elder ordination? One might expect Hood to insist on her right to ordination, that the individual bishops and annual conferences would follow the dictates of the law. Instead, the senior bishop made the ambiguous declaration: "I think it likely that a bishop would follow his own judgment regardless of any advice from those who are not authorized to advise him."[9] Given the context of the letter, Hood declared in so many words that even should a qualified woman candidate appear, it would be highly unlikely that any bishop would buck the apparent sentiment of the Zion membership or—at the very least—risk the severe dissension and acrimony that would erupt because of the ordination of a woman prior to the next General Conference. The bishops had heard the cries of dissension from the traditionalists!

The opponents of women's ordination realized the significance of Hood's letter and exulted. The *Star* editor, the Reverend J. W. Smith, called it "a significant opinion." He praised Hood for a "dignified, masterful" statement "equal to the cause and timely to the occasion." Smith agreed gratuitously with Hood that no one had the authority from the General Conference to meddle with the bishops by instructing them on the performance of their responsibilities (as Smith had done when he suggested that the bishops abstain from further ordination of women elders!). Smith was delighted to read that no women would be ordained prior to the General Conference "because the way the ministers feel now there will be none ordained after the adjournment of that body." Finally, Smith added that the lack of "necessity" of women elders of which Hood had spoken could be equally applied to women deacons.[10] One of the main critics of women's ordination, S. A. Chambers, boldly, simplistically, and imprecisely claimed that Hood had come out in defense of his position, dooming the issue to oblivion. "Gabriel will have to use extra force at his trumpet if he desires to bring it to judgment."[11] While Chambers might have intentionally misinterpreted Hood's letter, his read-

ing of the situation had the ring of truth to it. The fact that the senior and highly
regarded bishop of Zion had suggested that no more women would be ordained
prior to the General Conference reflected the simple fact that the traditionalists
had temporarily triumphed.

A number of weeks later Hood set the record straight by registering his strong
disapproval that certain individuals had misrepresented his statements. Hood
made it very clear that in principle he supported equal rights for women.[12] His
bold declaration of women's rights in principle, however, was qualified by the reality that currently women's ordination in practice would not be fully recognized
in Zion.[13] Hood proceeded to defend his declaration of women's equality. He disregarded the idea that women constituted "the weaker vessel." Regarding physical strength, such might be true. But there were many other aspects of the human
constitution. Regarding mental strength, women might actually be superior to
men, for example, by endurance in the watchful care of an ill family member.
Like his colleague Bishop Small, Hood claimed that woman and man in the Garden of Eden prior to the Fall originally enjoyed equal status, that woman's being
created from man did not represent subordination to him. Indeed, God created
woman from the rib in Adam's *side,* a clear indication that "she is to stand beside
him as his equal."[14] Interestingly, Hood's reading of Genesis regarding the status
of woman after the Fall differed somewhat from Small's argument. Small argued
that after the Fall, Adam, without God's authority, assumed domination over
Eve and that God since then had been gradually revealing that such was improper. Hood opined that God, not Adam, had originally cursed Eve with subordination to Adam, and hence every woman to every man. The mission of
Christ, however, revoked that curse, restoring humanity to the pre-Fall status
that included woman's equality with man. As a contemporary example, Hood
pointed to the recent sixty-year reign of Queen Victoria of England as a solid testament to women's capacity to function equally with men. Both blacks and
women, predicted the bishop, would eventually receive their proper rights under
the aegis of Christianity.[15]

WOMEN RESPOND TO THE ORDINATION ISSUE

Not only did Bishops Hood and Small come to the defense of the Reverend
Small, but some women offered their support in the pages of the denominational
newspaper. In 1896 Mrs. Sarah E. C. Dudley Pettey, wife of Bishop Pettey, started

a weekly "Woman's Column" in the *Star* as a voice for the Woman's Home and Foreign (now Overseas) Missionary Society, for which she had served as treasurer (1892–1896) and was current executive secretary.[16] In the June 23, 1898, issue, Mrs. Pettey did not directly join the debate over Small's ordination but hailed the connection as "progressive" regarding equal rights for women. Referring to the action of a previous General Conference that had eliminated gender descriptions from the discipline, Mrs. Pettey, like other proponents of women's ordination, praised the church for expanding opportunities for women. Her article spelled out Small's qualifications: her diaconate experience, eloquence, forcefulness, and "a most excellent record as an evangelist."[17]

Other Zion women endorsed the Reverend Small's ordination. Mrs. Carissa Betties in December 1898 offered strong words of support to Mrs. Small. She warned males not to oppose the will of God and encouraged the Reverend Small to remember that God had angels watching over God's children. Betties exhorted Small, "You are right; go, and as you go, preach." Male preachers who opposed her ordination had risen too late: Small had already been ordained according to church law. Reflecting the argument that women ministers were needed to perform ministries that some men left undone, Betties wrote to the men, "Let her alone; she is doing what you won't do." Nor did it matter that some male ministers subjected Small to name calling; her call to preach was more valid than that of some male preachers. "Some men heard a mule bray and said that God had called them to preach."[18] The comments of the woman editor of the *Bristol* (Tennessee) *Ship* reprinted in the *Star* during the summer of 1898 offered a curious blend of theological conservatism or at least uncertainty relative to women ministers, but a feminist commitment to women's rights. While she did not support the idea of women's ordination or preaching, the unnamed editor was greatly disturbed by the attempt of many male opponents to suppress Mrs. Small's ambition, especially given her rights under the church discipline, and blamed most male opposition on "envy, jealousy and fear" of women's progress.[19] The *Bristol Ship* editor insisted that women had the right to engage in the same vocational pursuits as their husbands. When the husbands were absent, wives should be able to step in. When the husbands were present, wives had the right to be companions. "[A]nd as long as you brethren let the women kill themselves working for the preachers, you ought not let fear of their surpassing you cause you to oppose their preaching, if they so desire." Besides, opposition to the ordination was coming too late since "Sister Small is already ordained. Ha, ha, ha!"[20]

ZION'S RESOLUTION AND AN ASSESSMENT OF THE ORDINATION DEBATE

The ordination of women to the ministry during these years faced tough opposition. It is surprising that Hood and Zion engaged the issue as much as they did. The only authority that most Protestants claimed was Scripture. To contradict the scriptures, in their opinion, was to call into question the very sovereignty of God. It would appear that no conclusive argument could have been made supporting the ordination of women without abandoning the traditional perspective that the Bible was the absolute, infallible Word of God. Just as there were passages that plainly portrayed women in roles of active leadership alongside and sometimes superior to men, there were also passages that clearly counseled women's subordination. No amount of contextual explanations, then or now, could render these passages so ineffectual as to provide an indisputable argument favoring women's ordination. To convince fully the traditionalists that women were eligible for *all* aspects of ministry, one would have to convince them to abandon some significant portions of their biblical traditionalism, a change that adherents on neither side of the debate were prepared to take. Even in the 1990s historical-critical approaches to biblical interpretation do not meet with universal favor among the traditionally religious populace, Zionite or otherwise. It would seem that the proponents of women's ordinations in those days were doomed to defeat.

Appearances, however, can prove deceptive. At the 1900 General Conference the Reverend A. J. Rogers introduced a resolution that apparently opposed the ordination of women. Five days later, a Saturday, May 19, when the matter finally came before the conference for consideration, the effort to outlaw the ordination of women went down to defeat, a development that perhaps caught even the supporters of women's ordination by surprise. The conference minutes provide no breakdown of the voting; thus, we have no way of knowing whether the margin of victory for the progressives was small or large. It is noteworthy that four bishops—Hood, Lomax, Harris, and Small—made qualifying statements after the defeat of the recommendation against ordination. In sum, the episcopal comments underscored that all women's ordinations hitherto had been carried out in accordance with church laws, that the female candidates had been fully qualified. Furthermore, no one should receive ordination to elder in the future unless she *or* he was fully qualified according to the stated specifications of church law.[21] Perhaps these comments were made both to clarify the denomination's position on the issue of ordination of women and to calm dissent or fear about the decision that the connection had just taken. Even though the conference did not take the *positive* step of passing a resolution with a ringing endorsement of female ordination, the progressives on gender had still scored a huge victory. Because of the commitment of Hood, other bishops, and progressive men and women, Zion became the first American Methodist or mainstream denomination, black or white, to recognize officially, unambiguously, and throughout its connection women's full equality in the ministry. As indicated previously, it would not be until the latter half of the twentieth century that women in mainline groups presented themselves as ministerial candidates in greater numbers and the actual practice of women pastors became more widely accepted.

There are other indications of the AMEZ's move toward greater gender equity during this era. An examination of the *Star of Zion,* the denomination's most prominent newspaper, will show that during the 1890s women began to play more active roles in its pages. For example, Sarah Pettey, who initiated a "Woman's Column," drew attention to women's personalities and issues in both the religious and secular realms. At least one of Hood's daughters, Margaret Hood Banks, wrote occasional articles on women's personalities in the Bible. There were also some prominent female evangelists, such as the Reverend Dr. Florence Randolph, who continued to have significant influence in the church. Bishop Hood and other progressives on women's issues, in addition, promoted the cause of women's advancement in other areas of church life, including strong recommendations and support of women for certain key missionary offices.

How do we account for the liberality of Hood, like-minded Zion leaders, and the overall denomination regarding the ordination of women? First, there have been, since the days of John Wesley, some women preachers in Methodism. Though not officially designated elders, their ministerial tradition helped to accustom at least some Zionites, like Hood and other Methodists, to the possibility that women could receive the call to preach. Second, Hood spent his earliest years in the Union Church of Africans, the first truly independent black denomination and one that provided women with a considerable degree of liberty in the pulpit, though not complete equality with male ministers. Third, Hood stood in a distinct Zion Methodist tradition supportive of women's ministry reaching back into antebellum times. As early as September 2, 1858, the connection recognized the right of women to preach, though not to be ordained as elders per se.[22] Fourth, at least one of Hood's sisters, the Reverend Mrs. Susan Walker Blackson, served as an evangelist in the AME Church. In addition, Hood spoke of a sister who had tremendous influence on his personal spiritual formation in the early years of his life. Thus, the senior bishop had close, intimate contacts with women preachers and spiritual leaders and was conditioned to the possibility of God's calling them to preach and using them to lead others.

Fifth, the AMEZ, compared to some other Methodist groups, had always granted a greater degree of freedom to its lay membership. One might wonder if this liberality toward the laity in general did not also nurture, wittingly or unwittingly, a liberality toward women in particular. Finally, the period between the years 1865 and 1920 was an exciting era of women's activity in public life, both in the secular and religious realms, a fact that probably encouraged liberality within some quarters of the Zion. From the religious perspective, the Methodist Protestant Church, a body that separated from the Methodist Episcopal Church, was organized in 1830 with great emphasis on the rights of the laity and other reforms. As early as 1880 the New York Conference of this connection ordained Anna M. Shaw as elder. Though the entire denomination failed to give its approbation, the New York Conference recognized her ordination. At the 1892 Conference at least four women requested recognition as ministerial delegates. Basically, the Methodist Protestant Church left the matter of women's ordination to the Annual Conferences, and this represented a great advancement over the practices of most other Methodist bodies.[23] Nor should we omit the fact that as early as November 1885 Henry McNeal Turner ordained Sarah Ann Hughes as deacon in the AME Church. The bishop did not find sufficient support to sustain his action or to bring greater gender equality to the AME ministry. While Hughes's ordination was later negated by the church at large, it succeeded in raising consciousness concerning the gender issue[24] and probably influenced the Zion membership. Zion retains the distinction, however, as the first major American religious body that recognized by church law, if not always in actual practice, complete gender equity within its body.

CONCLUSION

This chapter has examined the controversy over women's ordination to the orders of elder in the Zion Church during the late 1890s, particularly as it related to Hood's religious leadership and his management of the debate. Despite a difficult battle, progressives on gender equity won impressive victories in the areas of women's ordination as elder and other matters. However we might criticize Hood's political moderation and denominational positions, his firm, unwavering stance on gender equity in the church was both far-sighted and contributed immensely to greater gender freedom in theory and practice in American religious life during the twentieth century. Hood and the leaders of Zion worked assiduously to build a stronger denomination. Those efforts often entailed dealing with the relationship between religious leadership and racial progress, endeavoring to consolidate black Methodist forces to maximize their impact on religious and political issues, and examining the extent to which the principle of freedom that they read from the pages of the Bible and Christian history applied equally to women. Such assessments in general characterize all the major black denominations of the period, Baptist and Methodist, for they all were seriously engaged in making themselves relevant to both religious and secular spheres of life.

Chapter Ten

Hood's Leadership and Controversies
Regarding Zion's Episcopacy, 1888–1918

Behold, how good and how pleasant it is for brethren to dwell together in
unity!
  —Psalms 133:1, Holy Bible, King James Version{/epi}

A soft answer turneth away wrath: but grievous words stir up anger.
  —Proverbs 15:1, Holy Bible, King James Version

And he said unto them, The kings of the Gentiles exercise lordship over
them; and they that exercise authority upon them are called benefactors.
But ye *shall* not *be* so; but he that is greatest among you, let him be as the
younger; and he that is chief, as he that doth serve.
  —Luke 22:25, 26; Holy Bible, King James Version

In addition to controversy surrounding the spiritual and intellectual qualifications of black ministers, efforts to effect a union between Zion and Bethel, and
the internal debate in the AMEZ over the ordination of women as elders, there
were conflicts within Zion regarding its episcopacy. There were a number of issues subsumed under the various controversies over the episcopacy, all of which
involved Hood in some significant fashion: the nature of the episcopacy, the pro-
priety of personal ambition and campaigning for the bishopric, the adequacy of
the number of bishops currently serving the church, and, finally, the practical
question at the center of many of these vigorous debates, exactly who should be
elected bishop. These debates were numerous, involving clergy, laypeople, bish-

ops, women, and men. Again, because of limitations of space and because of the fruitfulness of the series of exchanges, this chapter will focus on Hood and the debate over the nature of the episcopacy, the conflict between Hood and the editor of *The Star of Zion,* John W. Smith, regarding the latter's candidacy for the episcopacy, and the debate between the AMEZ's "conservatives" and the "progressives" regarding the creation of new episcopal positions for the church. It is the last debate that proved to be the most important, occupied the greatest attention in the connection, and was most controversial and divisive. Thus, the chapter will focus mainly on the third issue.

The following pages demonstrate the aging Hood's continuing influential leadership in Zion Methodism, even as he moved toward forced retirement. Furthermore, the reader should be cognizant that these debates were not simply matters of theological arguments or contests regarding personal ambitions. Zionists with both progressive and conservative views on the nature and role of the episcopacy were greatly concerned about making Zion Methodism institutionally stronger for temporal as well as spiritual reasons. Both sides considered the building of a strong church as indispensable for the liberation and uplift of the race, however they might differ over strategies to accomplish said end. In this sense, even religious leaders such as Hood who eschewed political officeholding for themselves and focused on their religious vocations were seeking to advance the race politically. Furthermore, the conflicts within Zion mirrored similar debates and tensions in other black denominations as they struggled with self-definition and with deepening their institutional unity.

INCREASED EMPHASIS ON THE EPISCOPAL NATURE OF ZION METHODISM

The Zion historian Bradley has amply demonstrated that Zion Methodism witnessed the emergence of a stronger episcopacy from the days of its connectional origins in the early 1820s until the post–World War I era, but particularly in the post–Civil War decades. This stronger episcopacy is exemplified by the sole use of the title "bishop" and dropping "superintendent" to refer to these officers beginning around 1864. The 1880 decision by the General Conference made a number of changes that supported a heightened sense of the episcopacy in Zion: selecting bishops for life rather than quadrennially, specifying that candidates for the episcopacy must be between forty and sixty years old, and eliminating a conference committee previously charged with quadrennially examining the character of the bishops. In general, the Board of Bishops after the Civil War assumed greater supervisory responsibilities over denominational affairs between the meetings of the General Conferences.[1]

Along with these changes in church rules came a greater theological emphasis in some quarters on Zion's *episcopal* nature, that is, the emergence of a "high church" party within the AMEZ. Some proponents of this high-church view claimed a biblical basis for episcopacy and, advocating greater *episcopal* Methodism, looked on the bishop as one called by God to his office, regarding the office as a third ordination, in addition to those of deacon and elder. This was a distinct departure from Zion's tradition. During the earliest days of Zion, the superintendent or chief officer was an elder who had been set aside for a designated period of time to oversee the connection, with the clear understanding that at the next quadrennium he might be removed from office. Indeed, these pioneer Zionites apparently made a special effort to dissociate themselves from the more episcopal Methodism represented by the Methodist Episcopal Church, out of which they formed, and the African Methodist Episcopal Church, Zion's rival and with whom the AMEZ considered uniting from time to time. Like two other Methodistic counterparts, the African Union Church and the Methodist Protestant Church, Zionites placed greater stress on the rights of the laity and democracy (not episcopalianism) within the connection, objectives reflected in their deliberate decision to utilize the original nomenclature ("superintendent") of the Methodist founder, John Wesley, and to require the election or reelection of the leader quadrennially.

To be sure, there were outside influences on Zion's changes and debates regarding its episcopacy during the Civil War and postwar eras: the criticisms of the AME and the Methodist Episcopal church bodies that Zion did not have a true episcopacy, the possible influence of Roman Catholicism with its 1870 Vatican Council promulgation of papal infallibility (that the pope when exercising his office as teacher of the church makes infallible pronouncements related to faith and morality), the example of the Methodist Protestant Church with its limited, though mainly unsuccessful, efforts during this era to form a closer connectional organization and grant bishops greater powers, and the presence of persons within Zion who had come from family traditions of the Protestant Episcopal Church, such as Hood's third wife, Keziah P. Hood.

Another significant aspect of the historical-theological context of the debates over the episcopacy within Zion had to do with the declining economic and political fortunes of blacks from 1877 until well into the twentieth century. On one hand, the declining status of African Americans might have contributed directly or indirectly to a greater emphasis on a stronger episcopacy. The increased apathy and intolerance for the concerns of blacks, greater degrees of racial segregation and isolation, the disfranchisement of black voters, and an increase in overt acts of brutality and terrorism against African Americans, combined with the reality of a larger, more diverse church body, probably demanded in the minds of some Zion leaders, stronger governing and mediating roles for the church's chief officers. With the steady decline in the number of black political and economic leaders, the minister in general and the bishop in particular became for many blacks the symbols of leadership for the race, models who should be granted greater respect and power. Perhaps many of the clerical leaders compensated for declining opportunities in the secular realm with an increased emphasis on their power and position in church circles. In addition, the challenges to Christian orthodoxy brought by influences such as biblical criticism, Darwinism, and comparative religion probably increased the perceived need for learned (self or formally taught) leaders such as Hood to assume greater ecclesiastical supervision in the church.

On the other hand, the exclusion of blacks from politics in the South, economic setbacks, increased segregation, and innovative developments in religious thinking also influenced those who sought greater democracy within the church. Though blacks by and large did not receive invitations to participate in the political and literary discussion of white mainstream society, they could use the organs of their churches, such as newspapers, to express views on various issues, secular and religious. In addition, there were denominational leaders who believed that the church leaders should take stronger, more "radical" stances on issues facing the race. These Zionites could agree wholeheartedly on granting greater respect to the episcopal office while demanding that the leadership ranks be opened to more progressive-thinking individuals. Significantly, therefore, there were not strict lines of demarcation between factions in their debates over Zion's episcopacy. For example, an individual arguing in favor of biblical episcopacy might call for the election of a greater number of bishops. Another individual might speak regularly and approvingly of a "conservative" bishop but insist just as strongly that personal ambition regarding the attainment of church offices was a healthy trait. Rather than following rigid ideological lines, the Zion membership and its leaders generally made decisions based on current practical needs.

HOOD AND THE BIBLICAL EPISCOPACY DEBATE, 1897–1898

This debate over the episcopal nature of Zion Methodism is illustrated clearly in the 1897–1898 exchanges in the denominational newspaper between Bishop Charles Calvin Pettey, advocating the high-church perspective, and elder J. A. D. Bloice, a New Jersey pastor and candidate for deanship of Livingstone College, advocating the low-church position.[2] Though Hood did not intervene in the debate between the two learned individuals, an account of the exchange is important for illuminating Hood's own perspectives. Pettey was clearly a close associate of Hood's. Indeed, the catalyst of the debate was the sermon delivered by Pettey for the twenty-fifth anniversary of Hood's elevation to the episcopacy. Furthermore, Pettey's viewpoints reflected generally, if not exactly, the sentiments Hood expressed over the long term of his episcopacy (1872–1916). For example, in the spring of 1903 Hood wrote a series of articles to the *Star* focusing on the qualities of a bishop.[3] A perusal of these articles reveals that Pettey's high-church view of the episcopacy accorded quite well with Hood's. The exchange between Pettey and Bloice demonstrates the divisions in Zion circles over the nature of the episcopacy and pinpoints an occasion where each side systematically presented its arguments on the matter.

Pettey (1849–1900) was born into slavery in Wilkesboro, North Carolina, educated at Biddle University (renamed Johnson C. Smith) in Charlotte, North Carolina, ordained deacon in 1872 and elder in 1878 by Hood, pastored in a number of states in the South and California, and attained the episcopacy in 1888. A schoolteacher and versed in New Testament Greek, Pettey was widely recognized as a learned, forceful preacher and debater and one of the most educated bishops in the connection at the time. Available biographical information reveals the intellectual sharpness of J. A. D. Bloice. He pastored in Atlantic City, New Jersey, and during his life worked actively to establish a strong base for Zion in the area. Educated at Livingstone College, the Reverend Bloice was its first Bachelor of Arts graduate to pursue graduate-level studies. So impressed was the president of Boston University that he asked J. C. Price, Livingstone's president, to send more students as gifted as Bloice. Bloice also had an excellent command of New Testament Greek and at the time was a candidate for the deanship of Livingstone College.[4]

The controversy erupted when Bishop Pettey, in Fayetteville, North Carolina, in September 1897, delivered the silver-anniversary address, "Biblical and Patristic Episcopacy," commemorating Hood's elevation to the episcopacy. Speaking from the text of I Peter 3:15, Pettey enthusiastically sought to prove a biblically based episcopacy that was reflected in the writings of the Church Fathers, such as Irenaeus, Clement, Ignatius, Cyprian, and Polycarp. Drawing on the deutero-Pauline epistles of Timothy and Titus among other writings, Pettey claimed that Paul ordained persons such as Epaphroditus and Timothy as bishops by the laying on of hands. The North Carolina native claimed that Scripture recognized "apostles" as "bishops." During the first century, he claimed, the two terms were synonymous and used interchangeably. According to Pettey, the office of apostle or bishop had three functions. "First, to collect and compile the sayings and doings of Christ and bear testimony as eyewitnesses of the same. Second, to [go] into all the world and preach the gospel. Third, to oversee the church and ordain their own divine successors." Thus, Pettey was not only making the case for a biblically based episcopacy but also affirming the doctrine of apostolic succession. "I believe that Christ established a church episcopal in its polity, threefold in holy orders with a divine succession." The bishops of Zion, Pettey was arguing, were more than simply elders selected by the larger church to provide direction. They were spiritual inheritors of the third ordination, as established by Jesus Christ and practiced in the New Testament and Early Church. Pettey had arrived at these conclusions "[a]fter much research and a prayerful study of the Bible, coupled with a careful perusal of patristic history."[5]

Fortunately for the low-church party and loyalists to the older tradition in Zion Methodism, the Reverend Bloice of Atlantic City, New Jersey, rose to the occasion to combat Pettey's ecclesiology (or theory on the nature of the church and its organization). Citing Scripture, he argued that most of the gospel writings were not collected or written by the Apostles, that others besides the Apostles were entrusted with preaching the gospel, and he discounted the idea that the office of apostle and bishop constituted a synonymous ordination that was transferable by apostolic succession.[6] Bloice dismissed the high-church episcopal claims of Pettey with the bold declaration that "any average student who is able to read the Scriptures in the original [Greek language], and critically analyze Patristic literature in its native tongue, would throw to the winds the 'incontrovertible evidence' which he [Pettey] has by patient research gathered to establish" the bishop's argument. Bloice suggested that it would be more advantageous for Zion to base confidence in its leadership on loyalty to Jesus Christ rather than a claim of biblical episcopacy handed down by apostolic succession.[7]

The New Jersey minister wished to make it clear "to my humbler brethren in the ministry that the statements of a Bishop in the Methodist communion on questions of a doctrinal or theological nature, even though delivered *ex cathedra,* are not necessarily valid and reliable." Apparently, Bloice, by using the term "ex cathedra," sarcastically attempted to portray Pettey's supposed aspiration to force upon the connection the infallibility of his episcopal office, much as the Roman Catholic Vatican Council (1869–1870) had underscored the primacy of the pope when it employed the term in promulgating the doctrine of papal infallibility. Bloice was consciously combating any attempt of the bishops to exalt their positions at the expense of the connection's ministers. The elder saw Pettey's argument as a clear distortion of biblical teachings. Citing New Testament Scripture, Bloice argued that the episcopacy was not a position to which one was called to by other bishops, but an office to which one was elected by clergy and lay colleagues.[8] Bloice boldly offered a logical extension of Pettey's argument, the embracing of Roman Catholicism. "[T]he Roman Catholic idea of the Church being greater than the Bible lies encouched in this remark. 'Back to Rome!' seems to be the trend of the Bishop's argument."[9] Bloice might have been pushing his argument relative to Pettey's intent, but it contained a large grain of potential truth. John Newman, the Anglican priest and by this time a Catholic Cardinal, had argued earlier in the century the high-church position in the Church of England so forcefully that eventually he joined the Roman Catholic Church.

For a number of months the two learned personalities debated back and forth, often sinking to rather uncharitable levels in their depictions of each other's character and motivations.[10] It is not evident whether either side won adherents from the other camp. But a number of significant points suggest themselves regarding this exchange. Notwithstanding Pettey's attempt to defend the episcopal government of Zion in a historical context in which it was sometimes attacked by non-Zionites, and notwithstanding the possibility that he was genuinely convinced about his claim for the biblical and historical bases for the episcopal form of church government, Bloice helped to prevent a takeover of the connection by the high-church party. The elder countered the bishop's arguments clearly, vigorously, and directly. Second, this debate between a high-church bishop and a low-church elder might have set the stage for the overwhelming and deafening responses of traditionalist male ministers to the ordination of Mrs. Small, a controversy that developed as the Pettey-Bloice exchange was subsiding. In this latter debate was an opportunity for every minister, who opposed women's ordination and possessed a sufficient knowledge of the Bible, to remind the bishops that they—the bishops—were indeed fallible individuals subject to the Scriptures and the will of the General Conference. Third, this debate, aside from personal attacks, was one that reflected great learning on both sides. Utilizing their excellent command of New Testament Greek, analyses of New Testament scripture, and examining the writings of early church "fathers," such as Irenaeus, Polycarp, Ignatius, and the author of the recently discovered *Didache,* these two learned African American males impressed readers of the *Star,* blacks, whites, Zionites, and non-Zionites, with their scholarly debate on a theological issue of interest transcending the AMEZ. Finally, and to reiterate, Pettey's views fundamentally represented those of Hood's.

The Hood-Smith Controversy, 1898–1904

Another controversy, that between Hood and Elder John Wesley Smith, essentially revolved around the *Star* editor's ambition for the episcopacy and Hood's equally strong intention to bar him from the bishopric. The feud between these two influential leaders in Zion points to tensions between the older leaders in Zion, represented by Hood, and many younger ones, represented by Smith, who challenged the wisdom and judgment of their seniors. The relationship between the two individuals appears to have been much better in times past. As late as September 1889 Smith spoke glowingly of Hood as "a grand man" whose influence in the connection would long survive his earthly demise.[11] As Smith assumed the editorship of the *Star* in the 1890s and became a clear candidate for the episcopacy, that earlier relationship soured tremendously.

In Smith (1862–1910) the aging and sickly Hood met a formidable foe. Smith was eloquent, shrewd, a great preacher, and editor of the powerful denominational *Star* between 1896 and 1904.[12] A native of Fayetteville, North Carolina, Smith embraced the faith in 1880, became deacon and joined the Central North Carolina Annual Conference in 1881. Apparently, his home church was, like Hood's, the historic Evans Chapel (or Evans Metropolitan AMEZ Church) in Fayetteville, where Hood performed the marriage ceremony for Smith and his bride, Ida Thompson, in 1886. Interestingly, a Zion church in New Haven consented to have the then largely inexperienced Smith assume the pastorate, provided Bishop Hood would expedite his ordination as elder, which Hood and a group of elders did on September 4, 1882. In addition to Connecticut, Smith pastored churches in Arkansas, Kentucky, Maryland, Washington, D.C., and Pennsylvania, until he assumed the editorship of the *Star of Zion* from G. W. Clinton, a newly elected bishop.

Walls wrote that Smith carried the nickname "the left-handed Benjaminite"[13] because of his strong, courageous writings on behalf of the interests of ordinary people. The future bishop appears to have been a likable individual who truly cared about others. Smith's tenure at the newspaper proved to be a boon. He made marked improvement in the appearance and layout of the newspaper, converting it from a four-page paper with seven columns to an eight-page organ with five columns and bringing it praise from readers both within and without the Zion connection. Undoubtedly, editorship of the denominational newspaper proved instrumental in his successful campaign for the episcopacy as it would that of others. Indeed, if we exclude the first editor and layperson, John C. Dancy, four of the five minister-editors of the *Star* between 1885 and 1924 left the *Star* editorship for the bishopric: George W. Clinton, 1896; John W. Smith, 1904; George C. Clements, 1916; and William J. Walls, 1924.

The conflict between Hood and Smith moved through three crucial phases: the first period when Smith vigorously defended himself and sharply criticized Hood (1896–1900); the period after the 1900 General Conference, when Smith and Hood arrived at a truce and apparent conciliation(1900–1903); and the third phase, of active confrontation between the two Zion leaders (1903–1904).[14] Smith's interest in episcopal office emerged during his first term as editor. Smith had the support of some bishops, but not Hood. The editor's campaign approach appears to have varied. In March 1897 he and E. D. W. Jones were engaged in a dispute as to which of them had been more disrespectful toward the bishops.[15] Two years later Bishop Pettey, who was closely associated with Hood, announced that the church required more bishops and, despite his apparent differences with Smith over the issue of women's ordination, Pettey endorsed Smith for the episcopacy. Pettey's endorsement was not seconded by Hood, who made it clear in a host of articles during 1899 that Smith was not on his list of potential bishops. Hood particularly disliked what he perceived as Smith's use of the *Star of Zion,* the denominational newspaper that the senior bishop had helped establish, as a tool by which Smith and his supporters trumpeted his candidacy. Hood found the idea of a person's campaigning for the office of bishop very objectionable. The senior bishop suggested that Smith simply did not possess a character superior to all other possible episcopal candidates. Of course, Smith vigorously defended his editorial and his pastoral records, as did many other Zionites. Actually, few Zionites, if any, publicly shared Hood's strong distaste for Smith's candidacy, though some were actively supporting other candidates.[16]

The General Conference and other candidates for the episcopacy agreed in 1900 that the state of Alabama, a major stronghold of Zionism, deserved a seat on the Board of Bishops. The other candidates withdrew from contention and the assembly elected one bishop, J. W. Alstork (1852–1920), who had previously sought the office. After the conference Hood once again opposed the election of additional bishops. When it became apparent that general sentiment favored the election of more bishops in 1904, Hood, as he had done in previous years, agreed to the election of only one bishop. In September 1903 he recommended M. R. Franklin for the episcopacy. Hood praised Franklin as a dedicated church worker with high moral character, one who had sacrificed for the good of the church. In one newspaper issue the senior bishop spoke glowingly of Franklin's agreement to step down from a presiding eldership to assume the pastorate of a local congregation, but he did not bother to mention that he became pastor of the most prestigious church in the connection, the Mother AMEZ Church in New York City.[17] This move on the part of Hood in support of Franklin probably baffled both foe and friend. Apparently, some church leaders, including members of Hood's camp, had intimated in 1900 that they would support Josiah S. Caldwell, a candidate who, along with Smith, withdrew from contention for the episcopacy at that conference in favor of Alstork. Now Hood claimed that the church needed only one bishop and that he knew of no one with better qualifications than Franklin, not even, apparently, Caldwell.

Bishop Pettey died after the meeting of the General Conference at the end of 1900, thus creating another episcopal vacancy and helping to set the stage for another battle over episcopal elections. During his next term as editor, Smith, upon the advice of a number of bishops and church leaders, toned down considerably his criticisms of some of the bishops and sought to work out a truce with Hood. Though the available sources are not explicit about the matter, it appears that influential people in Zion had decided to give their support to Josiah Caldwell and Smith at the next General Conference. By the late summer or early fall of 1903 it was clear that Hood was not going to support Smith for the episcopacy; thus, controversy once again ensued between them. This time Smith's defense of himself was understood and encouraged by many in Zion. The editor and his supporters had sufficient strength to overcome Hood's opposition. By the fall of 1903 it was clear that Smith and Josiah Caldwell would probably be elected bishops at the 1904 General Conference. By that time it was also apparent to Hood that his campaign against Smith had failed, and while continuing his opposition to the editor, the bishop promised that, consistent with his modus operandi, he would gladly work in harmony with Smith as an episcopal colleague should the conference elect the newspaper editor.[18] The 1904 General Conference of the AMEZ

Church also rebuffed Hood on the question of the election of new bishops. Receiving the greater number of votes, Smith was elected the twenty-ninth bishop and served until his death in 1910. The General Steward of the AMEZ, Josiah S. Caldwell (1862–1935), became the thirtieth bishop and served for over thirty years. The senior bishop's favored candidate, M. R. Franklin, became the thirty-first bishop in 1908, but died in 1909.

THE CONSERVATIVE-PROGRESSIVE STRUGGLE
FOR THE EPISCOPACY

The conflict between Hood and Smith transcended the contest between a younger elder and the senior bishop of the church. This controversy fell against the backdrop of two major forces contending for power within Zion Methodism and represented on the Board of Bishops. The progressives (whom Hood termed "radicals") called upon the denomination to become more aggressive in utilizing its resources for church expansion. The conservatives cautioned a slower approach. Bishop Alexander Walters represented the progressives; and Hood, the senior bishop, led the conservative forces. Interestingly, Hood had promoted Walters for advancement in the ministry and to the episcopacy.[19] Each thought highly of the other and never appeared to clash openly over the issue of the expansion of the church or the number of bishops. Charles C. Pettey, also supported by Hood in his ministerial and episcopal career, probably represented a segment on the board and in the larger church that oscillated between conservatism and progressivism. Pettey, for example, at one point argued for a biblical episcopacy along with Hood and then, contrary to Hood, proposed the election of additional bishops. On the whole, it appears that the bishops guarded each other's honor, sought to maintain a high degree of harmony on the board, and individually were independent in thought. The controversy between Smith and Hood reflected the conservative-progressive debate but went far beyond it, sinking to the level of personal acrimony, especially, it seems, on the part of the senior bishop.

The progressives between 1888 and 1916 (as far as this study is concerned) argued for additional bishops for a number of reasons. First, they believed that additional bishops would help to expand the work of the denomination into new areas such as the Deep South and the western states. Second, and closely related to the above point, the progressives sometimes argued that additional bishops would give many people greater access to a bishop, that many people lived in remote places where they seldom had the pleasure of an episcopal visit. These people saw bishops only at the general conferences or very rarely, unlike people in other portions of Zion. One of the great attractions of Methodism for those inclined in that direction was the bishop, his symbol and presence. Without the episcopal presence it would be much harder to gain new members and to energize the connectional work. Third, the progressives pointed to the ailing health and advanced ages of a number of bishops. The connection required additional, younger, and healthier bishops who had the strength to perform the church's business. Fourth, from time to time the progressives spoke of a need for greater diversity on the board of bishops. Apparently, they believed that people with newer and bolder ideas would help chart more innovative paths for the connection. Fifth, there appeared to have been some correlation between ecclesiastical progressivism and political "progressivism." Both conservatives and progressives understood the church as a key institution working to uplift the race. The political progressives counseled a bolder, less accommodating insistence on political and economic justice. A stronger denomination would be a valuable instrument for uniting and energizing the black community around these progressive goals. But this political-ecclesiastical correlation is true only to a point. For example, Smith, though a denominational opponent of Hood, was closer to Hood politically than to Walters, the political progressive.

The conservatives, led by Bishop Hood, argued their points of opposition to an increased number of bishops with equal energy and determination. First, the strongest and most consistent argument advanced by the conservatives was the lack of sufficient funds to support a larger number of church officials. They bemoaned a top-heavy, increasingly bureaucratic denomination that used its limited funds to support additional officers rather than a connection that paid greater attention to other, more significant aspects of denominational work, like support for the denominationally sponsored Livingstone College, funds for retired or incapacitated ministers, and contributions to orphans and widows, especially those bereft of hardworking, sacrificial, deceased ministers and pastors. In some instances, Hood complained, not all the bishops had received their back salaries. Second, the conservatives argued that the present number of bishops, despite the age and sickness of some, were capable of handling the workload of the church. An increased number of bishops would be an excess that the church could ill afford. Third, the conservatives argued that it would be preferable to strengthen the denomination, help it to meet all of its present financial obligations, which were many, rather than attempting to expand into new areas. It would be better to have a smaller denomination that was internally strong than an overextended connection that would become a laughing stock because it was not able to meet the demands of its unreasonable ambitions and goals of an increased membership. Fourth, the conservatives insisted that there was already sufficient variety on the current board. Fifth, just as the progressives tended to connect their religious and political philosophies and approaches, so the conservatives argued that a cautious, well-managed, sober approach to both political matters and church expansion was preferable to the recommendations of the "radicals."

THE STRUGGLE OVER THE EPISCOPACY AND HOOD'S RETIREMENT, 1888–1916: RETROSPECT AND OVERVIEW

Let us now examine the historical development of the conservative-progressive contest. Alexander Walters, the progressive, offered an interesting and reliable sketch of this struggle between the years 1888 and 1916.[20] According to Walters, the 1888 General Conference, which met at St. Peter's Church in New Bern, North Carolina, proved to be the one in which the Zionites moved from a posture of "ultra-conservatism" to a more progressive stance. The progressive forces persuaded the conference to elect two additional bishops, Charles Calvin Pettey and Cicero R. Harris. Walters credited the superb orator and Livingstone College president, J. C. Price, with playing a key role in moving the conference forward in this way. When the Zion Conference assembled in Pittsburgh, Pennsylvania, in 1892, the progressives forces once again scored a victory. The conference selected two bishops, Alexander Walters and I. C. Clinton. In 1896 the General Conference returned South to Mobile, Alabama, and the progressive camp this time secured the election of three bishops: George W. Clinton, John B. Small, and Jehu H. Holiday. Unfortunately, from the progressives' standpoint, the General Conference did not vote an increase to one dollar per member assessment. Meeting in Washington, D.C., in 1900, the General Conference elected one bishop, John Wesley Alstork of Alabama. The assembly also approved Walters's recommendation to create a Connectional Council, a group composed of the bishops, other clergy, and laypersons that conducted business of the connection between the quadrennial conference meetings. In 1904 the General Conference assembled in St. Louis, Missouri, and elected two prominent leaders in Zion as bishops, John W. Smith, the editor of the *Star of Zion,* and Josiah S. Caldwell, the financial secretary of Zion. Additionally, Walters persuaded Hood to consent to an increase of the per member assessment to one dollar. In 1908 the conservatives and progressives engaged in a fierce battle that ranged back and forth at the

General Conference. The assembly, however, selected three new bishops: Martin R. Franklin, G. L. Blackwell, and A. J. Warner.

In 1912 the General Conference convened in Hood's home territory, Charlotte, North Carolina. The conservative forces, well organized and efficient, scored a major defeat of the progressives, the first since 1888, according to Walters. While no bishops were selected at this Conference, the progressives, contrary to an inference that could be drawn from Walters, gained a significant concession in that the conference, including the conservative leader Hood, agreed to elect two new bishops in 1916. The bishop issue proved to be such a prolonged and costly struggle that little legislation was enacted at this session. Indeed there were seven episcopal candidates who had suffered "suppressed ambitions": George C. Clements, R. B. Bruce, and W. L. Lee, all of whom would win election at the next General Conference; and J. S. Jackson, S. L. Corrothers, R. S. Rives, and J. B. Colbert, none of whom would ever ascend to the episcopacy. The General Conference minutes reported that a committee examining the credentials of the candidates reported that there were twelve additional contenders for the episcopal office, making a total of nineteen.[21] Furthermore, there was already serious consideration in some quarters that Bishop Hood be retired from the active bishopric. As early as September 1910, the Reverend E. Malcolm Argyle, editor of *The Zion Vidette* in Chattanooga, Tennessee, made some daring suggestions for the approaching General Conference: elect three bishops, retire Hood with his full salary, and commission the senior bishop as church historiographer with the duty to write a comprehensive history of the connection.[22] Interestingly, Mrs. K. P. Hood, the Bishop's wife, was defeated for presidency of the Woman's Home and Foreign Missionary Society in a close vote at the 1912 Conference by the Reverend Mrs. Mary J. Small, wife of Bishop J. B. Small. An observer might wonder whether Mrs. Hood's defeat foreshadowed what lay ahead for her husband.

THE 1916 CONFERENCE AND THE FORCED RETIREMENT OF HOOD

The fateful year for Hood regarding the episcopacy was 1916. Both sides, as usual, planned their strategies well ahead of the conference that was to meet in Louisville, Kentucky. In September 1915, Hood expressed his opinion on the wisdom and legality of forcibly retiring bishops. Hood's statements revealed three stances regarding this issue. First, the forced retirement of sitting bishops was against church law. Since 1880 Zion had elected its bishops for life based, of course, on "good behavior" and their ability to carry out duties. Second, the conference could retire *future* bishops, those "hereafter elected," not those already serving at the time of the conference's enacting a new law. Third, Hood pointed to the wisdom of retaining bishops for life. These episcopal officers, having such a guarantee, had proven well disposed to making generous, even sacrificial, contributions from their church salaries for the work of the connection. Hood pointed out that he had personally contributed "thousands of dollars" for the good of Zion. Fourth, should the conference enact retirement legislation applicable to future elected bishops, its language should be flexible, reading "may be" rather than "shall be retired at a stated age." Reflecting his postmillennialist theology, the aged prelate looked forward to the time when all humanity, including bishops, would have longer life spans and a bishop might be in the flower of productivity beyond 150 years of age![23]

Less than two months after the above entry by Hood, the Reverend E. D. W. Jones, who later assumed the episcopacy in 1924 and who had had his share of controversial exchanges with the senior bishop, called on all members of the General Conference to be independent in mind, not to accede automatically to recommendations simply because they derived from the Board of Bishops, but with seriousness and deliberation to follow their own best judgments.[24] Jones cautioned against permitting proposed legislation to die in committees before arriving on the floor of the General Conference, where it should be fully examined. The future bishop emphatically voiced his opinion that the serious business of this conference carried more import than that of any assembly over the past half century and required wise reflection and discourse, not social intermingling. Writing from San Francisco, California, Jones reminded his readers that each one of them, bishop, clergy, and laity, had equal suffrage, responsibility, and intelligence.[25] It appears that Jones's opposition to Hood stemmed from three main sources: disagreement concerning the need for additional bishops, family tensions traceable to the relations between Hood and the late Bishop S. T. Jones, the younger Jones's father, and the bishop's refusal to appoint the younger Jones to the prestigious parish of Mother AME Zion Church in New York City.

On May 3, 1916, the Twenty-Sixth Quadrennial Session of the African Methodist Episcopal Zion Church met at Broadway Temple AMEZ Church in Louisville, Kentucky, at noon, with Senior Bishop Hood presiding. A number of new bishops had been elected since 1888, but because of the heavy blows of death, the current number of active bishops stood at only eight: Hood, the senior bishop; Cicero R. Harris; Alexander Walters, secretary of the Board of Bishops; George

Wylie Clinton; John Wesley Alstork; Josiah Samuel Caldwell; George Lincoln Blackwell; and Andrew Jackson Warner. Four hundred delegates and representatives were present, a fourth of them women. Following custom, the Zionites recognized a number of distinguished guests, including Madame C. J. Walker, the first woman (who was also black) who became a millionaire in the United States, making her fortune from hair care products. Introduced by Bishop G. W. Clinton, Madame Walker pledged a thousand dollars to support a nondenominational school in Africa conditional upon a matching amount from the black Baptists and the Zionites. The conference accepted the challenge. Bishop C. H. Phillips of the Colored [later, Christian] Methodist Episcopal Church, a sister denomination of black Methodism, also addressed the assembly, on one occasion praising Hood for his length of episcopal service.[26] Other significant church dignitaries dropped by the conference, including Bishop Collins Denny of Richmond, Virginia, an official of the white Methodist Episcopal Church, South, and the Reverend H. K. Carroll of Washington, D.C., the secretary of the Federal Council of Churches, a forerunner to the National Council of Churches.[27] At the conclusion of their 1916 General Conference, the Zionites would have ten active bishops, two retired bishops on half salary, thirty general officers, three thousand clergy, and seven hundred thousand members.[28]

The focus of legislative activity fell upon the issue of the bishopric. On the eighth day of the conference, a Wednesday morning with Bishop Blackwell presiding, B. J. Bolding offered a motion to accept the recommendation from the Board of Bishops that two bishops be elected. W. D. Clinton, M.D., successfully modified the motion with a substitute amendment calling for four new prelates. Bishop Hood defended his intention to vote for two bishops since that had been the agreement at the 1912 General Conference. But the assembly voted 193 to 157 to accept Clinton's substitute motion.[29] On the eleventh day the conference began its balloting for the election of four new bishops from a list of forty-one candidates, an election that required a two-thirds vote to elect each new officer. At the afternoon session on May 15 and on the eleventh ballot, Dr. Lynwood Westinghouse Kyles finally secured election as Zion's thirty-fourth bishop. The following morning, a Tuesday, the twelfth balloting made Robert Blair Bruce eligible for consecration as Zion's thirty-fifth bishop, and on the fourteenth balloting that afternoon the conference selected William Leonard Lee and George Clinton Clements as the fortieth and forty-first bishops, respectively.[30]

Yet the action of far greater historic significance than the election of four new Zion bishops was the fact that this connection joined other Methodists and for the first time forcibly retired bishops for reasons other than improper behavior or dereliction of duties. On May 11, the day following the decision to elect four rather than two bishops and prior to the beginning of the episcopal balloting that afternoon, the conference took up the issue of retiring Hood and Harris at its morning session.[31] The decision by the conference did not come without some hesitation and agony on the part of the delegates. Both bishops enjoyed high favor among Zionites. Hood's situation probably posed the greater discomfort to the conference. The senior bishop, he had served as active bishop for forty-four years, was a prolific writer, church historian, defender of Zion, and admired by many. Some conference delegates were not old enough to recall a Zion Methodism without the episcopacy of Hood.

Evidently, Hood's own love for debate and his acerbic attack on Zionites who differed with him, more than the collective strength of the progressives, assured his episcopal downfall. The object of Hood's attack on this occasion was the Reverend Dr. John J. Smyer, pastor of Metropolitan Institutional AMEZ Church of Yonkers, New York, and a business partner of Hood's. In his report on the New York Conference to the General Conference (1916), Hood, who had served as episcopal overseer for the First Episcopal District (including the New York Conferences), made some very unflattering remarks concerning Smyer. The younger man took exception to that portion of Hood's report that reflected negatively upon his church and pastorate. Obtaining the floor on "a question of personal privilege," the highly respected Smyer spent two hours contradicting the "[misrepresentations] made by Bishop Hood and depicted the things which he and other ministers, also the church itself, had been made to suffer through what he termed the misuse of power on the part of the aged bishop." By all accounts Smyer's reply to the aged bishop was eloquent, masterful, and brilliant. Bishop C. R. Harris, the presiding bishop, then invited Hood to reply. Obviously, Hood's brief response was not satisfactory for the majority of the conference. Bishop Walters made the triumphant motion, seconded by Bishop Blackwell, that the contested material be obliterated from the report.[32] According to Walters, this fateful error by Hood solidified the progressive forces and resulted in his and Harris's removal from the active episcopacy.[33]

THE FATEFUL DAY ARRIVES, 1916

On May 11, on the ninth day of the conference, Dr. W. D. Clinton made the historic motion that Hood and Harris be retired. The Reverend A. P. Pettey seconded the motion. Bishop G. W. Clinton succeeded in amending the original motion to allow a one-hour discussion of the proposal, with both Harris and Hood having the opportunity to state their positions. It was a very heart-wrenching morning for both supporters and opponents of the two as they witnessed these aged shepherds of Zion fighting for their episcopal lives, having given so many years of sacrificial service for the upbuilding of the connection, but perhaps having done themselves and their splendid records disservice by not having vacated their offices earlier in their episcopal careers. The subsequent balloting revealed 187 votes for retirement and 168 in opposition, a relatively close vote but sufficient to retire the two Zion leaders on half salary.[34]

Also, the conference mandated seventy-four as the age of retirement for all bishops henceforth, with half salary as compensation, thus rejecting Hood's earlier suggestion that the conference adopt greater flexibility regarding forced retirement. The conference assigned Walters, a resident of New York City, to the First Episcopal District, previously under Hood's oversight. Hood's retirement also made Walters the new senior bishop, although the latter was thirty years Hood's junior.[35] Rather paradoxically, the four episcopal candidates had to undergo numerous ballots to attain the required two-thirds vote of the Zion Conference to be elected; but a *simple majority* at that same assembly forcibly retired two bishops, one of whom, Hood, had at that point served longer than any Methodist bishop of any American denomination, white or black. Evidently, the irony and, perhaps, injustice of these actions did not sufficiently register with the conference delegates.

Yet there are a number of facts and observations that might save Hood from a disgraceful finish in the eyes of his supporters and sympathizers. Jacob Wesley Powell drew two conclusions from the election of bishops at the 1916 Conference. One conclusion would not have necessarily pleased Hood: holding a denominational office was the best avenue to the episcopacy. The senior bishop would not necessarily have disagreed that this type of experience was helpful in preparing for the episcopacy, but he rebelled at the idea of people seeking offices. Offices were to seek the right persons. But as a major organizer of the work in North Carolina, Hood might have taken great delight in Powell's observation that that state still constituted "the storm center of Zion Methodism." One of Hood's enduring legacies, even as late as the 1990s, has been the great contribution he made in establishing North Carolina as the headquarters and major power in Zion. After the 1916 General Conference, North Carolina held the distinction of having been the current residence of three of the four successful episcopal candidates.[36] Powell also pointed out that the two bishops, though forcibly retired from active service, were awarded half their salaries ($1,000 at the time) and their services were used by the church as conditions dictated and their physical strength permitted.[37]

With the death of Bishop Walters in early 1917, Hood assumed Walters' episcopal duties. Indeed, it is ironic that Hood, who spent much of his life and career at death's door as a victim of severe bouts of influenza, fever, and other maladies, actually outlived many of his contemporaries, including some of his severest critics and church opponents, such as John W. Smith (who died in 1910), John J. Smyer (in 1916), and Alexander Walters (in 1917). As early as the 1890s some of these critics had actually advocated electing new, younger bishops based on the belief that Hood's death was imminent! Indeed, it is further ironic that the death of Bishop Walters, a leading progressive, occasioned the conservative Hood's resumption of active episcopal duties, which he evidently performed until sickness curtailed his activities. Furthermore, A. J. Warner, elected as a progressive bishop in 1908, died in 1920, two years after Hood. R. B. Bruce, one of the four bishops elected at the 1916 Conference, was severely ill when the Zionites convened in 1920 and died before the end of the year. Hood's fellow conservative and companion in the 1916 forced retirement, Cicero C. Harris, also died on June 24, 1917, a little over one year after that Conference.[38] Indeed, few Zion bishops approached Hood's longevity either in life or episcopal service. Undoubtedly the grueling travels and exacting demands of the high office took heavy tolls on persons who might otherwise have lived much longer lives. There were twenty bishops elected after Hood's consecration and prior to his death in 1918, from the year 1876 to 1916 inclusively. Of these twenty bishops, eleven died prior to Hood, with nearly half of them dead by 1911. Nine of these twenty bishops outlived Hood, but none elected prior to 1896 survived him. Of the twenty bishops elected during the 1876–1916 period, only Hood lived into his eighties.

On October 30, 1918, James Walker Hood died in Fayetteville, North Carolina, at the age of eighty-seven, having served as a minister for about sixty years and an active bishop for forty-four years. Mrs. K. P. Hood telegrammed Bishop George Wylie Clinton to deliver the eulogy. "Rest on old warrior, [l]ong and arduous were thy labors, but now thou canst rest. No traveling amid snow and rain, no more afflictions, no more misunderstandings, no more vexations[,] no more paralytic strokes. Thy tongue which was palsied by the stroke is no more needed where thou art now. . . ."[39] In 1991 Bishop J. Clinton Hoggard of Zion provided information regarding Hood's death given him by the Reverend Celeste F. Martin. At the time of Hood's death Fayetteville was in the grips of an influenza epidemic, which was very serious, given the fact that there were then no antibiotics. The federal government forbade group assemblies because of the epidemic. Hood's funeral was held at his home on Ramsey Street, with the sermon preached by Clinton from the porch (poetically just since Hood belonged to the whole community not only the church). From his home Hood's body was taken to a family plot in Cross Creek Cemetery near the historic Evans Memorial (now Evans Metropolitan) AMEZ Church in that city. This was the home church of the Hood family and was founded by and named in honor of the black Methodist Henry Evans, who had first established Methodism in the Fayetteville, North Carolina, area. Eulogies of Hood dominated the *Star of Zion*. All of Hood's children were deceased by the 1990s, having lived into their seventies, eighties, and nineties.[40]

Bishop G. L. Blackwell, who wrote and delivered the quadrennial address of the Zion bishops for the 1920 General Conference, noted sadly the passing since the last conference of Bishops Cicero R. Harris, Alexander Walters, and James W. Hood. Blackwell spoke highly of all three episcopal colleagues but especially elevated Hood with sober and accurate words. "His very busy life, his untold sacrifices for his church, rich contribution to the uplift of his race, and his long tenure of service, entitled him to the foremost place among his peers in the advancement of the church of his choice."[41]

CONCLUSION

In the last few chapters we have explored Hood's involvement in a several controversies that affected Zion during his episcopacy. These issues represent the types of struggles that all the major denominations during this era faced: the relationship between church duty and racial uplift, effecting greater black ecclesiastical unity, increased participation of, and leadership roles for, women in the historic denominations, and the attempts and necessity to define the faith and their denominational identity. Hood was always at the forefront of religious leadership. Some of the debates and controversies in which Hood was involved endeared him as a lover of Zion and a defender of the oppressed or circumscribed. Others represented him as an unreasonable opponent of change and a stifler of the ambitions of younger people. Hood's sarcastic, sharp style of argument and attack that appears to have come with advancing age eventually cost him the active bishopric, just as his personal piety, zeal, organizing skill and energy, devotion to the black race, and compassion for people had helped him to assume the episcopacy and build Zion into a major American denomination. Zion Methodism and the African American community as a whole at that time knew that Hood's death, whatever his shortcomings, cost them one of their most committed builders and protectors of the church and race. The concluding chapter will provide a summary on the life and leadership of Hood and his significance.

PART VI

HEADED FOR MOUNT ZION

Summary and Analysis of Hood's Leadership

CONCLUSION

A Summary and Some Assessments of the Leadership of James Walker Hood

Bishop Hood will never die in Zion.
—C. W. Winfield and M. N. Levy, Part IV, "The Hood Golden
Jubilee," in Hood, *Sketch of the Early History of the African Methodist
Episcopal Zion Church*

Bishop James W. Hood, of the African Methodist Episcopal Zion Church,
in his day [was] one of the most influential men of color in the United
States. . . .
—Carter G. Woodson, *History of the Negro Church*

Unborn generations shall yet rise up, and survey the expanse of his extensive and intensive labors, . . . and say: "Bless Father Hood, he [built] better
than he knew."
—The Reverend J. W. McDonald, *The Star of Zion*

This study of the religious and political leadership of James Walker Hood concludes with a summary of the enterprise and some assessment of this remarkable,
but largely forgotten individual. The preceding pages have demonstrated that
James Walker Hood, though long neglected and sometimes forgotten in scholarly circles, was a major political (especially in racial matters) and religious leader
during the nineteenth and early twentieth centuries. This study has recovered

the significance, both religious and secular, of Hood's contribution to the nation and the race during these momentous years, especially after his move from the Northeast to North Carolina and the commencement of his operations in the South. While researching and writing this book, I have received a great deal of support, a clear testimony to the fact that Hood's story must be told. Some of the most enthusiastic, helpful encouragement, primary data, and research suggestions came from members and scholars of the AME, Hood's rival denomination. By illustrating the significant religious and political leadership of this nineteenth and early twentieth century individual, this study will go far in preventing the error of unfairly and inaccurately relegating this great leader to the margins of historical importance.

Based on our present knowledge of African American religious history, Hood's life represents a microcosm of the development of the independent black denominations that originated in the Northeast, journeyed to the South during the Civil War era, and as a result of rapid growth in membership and organization became truly national religious bodies. This story of Hood's life has revealed that African American Christian leaders not only built churches, but also schools and businesses, and struggled to promote and safeguard civil liberties for their race. In other words, Hood and black denominational leaders in general, no matter how greatly they emphasized their commitment to the church and the gospel, also promoted the temporal interests and concerns of their people, regarding spiritual and temporal liberation as not only compatible, but to a major extent inseparable, goals. Thus, while I have focused on Hood's leadership and its importance, the reader, nonetheless, has been provided a case study, a prism, a reservoir of information regarding a larger historical picture, that is, the story of the struggle of African Americans, religiously and politically, during this crucial period of American history as the great majority of them advanced from human bondage to a greater measure of freedom.

SUMMARY

A portion of the introductory chapter outlined the emergence of independent black denominations during the nineteenth century. These groups emerged from white-controlled churches not because of serious doctrinal disputes over governance as such but to provide African American Christians with greater freedom, both religiously and temporally. Though only a minority of black Methodists withdrew from the multiracial but white-controlled Methodist Episcopal Church prior to the Civil War, they established churches that stood as powerful symbols and demonstrations to African Americans and whites of the ability of the race to endure and triumph. In addition, this section provided an overview of Hood's religious views, noting that he was very orthodox, evangelical, and of the temperance persuasion. Hood was a willing proponent of ecumenism and cooperation among religious bodies, but did not support African missions as strongly as some other bishops and denominational leaders within and outside the Zion connection. This chapter also noted that the religious conservatism of Hood did not equate with ignorance or with unconcern for the conditions of the less fortunate.

Chapter 1 examined the biography of Hood from his birth and childhood in southeastern Pennsylvania and his ministerial activities in Pennsylvania, New York, Connecticut, and Nova Scotia. Chapters Two treated Hood's religious activities in the South from 1864 to 1872. Under the missionary appointment of the great organizing bishop Joseph J. Clinton, Hood traveled South in the early part of 1864 and began a successful career of founding churches and preparing ministers for the upbuilding of Zion. The labors of Clinton, Hood, and others contributed immensely to making Zion a permanent ecclesiastical fixture in the southern states and establishing it as a major American denomination. In Chapter 3, we investigated Hood's participation in the first convention of free blacks in North Carolina in 1865 and the state Reconstruction convention in 1867–1868. The chapter also noted that Hood campaigned for the ratification of the new state constitution, served as Assistant Superintendent of Public Instruction for the state of North Carolina, served in a comparable capacity for the Freedmen's Bureau, acted for a while as a magistrate, played an active role in Republican politics, and assisted in the establishment of what is now Fayetteville State University and Livingstone College.

Chapters 4 and 5 chronicled Hood's rise to the episcopacy in 1872 and some major events during his early years as bishop. Undoubtedly, his contributions in the religious, political, and educational spheres during the 1864–1872 era made him a logical choice to serve as one of the episcopal leaders of the new and quickly growing black denominations. In these chapters we observed how he supported the candidacy and the episcopacy of a fellow North Carolinian, Thomas H. Lomax, and how he, acting in the interest of the AMEZ and the Christian faith, played a leading role in the disrobing of another bishop accused of immorality and drunkenness, William H. Hillery. Two case studies of his episcopal activities demonstrated his closeness to and respect for the people whom he served.

In Chapters 6 and 7 we examined Hood's philosophy, which in the context of black freedom thinking of the time might be characterized as "conservative" or "moderate." We must be careful, however, to observe that "conservatism" as applied to, and used by, Hood meant something fundamentally different than conservatism during the final decades of the twentieth century. It meant the pursuit of civil rights and justice in a spirit of cooperation and conciliation with the "better class of white people." The black conservatives or moderates were more apt to employ gentle persuasions and appeals to reason and the best interests of all concerned than the black progressives or "radicals" who directed more uncompromising denunciations of wrongs and brutalities inflicted on blacks by the acts of white reactionaries or the do-nothing approach of some white liberals and moderates. Mirroring the sentiments of the majority of blacks, Hood placed greater emphasis on voting rights and fidelity to what was perceived as the party of progress in racial matters, the Republican, than an insistence on racial integration *per se,* especially when it involved social matters.

Hood condemned lynching but, perhaps like most southern black leaders, not with the fierceness of many northern black spokespersons. Hood and the AMEZ as a whole—reflecting the stances of other black leaders, denominations, and the general African American populace—regretted and protested, mildly and forcefully, the continual erosion of black political and economic rights in the South. Hood represented the majority opinion of black leaders in counseling blacks to achieve despite negative circumstances by acquiring property, education, pursuing cooperation with the better elements of the white community, and by building strong moral and spiritual personalities. I have not found in Hood's thought any serious, prolonged disagreements with American foreign policy during this era. Hood supported the United States in the Spanish-American War, but advocated the granting of American citizenship rights to the populations brought under the sovereignty of the United States. Bishop Hood, probably reflecting the thinking of most black denominational leaders, had serious concerns about the mistreatment of African Americans, but held a generally appreciative attitude regarding the greatness of the nation, the latter attitude no doubt strongly influenced by the achievement of physical and civil liberties by blacks as a result of the Civil War. Overall, Hood, despite the painful setbacks to the race during the post-Reconstruction years, held an optimistic attitude regarding the future; he looked forward to the continued spread of the Christian gospel and with it the gradual arrival of the Millennium. This optimism in the eventual recognition by white America of black equality contrasted sharply with the more despondent perspective of Hood's AME counterpart, Bishop Henry M. Turner. But Hood's optimism, too, was probably a reliable reflection of the thinking of the majority of black denominational leaders during this era.

Chapters 8, 9, and 10 returned attention to Hood's religious leadership. In examining a select number of crucial controversies within and involving Zion Methodism during the 1872–1916 era, but especially the 1885–1916 years, we had an opportunity to observe both the admirable and the less admirable sides of Hood's leadership. Like the majority of black leaders of the time, secular and religious, Hood defended the black clergy in the South against the exaggerated, reckless attacks of Booker T. Washington during 1890. Washington pointed to some real problems afflicting some clergy, but he over generalized and even at this early date demonstrated his capacity to downgrade efforts of blacks while remaining painfully silent about the cruel behavior on the part of some racially reactionary and apathetic whites. Hood during the 1880s and 1890s was not personally hopeful that the highly desired union of black Methodist forces would materialize. Such would have been a major boon for the spread of the gospel and the advancement of the race, thought Hood and other denominational leaders. Hood, however, was determined that such union would not come at the expense of Zion's historical integrity or ecclesiastical rights. The senior bishop did not participate very intensely in the controversy over the ordination of the Reverend Mary J. Small as it raged in the pages of the denominational newspaper during 1898. Yet the bishop's own ministerial actions over the years and his comments as the debate subsided indicated that he clearly supported ordaining women and that he would continue to promote greater and equal opportunities for women in the church. His contributions to female equity in the church constitute one of his greatest legacies to American Christianity.

It was the controversies surrounding Zion's episcopacy that increasingly placed Hood in a very unfavorable light with many Zionites and that ultimately contributed to his forced retirement from the bench. Hood appears to have held a "high church" view of the episcopacy, believing that one should be called by God to the bishopric. Using his own life story, Hood believed that persons should not campaign for the office but should permit the office to seek them. On one hand, Hood was counseling ministers that their religious obligations left no time for secular political office holding. On the other, he insisted that personal ambition even in church circles must be circumscribed. Hood believed that the church should operate with as few bishops as necessary and thus conserve valuable and scarce financial resources. His critics argued that an increased number of bishops would provide the church with greater administrative means to expand the

church in new directions. Those seeking to establish a more "progressive" agenda
for the AMEZ succeeded in part at the 1916 General Conference when the Zionites set a mandatory retirement age for bishops, forcibly retiring Hood and C. R.
Harris as the active bishops. Upon the untimely death of another bishop, however, Hood returned for more active service prior to his death in 1918.

AN ASSESSMENT

How do we assess the leadership of such a significant individual? The much-
neglected Hood played major roles in both ecclesiastical and secular circles of
American society during the period under study. From the church perspective,
one could easily claim that Hood ranks as a founder of Zion Methodism. When
he entered the Zion's ministry, the denomination numbered fewer than five thousand. His organizing work of building churches, bringing in congregations, and
conducting revivals assisted tremendously in raising the membership to a half
million by 1900 and seven hundred thousand by the time of his death in 1918.
We might also mention some of his other contributions: support of denominational education, establishment of the church newspaper, endorsement of
women's rights, authorship of a number of significant works, including a comprehensive history of the Zion connection, and his charitable contributions and
sacrifices on behalf of members and clergy in the connection. Even those of a
more agnostic bent must acknowledge that the African American denominations
represented the capacity of blacks to manage, plan, and govern. Hood's powerful role in building up one of the major black denominations, therefore, has
earned him a well-deserved legacy for black institutional building; and this contribution alone more than merits a biography.

Hood insisted in later years that he was not a politician and that his services
for the state government must be viewed in a nonpolitical sense. Nonetheless, he
was a politician, and being a statesman does not detract from that fact. His postwar and Reconstruction activities in the South demonstrated a belief shared by
many black clergy from both the South and the North that the civil liberties of
blacks must be firmly established and perpetually defended. Historians have increasingly acknowledged that, contrary to earlier misrepresentations, the Reconstruction era was instrumental in bringing greater liberties and rights to both
blacks and whites in the South. Hood deserves appreciation for risking his health
and life to promote greater equity and justice for whites and blacks in North Carolina during the years 1864–1872. Even during his years as bishop, Hood never

completely left the political world. He still promoted individuals for political appointments, committed himself and the denomination to the interest of African Americans, and protested, however moderately, the injustices inflicted on blacks in the South.

Every individual, however, makes mistakes or operates without full knowledge of events, circumstances, or future dangers and possibilities. We can, thus, appreciate the secular and religious contributions of Hood without being uncritical of his modus operandi. In the religious sphere, one might criticize Hood for not being a greater supporter of African missions. Alexander Walters of the Zionites, Henry M. Turner of the AMEs, and Albert W. Pegues of the Baptists more forcefully demonstrated in their lives and activities the interconnected experiences and histories of continental Africans and their cousins in the Americas. Furthermore, it is unfortunate that in denominational debates over the episcopacy and other matters Hood sometimes demonstrated a tendency to be petty and self-righteous, a stifler of other persons' ambitions, inflexible, and close-minded. Given the weight of his mighty accomplishments in church and society, his faults do not invalidate his place among the great persons of the era. Indeed he enjoyed a greater reputation for being generous, kind to opponents in debate, deliberate and reasoned in exchanges, and not one to hold grudges. Unfortunately, this well-respected and aged figure was forcibly removed from the episcopal chair. His belated retirement might have contributed to his neglect in scholarly circles. He died, not at the height of his greatness, like Alexander Walters, but at a point when younger men and women were ascending to church power.

How we assess Hood politically depends perhaps on where we stand on the political spectrum. One could argue that Hood's moderation was the wisest and perhaps only practical course to follow in a post-Reconstruction South where black liberties were being inexorably curtailed and banished and in a nation that had decided that it had had enough of the "black problem." His more fervent supporters might contend that Hood was correct to be appreciative of the United States and to be optimistic about the future. With all of its faults, the nation, prodded by black leaders, had made tremendous progress in rectifying the conditions of blacks when the history of chattel bondage in all of its cruelty is acknowledged, notwithstanding a resurgence of white supremacist successes. Taking a broader view of history and its cycles, why should not blacks have reasonably hoped that better times would return? Hood did not simply counsel blacks to have faith in the future, he urged them to prepare themselves by taking full advantage of the economic and educational opportunities at their disposal. In the decade of the 1980s and 1990s many black leaders and white sympathizers have once again emphasized that governmental action and protection, especially when they cannot be politically guaranteed, must be accompanied by the development of economic and institutional resources and strong moral and spiritual values on the part of the victims of neglect and injustice. Whereas Hood's teachings in this regard might not have received a hearty reception among many during the 1960s and early 1970s, in latter decades such views rang with greater authenticity among increasing numbers of African Americans and white sympathizers. It should also be emphasized that Hood's thought reflected mainstream, contemporary black thinking by and large. Hood, like most black denominational leaders, did the best he could under the circumstances that African Americans encountered.

From the vantage point of the last decade of the twentieth century, we might express deep regret that Hood and other denominational leaders did not register greater outrage at the abuses heaped on blacks. The black community should have countered the terrorist tactics of the white supremacist and reactionary forces with their own means of armed self-defense. Why did not Hood and most black denominational leaders follow the leads of AME Henry M. Turner or an AMEZ M. D. Clinton, encouraging blacks to arm themselves for self-defense against lynching and violent intimidation of black voters? Hood had confidence that the hard work and loyalty of blacks, coupled with the continued spread of true Christianity, would in the not-too-distant future obliterate the distinctions of race and caste. It was not that Hood was completely naive about the reality of white supremacy or the manner in which it had gripped the minds and hearts of many white Americans. Nor did he believe that the efforts for disfranchisement of black voters were fueled by an ignorance of the capacity of blacks. Yet, it seems, he overestimated the opportunities of blacks to succeed economically in an environment where their political rights were continually eroded. Also, I suspect that Hood and other leaders, may have engaged in wishful thinking and, to some extent, false optimism regarding the plight of African Americans as being not as dismal as it truly was. They did not see that the very qualities of self-help, economic independence, educational enhancement, and moral virtue either did not matter to many racially reactionary or apathetic whites or were the very qualities that had occasioned oppressive measures in the first place.

We must not judge Hood and his contemporaries too harshly, however. They were dealing with a novelty: an entire race of people (at least 90 percent of them) had gained physical freedom and in a relatively short span of time had made tremendous accomplishments. They had few historical precedents for dealing with many of the momentous developments that occurred in the relatively short time after the event of freedom. According to the Bible, even the miraculously emancipated Hebrews, upon leaving Egyptian slavery, wandered forty years in the wilderness before entering the Promised Land. Indeed, one might argue that it was not that Hood and many of his contemporaries entertained misplaced optimism but that they treasured a firm faith in God and the ability of black people to overcome all obstacles and that their optimism and faith secured a hope and strength for the days when their descendants would successfully reclaim political rights and opportunities lost during these decades. Later generations should encounter stern judgment if they do not learn from the mistakes of black leaders of the past and remember that they must earn racial and any other freedoms and vigorously and eternally claim and defend them. They dare not permit moderation to appear as compromised principle. Furthermore, the spread of Christianity, Islam, or any other religion in and of itself is no panacea for social injustice. Religion in part is an organized, institutional response to God or the Sacred, usually colored by customs and habits of people. It tends to be only as useful as its adherents make it; and all peoples, including blacks and whites, have ways of creatively circumscribing religion's usefulness.

In sum, I agree with the Reverend McDonald's observation, cited at the beginning of this chapter. Bishop Hood built economically, educationally, politically, and, of course, religiously much better than he might have imagined. He was a crucial leader on all these fronts during a momentous era of changes and challenges in American history. In addition, his earliest days and family context, combined with his service to church and race down to World War I, connect us with the origins of independent black Christianity in the United States and reflect its amazing development. His faults notwithstanding, James Walker Hood has left a powerful legacy of devotion and contributions to church, race, and humanity.

Appendix A

	1821	1860	1884	1896	1916	1989	1990 Rank of Black Groups
Growth of the AMEZ Church, 1821–1989, U.S. Membership (Membership numbers designate every 1,000 members.)							
AMEZ	**1.4**	**4.6**	**300**	**350**	**700**	**1,200**	**2d largest black Methodist**
AME		20	400	450		2,200	largest black Methodist
CME				130		900	3d largest black Methodist
UM*						360	
NBC(I)**					3,000 (1915)	7,400	largest black denomination
COGIC***						3,700	2d largest black denomination
All black Methodist			210				
All black Baptist			400				

* Black members in the United Methodist Church
** The National Baptist Convention, Inc.
*** The Church of God in Christ

Sources: Lincoln and Mamiya, *The Black Church in the African American Experience*, 20–91. Richardson, *Dark Salvation,* 87, 143–48. Hill, ed., *Encyclopedia of Religion in the South,* 529. See the bibliography for full citations.

Appendix B

Bishops of AMEZ: A Partial Listing, 1822–1916

Name	Birth	Deacon	Elder	Bishop	Death
James Varick	1750	1806	1821	1822	?
Christopher Rush	1777	1822	1822	1828	1873
William Miller	1775	1808	1823	1840	1845
George Galbraith	1799	1830	1830	1848	1853
William H. Bishop	1793	1827	1828	1852	1873
George A. Spywood	1802	1843	1844	1853	1875
John Tappan	1799	1834	1835	1853	1870
James Simmons	1792	1833	1833	1856	1874
Solomon T. Scott	1790	1834	1835	1856	1862
Joseph J. Clinton	1823	1845	1846	1856	1881
Peter Ross	1809	1840	1842	1860	1890
John D. Brooks	1803	1843	1845	1864	1874
Jermain W. Loguen	1813	1843	1844	1868	1872
Samson D. Talbot	1819	1843	1844	1864	1878
John J. Moore	1804	1842	1843	1868	1893
S. T. W. Jones	1825	1850	1851	1868	1891
J. W. Hood	1831	1860	1862	1872	1918
J. Pascal Thompson	1818	1846	1847	1876	1894
William Hillery	1839	1864	1866	1876	1893
Thomas H. Lomax	1832	1867	1868	1876	1908
C. C. Pettey	1849	1872	1878	1888	1900
C. C. Harris	1844	1874	1874	1888	1917
I. C. Clinton	1830	1867	1867	1892	1904
Alexander Walters	1858	1879	1881	1892	1917
G. W. Clinton	1859	1882	1885	1896	1921
Jehu Holliday	1827	1862	1862	1896	1899
J. B. Small	1845	1872	1873	1896	1905
J. W. Alstork	1852	1882	1884	1906	1920
John W. Smith	1861	1881	1882	1904	1910
J. S. Caldwell	1862	1886	1888	1904	1935
M. R. Franklin	1853	1886	1888	1908	1909
G. L. Blackwell	1861	1884	1885	1908	1926
A. J. Warner	1850	1857	1857	1908	1920
L. W. Kyles	1874	1897	1901	1916	1941
R. B. Bruce	1861	1886	1892	1916	1920
W. L. Lee	1866	1893	1895	1916	1927
G. C. Clement	1871	1893	1895	1916	1934

Source: Walls, *The African Methodist Episcopal Zion Church*, pp. 565–97, see the bibliography.

Notes

Introduction

1. Carter G. Woodson, *History of the Negro Church,* 3d ed. (Washington, D.C.: Associated Publishers, 1972; originally published in 1921), 213.

2. Joyce D. Clayton, "Education, Politics, and Statesmanship: The Story of James Walker Hood in North Carolina, 1864–1890" (master's thesis, North Carolina Central University, 1978).

3. See Stephen Ward Angell, *Bishop Henry McNeal Turner and African-American Religion in the South* (Knoxville: University of Tennessee Press, 1992); Katherine L. Dvorak, *An African-American Exodus: The Segregation of the Southern Churches* (Brooklyn, N.Y.: Carlson Publishing, Inc., 1991); and Reginald F. Hildebrand, *The Times Were Strange and Stirring: Methodist Preachers and the Crisis of Emancipation* (Durham, N.C.: Duke University Press, 1995).

4. *The Black Church in the African American Experience* (Durham, N.C.: Duke University Press, 1990), see especially 56–60.

5. Dorothy Sharpe Johnson and Lula Goolsby Williams, *Pioneering Women of the African Methodist Episcopal Zion Church, 1796–1996* (Charlotte, N.C.: AME Zion Publishing House, 1996); George W. McMurray and Ndugu G. B. T'Ofori-Atta, *Mother Zion African Methodist Episcopal Zion Church: 200 Years of Evangelism and Liberation/The Birth Story of A Denomination* (Charlotte, N.C.: AME Zion Publishing House, 1996); Richard K. Thompson and Phyllis H. Galloway, *The Role of the Star of Zion in the African Methodist Episcopal Zion Church, 1796–1996* (Montgomery, Ala.: The Alabama/Florida Episcopal District of the African Methodist Episcopal Zion Church, 1996); Bishop Ruben L. Speaks, *Church Administration from the A.M.E. Zion Perspective* (Charlotte, N.C.: The AME Zion Publishing House, 1996); and the late Bishop William Jacob Walls, *The African Methodist Episcopal Zion Church: Reality of the Black Church* (Charlotte, N.C.: AME Zion Publishing House, 1974).

6. *Negro Thought in America, 1880–1915: Racial Ideologies in the Age of Booker T. Washington* (Ann Arbor: University of Michigan Press, 1963), see especially 161–89.

7. A major strength of the fine study by Lincoln and Mamiya, *Black Church,* is its treatment of a continuum of black religious thinking on political matters. See, for example, 164–235.

8. See Cain H. Felder's *Troubling Biblical Waters: Race, Class, and Family* (Maryknoll, N.Y.: Orbis Books, 1989); and his edited work, *Stony the Road We Trod: African American Biblical Interpretation* (Minneapolis: Fortress Press, 1991. Also consult Cyprian Davis, *The History of Black Catholics in the United States* (New York: Crossroads Publishing Company, 1990), especially

1–66; Frank M. Snowden, Jr., *Blacks in Antiquity: Ethiopians in the Greco-Roman Experience* (Cambridge, Mass.: Belknap Press of Harvard University Press, 1970); and St. Clair Drake, *Black Folk Here and There,* vol. 2 (Los Angeles: Center for Afro-American Studies, 1990).

9. For descriptions of evangelicalism during this era and African Americans' relationship to it, see Carter G. Woodson, *History of the Negro Church,* 3d ed. (Washington, D.C.: Associated Publishers, 1972), 1–60; Albert J. Raboteau, *Slave Religion: The "Invisible Institution" in the Antebellum South* (New York: Oxford University Press, 1978), 43–150; Lester B. Scherer, *Slavery and the Churches in Early America, 1619–1819* (Grand Rapids, Mich.: William B. Eerdmans, 1975), especially 82–103; Milton C. Sernett, *Black Religion and American Evangelicalism: White Protestants, Plantation Missions, and the Flowering of Negro Christianity, 1785–1865,* ATLA Monograph Series, No. 7 (Metuchen, N.J.: Scarecrow Press and the American Theological Library Association, 1975), especially 24–35. For a more general examination of evangelicalism and its impact on American culture and religion, see John B. Boles, *The Great Revival, 1787–1805: The Origins of the Southern Evangelical Mind* (Lexington, Ky.: University of Kentucky Press, 1972); and Donald G. Mathews, *Religion in the Old South* (Chicago: University of Chicago Press, 1977).

10. For accounts of the Methodist Episcopal–United Methodist tradition, see Frederick A. Norwood, *The Story of American Methodism: A History of the United Methodists and Their Relations* (Nashville: Abingdon Press, 1974); and Emory Stevens Bucke, general editor, *The History of American Methodism,* 3 vols. (New York and Nashville: Abingdon Press, 1964. To examine the substantial presence of blacks in that tradition throughout American history, see William B. McClain, *Black People in the Methodist Church: Whither Thou Goest?* (Cambridge, Mass.: Schenkman Publishing Company, 1984).

11. Warren Thomas Smith's *John Wesley and Slavery* (Nashville: Abingdon Press, 1986) elaborates on Wesley's adamant and unchanging opposition to human bondage, reveals the early involvement of blacks in Methodism, and illustrates Wesley's condemnation of racial prejudice. For a solid, one-volume treatment of Wesley's general religious thought, see the classic *John Wesley,* edited by Albert C. Outler (New York: Oxford University Press, 1964).

12. For historical accounts on the rise of independent black Christian denominations, see works such as Woodson, *Negro Church;* James Melvin Washington, *Frustrated Fellowship: The Black Baptist Quest for Social Power* (Macon, Ga.: Mercer University Press, 1986); Leroy Fitts, *A History of Black Baptists* (Nashville: Broadman Press, 1985); Othal Hawthorne Lakey, *The Rise of "Colored Methodism": A Study of the Background and the Beginnings of the Christian Methodist Episcopal Church* (Dallas: Crescendo Book Publications, 1972); Carol V. R. George, *Segregated Sabbaths: Richard Allen and the Emergence of Independent Black Churches, 1760–1840* (New York: Oxford University Press, 1977); Harry V. Richardson, *Dark Salvation: The Story of Methodism as It Developed among Blacks in America* (Garden City, N.Y.: Anchor Press/Doubleday, 1976); George A. Singleton, *The Romance of African Methodism: A Study of the African Methodist Episcopal Church* (New York: Exposition Press, 1952); James W. Hood, *One Hundred Years of the African Methodist Episcopal Zion Church* (New York: AME Zion Book Concern, 1895); Walls, *Zion;* David Henry Bradley, Sr., *A History of the AME Zion Church,* vol. 2,

1872–1968 (Nashville: Parthenon Press, 1970); Lewis V. Baldwin, *"Invisible" Strands in African Methodism: A History of the African Union Methodist Protestant and Union American Methodist Episcopal Churches, 1805–1980,* ATLA Monograph Series, No. 19 (Metuchen, N.J.: The American Theological Library Association and the Scarecrow Press, Inc., 1983); and Vinson Synan, *The Holiness-Pentecostal Movement in the United States* (Grand Rapids, Mich.: William B. Eerdmans Publishing Company, 1971).

13. See Richardson, *Dark Salvation.*

14. For a good description of antislavery and other race-related activities of the AMEZ Church and persons associated with them, see Walls, *Zion.* Walls's exhaustive work is valuable in pointing out the denominational connections of important antislavery campaigners. See pages 138–71 and 497–551.

15. *Star of Zion,* March 31, 1994, pages 1, 3, 4, and 6, for editorial comments. Hereafter the newspaper is cited as *Star.*

16. The following references are examples of Hood's views regarding the nature and mission of the Christian church in general and the black church in particular. See the *African Methodist Episcopal Zion Quarterly Review* 8 (1 and 2, 1899): 1–9. In some of the early issues of *AMEZ Quarterly Review* the exact months or volumes are not clearly indicated. Where this information is lacking, I have attempted to approximate the volume number by comparing the known publication dates of other issues. I have simply included information such as "Nos. 1 & 2" if more exact information was not available. Also see Hood's "The Character and the Persuasive Power of the Christian Religion," *Quarterly Review* 13 (January–March 1904): 11–19; *AMEZ Quarterly Review* 8 (April 1899): 6–7; and 59–66 of Hood's *Sketch.*

17. As a bishop in Zion, Hood had many occasions to give his perspectives on the nature and function of the ministry. The following are, of course, only a few examples of references concerning the bishop's views: Minutes, North Carolina Annual Conference, 1876, 7–8; 1878, 4, 18; 1880, 8; 1899, 24–25; Minutes, Central North Carolina Conference, 1881, 7–11; 1882, 11–12; 1899, 76–78, 85–87; Minutes, General Conference of the AMEZ Church, 1888, 18–19, 43, 57–58, 77; Minutes, New England Annual Conference, 1891, 36; Minutes, New York Annual Conference, 1913, 25; Minutes, West Central North Carolina Conference, 1914, 3–9; *Star of Zion,* March 24, 1904, 1; November 14, 1884, 1. Hood, *One Hundred Years,* 18–19; and Walls, *Zion,* 598–99.

18. Minutes, Virginia Annual Conference, 1875, quoted in Walls, *Zion,* 375–76. Also see Walls, *Zion,* 388–89; Sandy D. Martin, *Black Baptists and African Missions: The Origins of a Movement, 1880-1915* (Macon, GA: Mercer University Press, 1989), 41–72; Bradley, *History* 2:226; Minutes, Philadelphia and Baltimore Annual Conference, 1884, 12; and Hood's Address, Connectional Council, Boston, Massachusetts, August 14, 1907, printed in *AMEZ Quarterly Review* 6 (Fourth Quarter 1907): 22.

19. For Hood's evangelical and holiness views, see James W. Hood, *The Negro in the Christian Pulpit; Or, Two Characters and Two Destinies, As Delineated in Twenty-One Practical Sermons* (Raleigh: Edwards, Broughton & Company, Steam Power Printers and Binders, 1884), e. g., 7, 33–48, 51, 131–32, 188–204, 222–35, 249–58, 356–57. Other works provide insight on

the issue of holiness or sanctification as viewed by John Wesley, Hood, and some contempo-
raries of Hood's: *Star,* July 31, 1885, l; March 22, 1888, 2; October 17, 1889, 1; June 28, 1894, 2;
Julia A. Foote, *A Brand Plucked from the Fire: An Autobiographical Sketch* (Cleveland, Ohio:
Printed by W. F. Schneider, 1879), reprinted in William L. Andrews, ed., *Sisters of the Spirit:
Three Black Women's Autobiographies of the Nineteenth Century,* Religion in North America Series, edited by Catherine L. Albanese and Stephen J. Stein (Bloomington: Indiana University
Press, 1986), 161–234. For other references to Foote, see *Star,* July 31, 1885, 1; and Walls, *Zion,*
111–12. For an excellent treatment of the religious thought of John Wesley, see Albert C. Outler, ed., *John Wesley,* especially his explication of Wesley's view of Christian perfection on pages
29–33, 251–53. See Wesley's sermons and explanations of the doctrine on pages 254–71 and
283–98. There were Baptists who shared the holiness perspective. See Virgin W. Broughton,
Twenty Year's Experience of A Missionary (Chicago: Pony Press, 1907), reprinted in *Spiritual Narratives* edited by Louis Gates with an Introduction by Sue E. Houchins, The Schomburg Library of Nineteenth-Century Black Women Writers Series (New York: Oxford University
Press, 1988).

    20. For some excellent surveys and insights concerning the intellectual challenges facing
historic and traditional Christianity during the period 1860–1920, see, e.g., Robert T. Handy,
ed., *Religion in the American Experience: The Pluralistic Style* (New York: Harper & Row, 1972),
116–29; Handy et al., eds., *American Christianity: An Historical Interpretation with Representative Documents,* vol. 2, 1820–1960 (New York: Charles Scribner's Sons, 1963), 213–416; Sydney
E. Ahlstrom, *A Religious History of the American People* (New Haven, Conn.: Yale University
Press, 1972), 731–872; and Winthrop S. Hudson and John Corrigan, *Religion in America: An
Historical Account of the Development of American Religious Life,* 5th ed. (New York: Macmillan Publishing Company, 1992), 203–311.

    21. Regarding Hood's position that Christianity is the unique pathway of salvation, see,
e.g., Hood, *Pulpit,* 105–21.

    22. For Hood's views regarding blacks in antiquity, see, e.g., *Star,* November 16, 1893, 2.
During the 1980s, if not before this time, professionally trained black scholars of the Bible
began ongoing critical assessments of biblical interpretation as it related to African American
life. See, e.g., Felder, *Troubling Biblical Waters* and his edited work, *Stony the Road.* These are
indispensable, groundbreaking texts that represent scholarly efforts among African American
scholars to make the Christian canon and its interpretation more relevant to the liberation
struggles of peoples of color, women, and the poor. Also, see Snowden, Jr., *Blacks in Antiquity,*
Martin Bernal, *Black Athena: The Afroasiatic Roots of Classical Civilization, Volume 1, The Fabrication of Ancient Greece 1785–1985* (New Brunswick, N.J.: Rutgers University Press, 1987);
John G. Jackson, *Introduction to African Civilizations* (Secaucus, N.J.: The Citadel Press, 1970);
and Cheikh Anta Diop, *The African Origin of Civilization: Myth or Reality* (New York:
Lawrence Hill & Company, 1974). All of the above sources are significant for this study since
they highlight not only the presence but the powerful influence of Africans in the ancient world
and early Christianity.

    For a historical analysis of white attitudes toward the personhood of blacks, see George M.

Fredrickson, *The Black Image in the White Mind: The Debate on Afro-American Character and Destiny, 1817–1914* (New York: Harper Torchbooks, Harper & Row, 1971). The following chapters might prove of particular relevance to this discussion: chapter 3, "Science, Polygenesis, and the Proslavery Argument," 71–96; chapter 8, "The Vanishing Negro: Darwinism and the Conflict of the Races," 228–55; chapter 9, "The Negro as Beast: Southern Negrophobia at the Turn of the Century," 256–82.

23. For examples of Hood's ecumenism and views of Catholicism, see Hood, *Plan of the Apocalypse* (York, Pa.: Anstadt & Sons, 1900), 104, 115, 135, 195; and Hood, *One Hundred Years,* e.g., 130–31.

24. For an examination of social gospel, Christian socialists, and Hood's millennial perspectives, see Ronald C. White, Jr., *Liberty and Justice for All: Racial Reform and the Social Gospel (1877–1925)* (New York: Harper & Row, Publishers, 1990); especially 268–75; Robert T. Handy, editor, *The Social Gospel in America, 1870–1920* (New York: Oxford University Press, 1966); Walter Rauschenbusch, *The Theology of the Social Gospel* (Nashville: Abingdon Press, Copyright renewed, 1945; latest printing 1987). Also see Philip S. Foner, ed., *Black Socialist Preacher: The Teachings of Reverend George Washington Woodbey and his Disciple, Reverend G. W. Slater Jr.* (San Francisco: Synthesis Publications, 1983); Reverdy C. Ransom, "The Race Problem in a Christian State, 1906," in *Afro-American Religious History: A Documentary Witness,* edited by Milton C. Sernett (Durham, N.C.: Duke University Press, 1985), 296–305; and David Wills, "Reverdy C. Ransom: The Making of an A. M. E. Bishop," in *Black Apostles at Home and Abroad,* edited by Randall K. Burkett and Richard Newman (Boston: G. K. Hall, 1978), 57–75. For Hood's millennialist views, see the *Daily Star of Zion* (Washington, D.C.), May 2 and 3, 1900, 1–3; May 4, 1900, 1–3; Hood's episcopal address in Minutes, New England Annual Conference, 1891, 27–28; Minutes, Central North Carolina Annual Conference, 1899; 82 Minutes, New York Annual Conference, 1913, 26–27.

The connection between evangelical Christianity and the quest for social progress is illustrated in David O. Moberg, *The Great Reversal: Evangelism versus Social Concern* (Philadelphia: Lippincott, 1972); and Ralph E. Luker, *The Social Gospel in Black and White: American Racial Reform, 1885–1912* (Chapel Hill: University of North Carolina Press, 1991). Peter J. Paris has laid a firm foundation for further historical exploration of social teachings in the major black denominations since the Civil War. See his *The Social Teaching of the Black Churches* (Philadelphia: Fortress Press, 1985). For an overall analysis of the Social Gospel Movement, see Donald K. Gorrell, *The Age of Social Responsibility: The Social Gospel in the Progressive Era, 1900–1920* (Macon, Ga.: Mercer University Press, 1988). Although most of the above-cited works do not focus on fundamentalism and/or evangelicalism, they all amply demonstrate that evangelical ministers and laity were involved in the efforts to reform society.

Chapter One: James Walker Hood

1. James Walker Hood, *One Hundred Years,* 140–42. Another helpful reference for Hood's early life is R. M. Bolden, "Biography of Bishop James Walker Hood, D. D., LL.D.," in *Sou-*

venir Programme—Hood Thank[s] Offering (New York: Printing by Author of Activities at Mother AMEZ Church, May 28–30, 1911).

2. See *Star* (Charlotte, N.C.), January 25, 1900, 5.

3. Clayton, "Hood," 106.

4. See Haygood's introduction to *Pulpit* by Hood, 4; and *Souvenir,* 8.

5. Hood, *One Hundred Years,* 185.

6. *Star,* January 5, 1899, 5.

7. *Star,* December 20, 1888, 1.

8. Edward Raymond Turner, *The Negro in Pennsylvania: Slavery, Servitude, Freedom, 1639–1861* (Washington: American Historical Association, 1911); see especially 247–49, 253.

9. Hood's "Sketch/Personal Reminiscence" of his life, first page, in James Walker Hood Collection or Papers, in Carter G. Woodson Papers, Microfilmed, Auburn University, Auburn, Alabama. The Woodson Papers are henceforth referred to as CGW Papers, or CGW.

10. See Hood's Papers, CGW Papers; and *Star,* February 14, 1901, 1. In the *Star* article Hood recalled the song in memory of Queen Victoria of Britain upon her death and what he saw as her significance for the freedom of the black race.

11. See Hood's handwritten reply to biographical sheet in Hood Collection, CGW Papers; and *Souvenir,* 6–7.

12. Hood's "Bishop J. W. Hood, D. D., L.L.D.," a biographical sketch, first page, Hood Collection, in CGW Papers.

13. See *Star,* February 1, 1917, 1. This article is a reprint of an editorial that appeared in the *Southwestern Christian Advocate.*

14. Bolden, *Souvenir,* 7.

15. Hood, *One Hundred Years,* 186 for quote; also see 185.

16. Hood's "Personal," 1, CGW Papers.

17. Hood, *One Hundred Years,* 186. According to R. M. Bolden, who wrote a brief biographical sketch of Hood, the young minister joined the Mother AMEZ Church congregation, became a class leader, and was granted a local preacher's license shortly after his affiliation. Hood's personal handwritten account, however, speaks in clear, detailed terms about not joining the AMEZ connection until his move to Connecticut in 1857. Perhaps Bolden, in 1911, was anxious to have the Senior Bishop Hood connected with the Mother AMEZ Church, which Bolden then pastored. See Bolden, *Souvenir,* 7.

18. Hood, "Personal," 2, CGW Papers.

19. See Robert T. Handy's *History of the Churches in the United States and Canada* (New York: Oxford University Press, 1977).

20. Hood, "Personal," 2, CGW.

21. Ibid.

22. See Minutes, New England Annual Conference, 1862, 3, 6–7.

23. Ibid., 6.

24. Ibid., 7.

25. R. H. Simmons, "Rt. Rev. J. W. Hood, D. D., LL. D.," in *Negro Stars in All Ages of the*

World, 2d ed., edited by W. H. Quick (Richmond, Va.: S. B. Adkins & Co., Printers, 1898), 157. The entire article is found on 155–63.

26. Hood, "Personal," 2–3, CGW; Hood, *One Hundred Years,* 187.

27. Hood, "Personal," 3, CGW.

28. Ibid.

29. See, Minutes, New England Annual Conference, 1863, especially 2, 6, 9–11, 17, 21–22, 28, 31–32.

30. Ibid., 6, 10–11.

31. Ibid., 17.

32. Ibid., 24, 28.

33. Ibid., 32.

34. See Sandy Dwayne Martin, "Black Churches and the Civil War: Theological and Ecclesiastical Significance of Black Methodist Involvement, 1861–1865," in *Methodist History* 32 (April 1994): 174–86, especially 176–79; and Daniel Alexander Payne, "Welcome to the Ransomed," in Sernett, *Afro-American,* 217–26.

35. Hood, "Personal," 3, CGW.

36. Hood's Quadrennial Report for the First Episcopal District, 2, located in his *Sketch;* and Hood, "Personal," 3, CGW.

37. For biographical sketches of Ross, see Walls, *Zion,* 572; and Hood's article in *Star,* August 14, 1890, 2. For an account of the schism within Zion during 1852–1860, see Carter G. Woodson, *Negro Church,* 92–93.

38. *Star,* August 14, 1890, 2.

39. Hood's Quadrennial Report of the First Episcopal District, 21, in *Sketch.*

40. Walls, *Zion,* 571–72.

41. Hood's "Personal," 4, CGW.

42. Ibid., 5.

43. See, Minutes, North Carolina Central Conference, 13, where Hood's son is listed as a financial contributor to connectional work.

44. *Star,* November 16, 1899, 1.

45. Ibid.

46. Ibid.

47. Hood's handwritten answer to biographical questionnaire in CGW.

48. The Reverend J. Harvey Anderson's editorial comments eulogizing Hood, *Star,* October 31, 1918, 4.

49. Ibid.

50. Ibid.

51. For biographical sketches and references to Keziah P. Hood, see Hood, *One Hundred Years,* 282–85; "The Hood Golden Jubilee," 73–74, 81–82. (See pages 78 and 80 of "The Hood Golden Jubilee" for brief references to Gertrude and Maude Hood respectively.) *Star,* October 29, 1896, 2, is another reference to Keziah Hood.

52. For references to, or articles by, the children of Hood, see, e.g., *Star,* June 12, 1890, 1;

December 3, 1896, 1; September 14, 1899, 2; April 19, 1900, 5; February 7, 1901, 1; September 26, 1901, 5; December 19, 1901, 1; April 3, 1902, 6; October 11, 1917, 4. I am also grateful to Bishop J. Clinton Hoggard of the AMEZ Church, now retired, for information regarding Hood's children revealed in a spring 1991 telephone interview with him.

Chapter Two: Hood's Religious Activities in the South, 1864–1872

1. Forest G. Wood, *The Arrogance of Faith: Christianity and Race in American from the Colonial Era to the Twentieth Century* (Boston: Northeastern University Press, 1990), 140–43.

2. See, e.g., Raboteau, *Slave Religion;* and Mathews, *Religion in the Old South* (Chicago: University of Chicago Press, 1977), especially chapters 5 and 6.

3. See Angell, *Turner;* Dennis C. Dickerson, "William Fisher Dickerson: Northern Preacher/Southern Prelate," *Methodist History* 23 (April 1985): 135–52; Dvorak, *Exodus;* William E. Montgomery, *Under Their Own Vine and Fig Tree: The African-American Church in the South, 1865–1900* (Baton Rouge: Louisiana State University Press, 1993); Alonzo Johnson and Paul Jersild, *Ain't Gonna Lay My 'Ligion Down: African American Religion in the South* (Columbia: University of South Carolina Press, 1996); Washington, *Frustrated Fellowship;* and Martin, "Black Churches," 174–86.

4. Hood's Quadrennial Report of the First Episcopal District, 2, in *Sketch.*

5. Hood, *One Hundred Years,* 292.

6. Ibid.

7. Dennis C. Dickerson, "'I Seek My Brethren': A Commentary on Religious Leadership and Black Church Development in the Carolinas," delivered at the 81st Annual Meeting of the Association for the Study of Afro-American Life and History, Charleston, South Carolina, October 5, 1996, 3.

8. Hood, *One Hundred Years,* 293.

9. Quotation found in Ibid., 293.

10. Hood, *Sketch;* see Hood's "A Supplemental Statement," 89–92, especially 89–90.

11. Ibid., 90.

12. Hood, *One Hundred Years,* 293.

13. Hood's "A Supplemental Statement," 89, in *Sketch.*

14. Hood, *One Hundred Years,* 294.

15. Ibid., 295.

16. Also see Barbara W. Howlett, "Saint Peter's A. M. E. Zion Church," *Journal of the New Bern Historical Society* 1 (May 1988): 31–34, see especially 31.

17. Ibid., 296.

18. Hood, 91 of "A Supplemental Statement," *Sketch.*

19. Minutes, North Carolina Annual Conference (NCC), 1880, 8.

20. Bolden, *Souvenir,* 9. For information regarding the highway marker, see the program for the "Dedication of Highway Marker for Bishop James Walker Hood," with Alfred G. Dunston, Jr., host and presiding bishop, and J. J. Reece, host pastor of Saint Peter's AMEZ

Church, Hood Papers, Walls Heritage Center, Salisbury, North Carolina.

21. Minutes, North Carolina Central Conference, 1880, 8.

22. Hood, *One Hundred Years,* 298.

23. Hood, *One Hundred Years,* 297.

24. See the two-page "Historical Sketch of St. Luke A.M.E. Zion Church," an unpublished synopsis of the congregation's history, in the official records of St. Luke, Wilmington, North Carolina.

25. Walls, *Zion,* 188–89.

26. Hood's Quadrennial Report of the First Episcopal District; see page 3 for quote and pages 2–3 for discussion of the transfer from New Bern to Fayetteville.

27. Simmons, "Hood," in *Negro Stars,* 159.

28. Ibid., 159.

29. E. A. Armstrong, W. E. Murphy, and Sara Chestnut, "History of Evans Metropolitan A. M. E. Zion Church," in the *One Hundred Fiftieth Anniversary Celebration and Rededication of the Evans Metropolitan African Methodist Episcopal Zion Church* (Fayetteville, N.C.: October 1951), 7–10, especially 9.

30. See Hood's handwritten copy of "Some Incidences in the Life of Bishop J. W. Hood," 2–3, in the CGW Papers. This incident involving Price will be explored further in a subsequent chapter dealing with Hood's rise to the episcopacy.

31. See 92 of "A Supplemental History," in Hood's *Sketch.*

Chapter Three: Hood's Political and Educational Leadership in the South, 1864–1872

1. See letter from Mrs. G. V. Grace of Evergreen, Alabama, dated January 22, 1983, to Mrs. Catherine McNeil, archivist, Evans Metropolitan AMEZ Church, Fayetteville, N.C., located in the church's archives; and Minutes, Central North Carolina Annual Conference, 1899, 82.

2. Simmons, *Men of Mark,* 136.

3. Simmons, *Men of Mark;* the quotes are taken from page 136; see 135–36 for discussion.

4. Leon F. Litwack, *Been in the Storm So Long: The Aftermath of Slavery* (New York: Vintage Books, division of Random House, 1979), 507.

5. Ibid., 502–3.

6. "Some Criticisms and Suggestions by Bishop Hood, Letter No. 3," circa 1899, 3 and 4, unpublished manuscript, probably prepared for the *Star,* located in CGW.

7. Litwack, on page 503 of *Storm,* quotes from the Minutes of the Freedmen's Convention of North Carolina, 1865.

8. Simmons, *Men of Mark,* 135.

9. Woodson, *Negro Church,* 214.

10. Ibid., and Litwack, *Storm,* 105.

11. Litwack, *Storm,* 504–7.

12. W. E. Burghardt Du Bois, *Black Reconstruction in America: An Essay Toward A History*

of the Part Which Black Folk Played in the Attempt to Reconstruct Democracy in America, 1860–1880 (New York: Russell & Russell, 1963), 529.

13. Woodson, *Negro Church,* 214.

14. Leonard Bernstein, "The Participation of Negro Delegates in the Constitutional Convention of 1868 in N.C.," *Journal of Negro History* 34 (October 1949): 391–409.

15. Ibid., 392. For Woodson's remarks, see *Negro Church,* 237.

16. Ibid., Bernstein, "Participation." For a biographical sketch of Galloway, see page 392; for Harris's biographical sketch see pages 392–94.

17. Ibid., 400–2.

18. Clayton, "Hood," 30–31.

19. For a solid account of the status of free African Americans in southern states before the Civil War, see Ira Berlin, *Slaves without Masters: The Free Negro in the Antebellum South* (New York: Oxford University Press, 1974).

20. James Walker Hood, *Speech of Rev. James W. Hood of Cumberland County on the Question of Suffrage, Delivered in the Constitutional Convention of North Carolina, February 12th, 1868* (Raleigh, N.C.: W. W. Holden & Son, Printers, 1868), 1–9. Also see Glenda Elizabeth Gilmore, *Gender and Jim Crow: Women and the Politics of White Supremacy in North Carolina, 1896–1920* (Chapel Hill: University of North Carolina Press, 1996), 203–24.

21. Ibid., 402–7.

22. Clayton, "Hood," 32–35.

23. Ibid., 405.

24. Ibid., 394–95.

25. Simmons, *Mark,* 137. This statement credited to Hood closely resembles a statement by Williams Wells Brown in his 1863 book *The Black Man: His Antecedents, His Genius, and His Achievements* made in response to Lincoln's claim that blacks should be colonized elsewhere and implying the superiority of the white race. See *The Negro's Civil War,* 101–9. A common tactic of blacks in the nineteenth century was to remind whites of their "less civilized" history and connect that observation with the insistence that not only have blacks been great in the past but with Christian religion and culture they would be great again.

26. Hood, *Speech,* 9–12.

27. Hood, *Speech,* 4–6.

28. Ibid., *Mark,* 137–39; and Woodson, *Negro Church,* 237.

29. Hood, "Personal," 6, Hood Folder, CGW.

30. Woodson, *Negro Church,* 237.

31. Simmons, *Mark,* 139.

32. Clayton, "Hood," 51–52.

33. Hood, "Some Incidences in the Life of Bishop J. W. Hood, Written by Himself," 1–2, CGW. Prior to his death, Hood had begun the task of writing his autobiography. This manuscript covers the years ca. 1868–1880. I have been unsuccessful in locating that portion of the manuscript covering the pre-1868 years.

34. Simmons, *Mark,* 140.

35. Quoted Quick's *Negro Stars,* 160–61.

36. Ibid., 161.

37. Ibid.

38. Hood, "Incidences," 1, CGW Papers. For an account of northern missionary teachers and ministers and their work among African Americans in the South during the Civil War and immediate post war period, see Litwack, *Storm,* 450–501. For a firsthand description of missionary work in the South by a black woman, see Ray Allen Billington's edited work, *The Journal of Charlotte L. Forten: A Free Negro in the Slave Era* (London: Collier Books, Collier-Macmillan Ltd., 1953).

39. Hood, "Personal," 6–7, CGW Papers.

40. Ibid.

41. Eric Anderson, *Race and Politics in North Carolina, 1872–1901: The Black Second* (Baton Rouge: Louisiana State University Press, 1981), 94–95.

42. Ibid., 97.

43. Frenise A. Logan, *The Negro in North Carolina, 1876–1894* (Chapel Hill: University of North Carolina Press, 1964), 43.

44. Ibid., 121, 132.

45. See Hood Papers, CGW.

Chapter Four: Hood's Early Episcopal Leadership, Part I

1. See Hood, "Incidences," CGW.

2. Ibid., 2–4.

3. For a recent history of the CME Church, see (Bishop) Othal Hawthorne Lakey, *The History of the CME Church* (Memphis, Tenn.: The CME Publishing House, 1985). An article of interest relative to the origins of the CME is Glen T. Askew's "Black Elitism and the Failure of Paternalism in Postbellum Georgia: The Case of Bishop Lucius Henry Holsey," *Journal of Southern History* 58 (November 1992): 637–66.

4. Walls, *Zion,* 572–73.

5. Ibid., 572.

6. Albert G. Miller, "Striving to Reconcile the World: A Glimpse of the Life and Writings of Theophilus Gould Steward," in *The AME Church Review* 91 (April–June 1996), 38–53. See page 41 for the Steward-Cain conflict.

7. Dickerson, "Dickerson," 135–52, especially 149–50.

8. Ibid.; for Hood's description of Price's attempts, see Hood's "Incidences" 2–5, CGW.

9. Ibid., 5.

10. Ibid., 3.

11. Ibid., 5–6.

12. Ibid., 10.

13. Hood, "Incidences," 10–11, CGW.

14. Ibid. See pages 10–13, for Hood's South Carolina episcopal journey.

15. For Hood's Virginia episcopal journey, see Ibid., 13–16.

16. Ibid., 19–20.

17. Ibid., 16–18.

18. For Hood's accounts of camp meetings, see Ibid., 24–28.

19. See John W. Smith's letter in *Star* (Petersburg, Virginia), August 7, 1885, 2, for insights into how some Zionites regarded the importance of camp meetings during this era. Andrews, ed., *Sisters,* for example, contains accounts of camp meetings during the nineteenth century. These accounts point to the often interracial, interdenominational, and to some degree female-led, aspects of many of these events. Some excellent treatments of black and white evangelical religion in the Antebellum South are Raboteau, *Slave Religion,* Mathews, *Old South;* Scherer, *Slavery;* and Sernett, *Black Religion.* For important insights and analyses of Southern white religion after the Civil War, see Kenneth K. Bailey, *Southern White Protestantism in the Twentieth Century* (New York: Harper & Row, 1964. Reprint: Gloucester, Mass.: Peter Smith, 1968); John Lee Eighmy, *Churches in Cultural Captivity* (Knoxville: University of Tennessee Press, 1978); and Charles Reagan Wilson, *Baptized in Blood: The Religion of the Lost Cause, 1865–1920* (Athens: University of Georgia Press, 1980).

20. Sources on the life and ideas of Bishop Daniel Alexander Payne of the AME Church include Daniel A. Payne, *Recollections of Seventy Years* (Nashville: AME Sunday School Union, 1888); Singleton, *Romance,* e.g., 88–104, 122–23; and Charles Killian, ed., *Daniel Alexander Payne: Sermons and Address, 1853–1891* (New York: Arno Press, 1972).

21. Hood describes his response to the death of Mrs. Sophia Hood in "Incidences," 28–36, CGW.

22. Ibid., 18–19, 24.

23. For a summary of the General Conference of 1876, see Bradley, *History,* 2:48–50.

24. Bradley, *History,* 2:49.

25. For Hood's account of Lomax's elevation to the bishopric, see "Incidences," 36–40, CGW. While the context clearly indicates that this account continues past page 40 of Hood's manuscript, the remainder of the manuscript is not extant.

26. For the Turner and Cain challenges, see Dickerson, "Dickerson," 140–46; see Miller, "Steward," 45 for the Gaines and Grant elections; see Washington, *Frustrated Fellowship,* for an account of the rise of black Baptist denominational unity; Martin, *Black Baptists,* 139–85 treats the Baptist foreign missions conflict; and, finally, Leroy Fitts, *Black Baptists,* provides an excellent overview of the history of African American Baptists.

Chapter Five: Hood's Early Episcopal Leadership, Part II

1. Walls, *Zion,* 579.

2. Bradley, *History,* 2:397–403.

3. Ibid., 400.

4. Ibid., 401.

5. Ibid., 402

6. *Star,* March 5, 1886, 2.

7. For Hood's analysis of the Hillery episode, see Minutes, Philadelphia and Baltimore Annual Conference, 1885, 13–15.

8. Ibid., 13–14.

9. Ibid.

10. Ibid., 15.

11. Ibid., 14–15.

12. Ibid., 15.

13. *Star,* November 29, 1888, 1.

14. Minutes, AMEZ General Conference, 1884, 28, quoted in Bradley, *History,* 2:398.

15. Bradley, *History,* 2:403.

16. During the post–Civil War years there was a great exodus of blacks to the western states. For a discussion of this phenomenon, see Nell Irvin Painter, *Exodusters: Black Migration to Kansas after Reconstruction* (Lawrence: University Press of Kansas, 1976/1986). Of course there were also movements among African Americans to "return" to the African continent. See, e.g., Edwin S. Redkey, *Black Exodus: Black Nationalist and Back-to-Africa Movements, 1890–1910* (New Haven, Conn.: Yale University Press, 1969).

17. *Star,* June 26, 1885, l.

18. Ibid.

19. *Star,* August 14, 1885, 1.

20. *Star,* June 26, 1885, 1.

21. For a discussion of ecclesiastical affairs in Portland, see *Star,* July 24, 1885, 1.

22. Ibid.

23. *Star,* July 31, 1885, 1.

24. For an account of Hood's travels and activities in San Francisco, see Ibid.

25. Ibid.

26. Ibid.

27. Bradley, *History,* 2:386; and Walls, *Zion,* 571–71, 583.

28. *Star,* July 31, 1885, 1.

29. Ibid., August 7, 1885, 1.

30. For accounts of women preachers and missionaries active in the nineteenth and early twentieth centuries, see, e.g., autobiographical accounts of women such as Julia Foote, Jarena Lee, Zilpha Elaw, Maria Stewart, and Virginia Broughton in the following works: Andrews, ed., *Sisters;* and Sue E. Houchins, ed., *Spiritual Narratives* (New York: Oxford University Press, 1988). A historical account of black women's involvement in the black Baptist churches during the turn of the century is Evelyn Brooks Higginbotham, *Righteous Discontent: The Women's Movement in the Black Baptist Church, 1880–1920* (Cambridge, Mass.: Harvard University Press,

1993). Women had more ecclesiastical freedom on the mission fields, especially in areas overseas; see, e.g., Sandy Dwayne Martin, "Spelman's Emma B. Delaney and the African Mission," *Journal of Religious Thought* 41 (spring–summer 1984): 22–37; and "Black Baptist Women and African Mission Work, 1870–1925," *SAGE: A Scholarly Journal on Black Women* 3 (spring 1986): 16–19.

31. *Star,* July 31, 1885, 1.

32. Ibid.

33. Ibid., August 7, 1885, 1.

34. *Star,* August 14, 1885, 1; and September 4, 1885, 1.

Chapter Six: Hood and Black America during the Post-Reconstruction Years

1. For a splendid overview of the range of black social thought during the 1880–1915 period, see August Meier, *Negro Thought in America, 1880–1915: Racial Ideologies in the Age of Booker T. Washington* (Ann Arbor: University of Michigan, Press, 1963), especially chapter 10, "Radicals and Conservatives," 171–89.

2. Hood's Episcopal Address, Minutes, New York Annual Conference, 1888, 6–12; see page 9 for quote.

3. Minutes, General Conference of the AMEZ Church of America, May 2, 1888, 18–19.

4. Ibid., 19.

5. *Star,* November 29, 1888, 1.

6. Minutes, Central North Carolina Annual Conference, 1900, 20.

7. Ibid., 23–24.

8. *Star,* September 4, 1885. See Hood's letter regarding his return from California on page 1.

9. Minutes, Central North Carolina and West Central North Carolina Conferences, 1910, 6.

10. This address is located in the papers of Hood found in the Carter G. Woodson Collection, microfilm. The exact date of this speech is unknown.

11. Ibid., 5.

12. Ibid., 5–6.

13. Hood's Episcopal Address in Minutes, North Carolina Annual Conference, 1878, 4–8; see especially 4–6.

14. Bishop's Address, Minutes, North Carolina Annual Conference, 1899, 21–22.

15. Bishop's Address, New York Annual Conference, 1904, 21.

16. See, e.g., "Report on the State of the Country," in *AMEZ Quarterly Review* (October–December 1900): 39–40.

17. Minutes, Central North Carolina Annual Conference, 1882, 12–13.

18. Minutes, Central North Carolina Conference, 1912, 32–33.

19. Hood's Address, printed in *Star,* November 14, 1884, 1.

20. Hood Address Continued, printed in *Star,* November 21, 1884, 1.

21. Minutes, Central North Carolina Conference, 1882, 28.

22. Bishop Hood's Address, Minutes, New England Annual Conference, 1891, 26.

23. Minutes, Central North Carolina Conference, 1899, 63. Also, see "Report on the State of the Country," General Conference of AMEZ, printed in *AMEZ Quarterly Review* (October–December 1900): 35–43.

24. For an account of Wells-Barnett, see Mildred I. Thompson, *Ida B. Wells-Barnett: An Exploratory Study of An American Black Woman, 1893–1930,* Black Women in United States History Series edited by Darlene Clark Hine, *et. al* (Brooklyn, N.Y.: Carlson Publishing Inc., 1990).

25. Glenda Elizabeth Gilmore, *Gender,* 62–88.

26. Minutes, AMEZ General Conference in *AMEZ Quarterly Review* (October–December 1900): 40–41; and Elias C. Morris, "1899 Presidential Address to the National Baptist Convention," Sernett, ed., *Afro-American, 277.*

27. *Star,* September 9, 1897, 1.

28. See Bishop Walters' Episcopal Address, New England Annual Conference, 1906, published in *AMEZ Quarterly Review* (Third Quarter 1906): 1–15.

29. Minutes, AMEZ General Conference, 1896, 53–54.

30. For accounts of the Payne incident, see *Star,* June 12, 1902, 1, 4.

31. Walters's Address, *AMEZ Quarterly Review* (Third Quarter 1906): 13–14; and Quadrennial Address of the AMEZ Bishops, Minutes, General Conference of the AMEZ Church, 1912, 139.

32. Gilmore, *Gender,* 92–117.

33. Episcopal Address, North Carolina Annual Conference, 1899, 32–33.

34. Gilmore, *Gender,* 115–16.

35. Episcopal Address, North Carolina Annual Conference, 1899, 33.

36. *Star,* January 5, 1899, 5; and February 2, 1899, 4;

37. *Star,* January 5, 1899, 5.

38. *Star,* February 2, 1899, 4.

39. Minutes, Central North Carolina Conference, 1901, 25.

40. Ibid., 26.

41. For some accounts and analyses of Booker T. Washington's life and influence, see Louis Harlan et al., eds., *Booker T. Washington Papers,* 14 vols. (Urbana: University of Illinois Press, 1972–1989) and Harlan's *Booker T. Washington: The Wizard of Tuskegee, 1901–1910* (New York: Oxford University Press, 1985).

42. Hood's Address, *AMEZ Quarterly Review* (Third Quarter: 1909): 10–11.

43. See, e.g., Minutes, Central North Carolina Annual Conference, 1899, 82–85 for Hood's entire discussion of the disfranchisement proposal; *AMEZ Quarterly Review* (January–March 1901): 22; and Hood, "The Enfranchisement of the Negro Race A Benefit to the State," *AMEZ Quarterly Review* (July–September 1902): 84–89. For two examinations of race relations and politics in North Carolina from the Reconstruction period to the turn of the century, see: An-

derson, *North Carolina,* especially 94–95, 97; and Logan, *North Carolina,* especially 43, 99, 121, 132, 143, 171–72. See the respective listings of pages in Anderson's and Logan's works for references to the activities of Bishop Hood.

44. Minutes, West Central North Carolina Annual Conference, 1913, 7.

45. Minutes, AMEZ General Conference, 1912, 138.

46. See, e.g., Minutes, Central North Carolina Conference, 1899, 62; Virginia Annual Conference, 1911, 22–23; AMEZ General Conference, 1912, 138–39; and AMEZ General Conference, 1916, 35–36.

47. Hood's Address, Minutes, New England Annual Conference, 1886, 14–15.

48. Minutes, Report on the State of the Country, Philadelphia and Baltimore Conference, 1891, 101.

49. *Star,* May 5, 1898, 2.

50. Minutes, Central North Carolina Conference, 1899, 65; and Minutes, General Conference of the AMEZ Church, 1900, located in the *AMEZ Quarterly Review* (October–December 1900): 36.

51. Hood's Episcopal Address, Minutes, Central North Carolina Annual Conference, 1899, especially 79–82.

52. Ibid., 82.

Chapter Seven: The Loyal Republican

1. For a look at black political, social, and economic thought during the 1880–1915 period, see Meier, *Negro Thought.* Chapters 2 and 10 are particularly relevant for the present discussion of political alignments.

2. Minutes, Philadelphia and Baltimore Annual Conference, 1885, 16.

3. Minutes, New York Annual Conference, 1887, see page 12 for quote and 12–13 for entire report.

4. An excellent source on the life and work of Walters is George Mason Miller's "'A This Worldly Mission:' The Life and Career of Alexander Walters (1858–1917)" (Ph.D. diss.: State University of New York at Stony Brook, 1984). This work especially chronicles Walters' fight for civil rights. See chapters 6, "New Approaches to Old Problems, 'Contending for His Civil and Political Rights' 1908–1912; and chapter 7, "'A Dream Again Deferred': 1912–1915"; and chapter 8, "'Being Strong': 1915–1917." These chapters provide significant information and insight into Walters' support of William J. Bryan and Woodrow Wilson. Equally compelling is the bishop's autobiography, *My Life and Work.* See biographical sketches of Walters in Walls, *Zion,* 583; and David Henry Bradley, Sr. *History,* 2:386

5. See Walls, *Zion,* 350–51, and 596; and Bradley, *History,* 2:409–10.

6. Walls, *Zion,* 350–51.

7. See John C. Dancy's editorial comments in *AMEZ Quarterly Review* (October–December 1908): 46–50.

8. Meier, *Negro Thought,* 164–65. Also, see Miller, *This Worldly,* 297–300.

9. See Miller, *This Worldly,* 307–15; and Meier, *Thought,* 164–65.

10. Bradley, *History,* 2:477; and *AMEZ Quarterly Review* (July–September [1908]): 41–49.

11. *Quarterly Review* (July–September [1908]): 23–40. Hood's article is found on 23–26.

12. Ibid., 25.

13. Ibid., 26.

14. Ibid., Dancy's editorial comments are found sprinkled throughout the editorial section, 41–49.

15. Ibid., 47.

16. John A. Garraty and Robert A. McCaughey, *The American Nation: A History of the United States,* Sixth Edition (New York: Harper & Row, Publishers, 1987), 958–59.

17. Dancy's editorial comments, *AMEZ Quarterly Review* (October–December 1908): 46–57.

18. Ibid., 53–54.

19. See, e.g., "Bishop Hood's Address to the New York Conference," *AMEZ Quarterly Review* (Third Quarter, 1909): 1–13.

20. Meier, *Negro Thought,* 164–65.

21. Ibid., 187–88.

22. Garraty and McCaughey, *American Nation,* 959.

23. Meier, *Negro Thought,* 187–89.

24. Manuscript copy of Hood's article, "Bishop J. W. Hood Gives Some Reasons for Supporting Taft," 3 pages, in CGW. The article was prepared for the North Carolina (?) newspaper, *The Independent,* and is dated September 23, 1912.

25. Ibid., 1.

26. Ibid., 1–2.

27. Ibid., 2.

28. Minutes, New York Annual Conference, AMEZ, June 11–16, 1913, 19–27. This quote is found on page 26. The totality of Hood's comments on the state of the country is found on pages 25–27.

29. Ibid.

30. "The State of Country" Report, Ibid., 18.

31. Meier, *Negro Thought,* 189; See 188–89 for a discussion of Wilson's presidency.

32. Minutes, New York Conference, AMEZ, 1915, 49–50.

33. Minutes, General Conference of the AMEZ Church, 1916, 36.

Chapter Eight: Hood as Leader in Religious Controversies, 1872–1916

1. This article, "The Colored Ministry: Its Defects and Needs," is included in *The BTW Papers,* vol. 3: 1889–95 (*BTW,* 3), edited by Harlan, 71–75. It was originally published in *Christian Union* 42 (August 14, 1890): 199–200.

2. Ibid., *BTW,* 3:72.

3. Ibid., 72–73.

4. Ibid., 73.

5. Ibid., 74–75.

6. See Payne's correspondence in Ibid., 97–99, especially 98. For biographical details of Payne, see Singleton, *Romance,* 34, 43, 63, 69, 88, 90, 100–101, 103–104, 122. Also see Daniel A. Payne, *Recollections.*

7. *Star,* January 15, 1891, 4.

8. Ibid.

9. Ibid.

10. Ibid.

11. *Star,* February 26, 1891, 2.

12. *Star,* March 17, 1892, 2.

13. See, e.g., the *BTW* Papers.

14. *Star,* February 17, 1904, 1.

15. For a description of Washington's viewpoint of religion, see Robert Michael Franklin, *Liberating Visions: Human Fulfillment and Social Justice in African-American Thought* (Minneapolis: Fortress Press, 1990), 11–42, but especially 24–30.

16. Orishatukeh Faduma, "The Defects of the Negro Church," in *The American Negro Academy Occasional Papers,* No. 10 (Washington, D.C.: The American Negro Academy, 1904), 3–17. Moses Nathaniel Moore has thoroughly researched the life of this significant figure. See Moore's *Orishatukeh Faduma: Liberal Theology and Evangelical Pan-Africanism, 1857–1846* (Landham, Md., and London: American Theological and Library Association and Scarecrow Press, Inc., 1996); and his "Orishatukeh Faduma and the New Theology," in *Christian History* (March 1994): 60–80. For Du Bois's analyses of religion, see, e.g., Franklin, *Visions,* 43–73, especially 63–68.

17. Angell, *Turner,* 196–97.

18. See, e.g., Hudson and Corrigan, *Religion in America,* 213–16.

19. Black Baptists also sought (and attained) unity among themselves in post–Civil War America, culminating in the establishment of the National Baptist Convention (NBC) in 1895. For an excellent account of the rise of the NBC, see Washington, *Frustrated Fellowship.*

20. Ibid., 145–53.

21. Angell, *Turner,* 64–65.

22. For Zion's efforts to effect organic union with other Methodist bodies, see Bradley, *History,* 2:314–68; and Walls, *Zion,* 459–77.

23. *Star,* September 25, 1885, 1; January 15, 1886, 1.

24. *Star,* January 15, 1886, 1.

25. *Star,* July 30, 1886, 1; August 20, 1886, 1, 3.

26. *Star,* April 9, 1886, 2; August 13, 1886, 3.

27. See *Star,* August 13, 1886, 2–3; September 10, 1886, pages 1 and 2 for Turner's, Hood's, and the *Star* editor's opinion.

28. *Star,* August 13, 1886, 2.

29. *Star,* September 10, 1886, 1.

30. Ibid.

31. *Star,* September 10, 1886, 1.

32. Ibid.

33. *Star,* May 2, 1889, 2.

34. *Star,* December 22, 1892, 3.

35. *Star,* May 25, 1892, 2.

36. Hood,*One Hundred Years,* 130–53.

Chapter Nine: The Women's Ordination Controversy, the AMEZ Church, and Hood's Leadership, 1898–1900

1. For examinations of women's presence and activity within early Christianity, see, e.g., Elizabeth A. Clark, *Women in the Early Church* (Wilmington, Del.: Michael Glazier, Inc., 1983), Elisabeth Schussler Fiorenza, *In Memory of Her: A Feminist Theological Reconstruction of Christian Origins* (New York: Crossroad, 1983); and Karen Jo Torjesen, *When Women Were Priests: Women's Leadership in the Early Church and the Scandal of Their Subordination in the Rise of Christianity* (San Francisco: Harper SanFrancisco, 1993).

2. For information regarding women ministers in American Christianity and Judaism, see Catherine Wesinger, ed., *Religious Institutions and Women's Leadership* (Columbia: University of South Carolina Press, 1996). While Rosemary Skinner Keller and Rosemary Radford Ruether's edited work does not limit itself to women in the ministry, there is good information relative to Christian and Jewish women ministries in *In Our Own Voices: Four Centuries of American Women's Religious Writing* (San Francisco: Harper SanFrancisco, 1995). Given the historical and sometime rival relationship between the AMEZ and the AME, Jualynne E. Dodson's "Women's Ministries and the African Methodist Episcopal Tradition," 124–38, is of special interest for this study. Judith Weisenfeld and Richard Newman's edited volume *This Far by Faith: Readings in African-American Women's Religious Biography* (New York: Routledge, 1996), is also very useful.

3. Walls, *Zion,* 111–12, provides a brief overview of the enhancement of women's status in the Zion Church during this era.

4. For sketches of Mary J. Small, see the reprint of a *York* (Pa.) *Daily* article, in *Star,* November 17, 1898, 7; Wall, *Zion,* 111–12, 260, 404, 586; Bradley, *History,* 2:78, 233, 236, 384, 393–94; and Johnson and Williams, *Pioneering Women,* 23–24.

5. For these moderate perspectives, see the *Star,* June 23, 1898, 6; July 21, 1898, 1; and August 8, 1898, 4.

6. Bishop Small is an excellent representative of the progressive position. See his arguments in the *Star,* June 16, 1898, 6; July 28, 1898, 6; August 11, 1898, 1; August 18, 1898, 1; August 25, 1898, 2, 5; and September 1, 1898, 6.

7. For exchanges between the traditionalist Chambers and his critics, see the *Star,* June 16, 1898, 1; June 30, 1898, 5; July 21, 1898, 5; July 28, 1898, 2; and August 18, 1898, 1.

8. *Star,* July 14, 1898, 1.

9. *Star,* October 27, 1898, 5.

10. Ibid., 4.

11. *Star,* November 10, 1898, 1.

12. *Star,* January 12, 1899, 1.

13. Ibid.

14. Ibid.

15. Ibid.

16. For biographical details about Sarah Pettey, see Walls, *Zion,* 408–9, 413, 421; and Johnson and Williams, *Pioneering Women,* 19. In addition, the political activities and philosophy of Sarah Pettey play a central role in Gilmore's *Gender and Jim Crow.*

17. *Star,* June 23, 1898, 5.

18. *Star,* December 22, 1898, 6.

19. Reprinted in *Star,* August 11, 1898, 1.

20. Ibid.

21. Minutes, General Conference, AMEZ Church, 1900, 56, 76.

22. Minutes, Genesee Annual Conference of the AMEZ Church, 1858, 4–5.

23. Bucke, general editor, *American Methodism,* 2:405–6.

24. Angell, *Turner,* 181–84.

Chapter Ten: Hood's Leadership and Controversies Regarding Zion's Episcopacy, 1888–1918

1. See Bradley, *History,* 2:120–48, for two insightful chapters on "The Development of the Episcopacy."

2. *Star,* September 30, 1897; October 28, 1897, 1; December 9, 1897, 1, 4; February 3, 1898, 1; February 10, 1898, 1; February 17, 1898, 1; February 24, 1898, 1, 2; March 3, 1898, 1; March 10, 1898, 1, 2; and March 24, 1898, 1.

3. See *Star,* February 26, 1; March 5, 1; March 12, 1; March 19, 1; March 26, 1; April 2, 1; and April 9, 1903, 1.

4. For biographical sketches of these two individuals, see Bradley, *History,* 2:385; Walls, *Zion,* 203, 315; 580–81; and *Star,* March 10, 1898, 2.

5. *Star,* September 30, 1897, 1.

6. *Star,* December 9, 1897, 1, 4.

7. *Star,* October 28, 1897, 1.

8. *Star,* December 9, 1897, 1, 4; quotes from page 1.

9. *Star,* February, 3, 1898, 1.

10. In addition to those issues of the *Star* already cited, see February 10, 1898, 1; February 17, 1898, 1; February 24, 1898, 1, 2; March 3, 1898, 1; March 10, 1898, 1, 2; and March 24, 1898, 1.

11. *Star,* September 19, 1889, 3.

12. For biographical accounts of Smith, see Bradley, *History,* 2: 390–91; Walls, *Zion,* 350, 587–89; and *Star,* June 4, 1886, 1.

13. Walls, *Zion,* 588.

14. To follow this series of conflicts articles written by the major players in the *Star* between April 1899 and March 1904.

15. *Star,* March 4, 1897, 2.

16. *Star,* October 29, 1903, 4.

17. *Star,* September 3, 1903, 1, 5.

18. *Star,* October 22, 1903, 1, 5. The quote is located on page 5.

19. For a look at Bishop Walters's ministerial career prior to his episcopacy and the role of Hood in Walters's ministry, see Chapter 2, "A 'This Worldly Mission:' In the Black Man's Church, 1877–1892," in George Mason Miller's "This Worldly," 44–86, including note 32 on page 79.

20. Walters, *My Life and Work;* see pages 141–48 for a discussion of the conservative-progressive struggle in the Zion church between the years 1888 and 1916.

21. Minutes, General Conference of the AMEZ Church, 1912, 90–93.

22. *The Zion Vidette* (Chattanooga, Tennessee), September 1910, 7.

23. *Star,* September 30, 1915, 1.

24. *Star,* November 4, 1915, 1.

25. Ibid.

26. *Star,* May 18, 1916, 1, 4; and Minutes, General Conference of AMEZ, 1916, 2.

27. *Star,* Ibid.

28. *Star,* June 8, 1916, 3.

29. *Star,* May 18, 1916, 1.

30. Minutes, General Conference of AMEZ, 1916, 20–21, 23, 25–26. The partial quote is on page 23.

31. Minutes, General Conference of AMEZ, 1916, 16–17.

32. *Star,* June 8, 1916, 3.

33. Walters, *My Life and Work,* 148.

34. Minutes, General Conference of the AMEZ, 1916, 16–17. The quote is located on page 17.

35. *Star,* June 8, 1916, 3.

36. Jacob W. Powell, *Bird's Eye View of the General Conference of the African Methodist Episcopal Zion Church with Observations on the Progress of the Colored People of L'Ville, Kentucky and A History of the Movement Looking Toward the Elevation of Rev. Benjamin W. Swain, D. D. to the Bishopric in 1920* (Boston: LaValle Press, 1918), 9.

37. Ibid., 9.

38. Minutes, General Conference of AMEZ, 1920, 55.

39. *Star,* October 31, 1918, 8. Obviously, this issue of the *Star* began circulation after its publication date.

40. Ibid. There were other eulogies recorded in the *Star* besides that of Clinton. See pages 1, 4, 5, and 8. Bishop Hoggard and I spoke by telephone during the spring of 1991.

41. Minutes, General Conference of AMEZ, 1920, 54–55. See page 55 for quotes.

Bibliography

I. Primary Sources

A. Minutes, General Conference of the AMEZ Church, 1852 (Synopsis), 1856, 1880, 1884, 1888, 1892, 1896, 1900, 1904, 1908, 1912, 1916, 1920

B. Minutes of Annual Conferences in the AMEZ Church

Central North Carolina Conference, 1876, 1878, 1880, 1881,1886, 1887, 1899, 1907, 1912
Central and West Central North Carolina Annual Conference, 1910, 1915
Genesee Annual Conference, 1858
New England Annual Conference, 1856, 1862, 1863, 1867, 1886, 1889, 1890, 1891
New York Annual Conference, 1856, 1887, 1888, 1890, 1892, 1903, 1904, 1910, 1912–1915
New York and New England Annual Conference, 1855
North Carolina Annual Conference, 1876, 1878, 1880, 1881, 1886, 1887, 1892, 1899, 1907, 1912
Philadelphia and Baltimore Annual Conference, 1884, 1885, 1891
Virginia Annual Conference, 1911
West Central North Carolina Annual Conference, 1910, 1913–1915
West Central and North Carolina Annual Conference, 1913

C. Periodicals

AME Christian Recorder (Philadelphia), June 1861–December 1864; March 1869–June 1877.
The African Methodist Episcopal Zion Quarterly Review, 1 (1891, Only Fragment of Issue, Unidentifiable); 9 (January–March 1899); 9 (April–June 1899); 9 (October–December 1899); 10 (July–September 1900); 10 (October–December 1900); 11 (January–March 1901); 12 (July–September 1902); 13 (July–September 1903); 14 (January–March 1904); 16 (April–June 1906); 16 (July–September 1906); 17 (October–December 1907); 18 (July–September 1908); 18 (October–December 1908); 19 (January–March 1909); 19 (July–September 1909); 29 (April–June 1919); 31 (January–March 1921).
The Daily Star of Zion (Washington, D.C.), May 2–3, May 4, May 10, May 12, and May 18, 1900.
The Star of Zion (Published in Petersburg, Virginia, 1884–1885; in Salisbury, North Carolina,

1886–1895; and in Charlotte, North Carolina, 1896–Present); September 1884–October 1910 (Some items are missing, especially between the years 1904 and 1910.); January 1915–January 1919.

The Zion Vidette (Chattanooga, Tenn.), September 1910.

II. Other Contemporary Sources

Acornley, John H., *The Colored Lady Evangelist—Being the Life, Labors and Experiences of Mrs. Harriet A. Baker.* Brooklyn, N.Y.: 1892. Reprint: New York: Garland Publishing, 1987.

Allen, Richard. *The Life Experience and Gospel Labors of the Rt. Rev. Richard Allen, Written by Himself.* Philadelphia: AME Book Concern, 1887.

Andrews, William R., ed. *Sisters of the Spirit: Three Black Women's Autobiographies of the Nineteenth Century.* Bloomington: Indiana University Press, 1986.

Atkins, S. G. "The AME Zion Church as a Factor in the Elevation of the Negro Race." In *The African Methodist Episcopal Zion Quarterly Review* [15] (April–June 1905): 6–15.

Binga, Anthony, Jr. *Sermons on Several Occasions.* vol. 1. Washington, D.C.: n.p., 1889.

Chambers, Reverend S. A. *The Star of Zion,* June 16, 1898, 1.

Clinton, Bishop George W. *Christianity Under the Searchlight.* Nashville: National Baptist Publishing Board, 1909.

———. Eulogy for Hood, *The Star of Zion,* October 31, 1918, 1.

Colbert, Jesse B., ed. *History of the Varick Christian Endeavor Society, AME Zion Church.* N.p., n.d.

Dowd, Jerome. *Negro in American Life.* New York: Century Company, 1926.

Historical Documents in the Archives of Evans Metropolitan AMEZ Church. Fayetteville, N.C.

Historical Documents in the Library of St. Luke AMEZ Church. Wilmington, N.C.

Hood, James Walker. *The Negro in the Christian Pulpit: Twenty-one Practical Sermons.* Raleigh, N.C.: Edwards & Broughton Co., 1884.

———. *One Hundred Years of the African Methodist Episcopal Zion Church.* New York: AME Zion Book Concern, 1895.

———. *The Plan of the Apocalypse.* York, Pa.: Anstadt & Sons, 1900.

———. *Sermons.* vol. 2. York, Pa.: Anstadt & Sons, 1908.

———. *Sketch of the Early History of the African Methodist Episcopal Zion Church.* Vol. 2. N.p., 1914.

———. "Will It Be Possible for the Negro to Attain, in This Country, Unto the American Type of Civilization?" In *Twentieth Century Negro Literature . . . By One Hundred of America's Greatest Negroes,* edited by D. W. Culp. Atlanta, Ga.: J. L. Nichols & Co., 1902, 50–56.

Houchins, Sue E., ed. *Spiritual Narratives.* Schomburg Library of Nineteenth-Century Black Women Writers Series. Henry Louis Gates, general editor. New York: Oxford University Press, 1988.

Johnson, W. Bishop. *The Scourging of a Race and Other Sermons and Addresses.* Washington, D.C.: Beresford Printer, 1904.

McDonald, Reverend J. W. *The Star of Zion,* January 23, 1919, 1.

Moore, Bishop John J. *A Scripture Catechism for Bible Scholars and Sunday Schools for the AME Zion Church, Also with the Principles of Methodism as a Religious Sect . . .* Salisbury, N.C.: Livingstone College Printer, n.d.

―――. *History of the AME Zion Church in America.* York, Pa.: Teachers Journal Office, 1884.

Powell, Jacob W. *Bird's Eye View of the General Conference of the AME Zion Church at Louisville, Kentucky, 1916.* Boston: Lavelle Press, 1918.

Rush, Christopher. *The Rise and Progress of the African Methodist Episcopal Zion Church in America.* New York: The Author, 1843.

Simmons, William J. *Men of Mark: Eminent, Progressive and Rising.* New York: Arno Press, 1968.

Small, Bishop John Bryan. *Code on the Discipline of the African Methodist Episcopal Zion Church..* Originally Published 1898. Reprint, Copyright, and Introduction by Bishop J. Clinton Hoggard, Washington, D.C., 1990.

―――. *The Star of Zion,* August 18, 1898, 1.

Walters, Alexander. *My Life and Work.* New York: Fleming H. Revell Company, 1917.

Woodson, Carter G., Collection of Papers. Library of Congress. Microfilmed 1975. Available from Auburn University, Alabama.

III. Secondary Sources

Ahlstrom, Sydney E. *A Religious History of the American People.* New Haven, Conn.: Yale University Press, 1972.

Albanese, Catherine L. *America: Religion and Religions.* Belmont, Calif.: Wadsworth Publishing, 1981.

Anderson, Eric. *Race and Politics in North Carolina, 1872–1901: The Black Second .* Baton Rouge: Louisiana State University Press, 1981.

Angell, Stephen Ward. *Bishop Henry McNeal Turner and African-American Religion in the South.* Knoxville, Tenn.: University of Tennessee Press, 1992.

Backman, Milton V., Jr. *Christian Churches of America: Origins and Beliefs.* Rev. ed. New York: Charles Scribner's Sons, 1983.

Bacon, Margaret Hope. *Mothers of Feminism: The Story of Quaker Women in America.* San Francisco: Harper and Row, 1986.

Baldwin, Lewis V. *"Invisible" Strands in African Methodism: A History of the African Union Methodist Protestant and Union American Methodist Episcopal Churches, 1805–1980.* Metuchen, N.J.: Scarecrow Press, 1983.

Bennett, Lerone, Jr. *Before the Mayflower: A History of Black America.* 5th ed. New York: Penguin Books and Johnson Publishing Company, 1982.

Benson, Donna Johanna. "'Before I Be A Slave': A Social Analysis of the Black Struggle for Freedom in North Carolina, 1860–1865." Ph.D. diss., Duke University, 1984. University Microfilms International, Ann Arbor, Mich.

Berlin, Ira. *Slaves without Masters: The Free Negro in the Antebellum South.* New York: Oxford University Press, 1974.

Bernal, Martin. *Black Athena: The Afroasiatic Roots of Classical Civilization.* Vol. 1: *The Fabrication of Ancient Greece, 1785–1985.* New Brunswick, N.J.: Rutgers University Press, 1987.

Berry, Mary, and John Blassingame. *Long Memory: The Black Experience in America.* New York: Oxford University Press, 1982.

Billington, Ray Allen, ed. *The Journal of Charlotte L. Forten : A Free Negro in the Slave Era.* First published by the Dryden Press in 1953. Reprint: London: Collier Books, Collier-Macmillan Ltd., 1961.

Blassingame, John W. *The Slave Community: Plantation Life in the Antebellum South.* New York: Oxford University Press, 1972.

Boles, John B. *The Great Revival, 1787–1805.* Lexington: University of Kentucky Press, 1972.

———. *Masters and Slaves in the House of the Lord: Race and Religion in the American South, 1740–1870.* Lexington: University of Kentucky Press, 1988.

Bowden, Henry Warner. *Church History in the Age of Science: Historical Patterns in the United States, 1876–1918.* Reprint: Carbondale: Southern Illinois University Press, 1991.

Bracey, John H., Jr., August Meier, and Elliot Rudwick, eds. *Black Nationalism in America.* New York: Bobbs-Merrill Company, 1970.

Bradley, David Henry, Sr. *A History of the AME Zion Church.* Vol. 2. Nashville: Parthenon Press, 1970.

Brauer, Jerald C., et al., eds. *The Westminster Dictionary of Church History.* Philadelphia: Westminster Press, 1971.

Brekus, Catherine A. "Harriet Livermore, the Pilgrim Stranger: Female Preaching and Biblical Feminism in Early Nineteenth Century America." *Church History* 65 (September 1996): 389–405.

Brotz, Howard. *Negro Social and Political Thought, 1850–1920: Representative Texts.* New York: Basic Books, 1966.

Bucke, Emory Stevens, general editor. *The History of American Methodism.* 3 vols. New York: Abingdon Press, 1964.

Burkett, Randall. *Garveyism as a Religious Movement.* Metuchen, N.J.: Scarecrow and ATLA, 1978.

Burkett, Randall K., and Richard Newman. *Black Apostles: Afro-American Clergy Confront the Twentieth Century.* Boston: G. K. Hall, 1978.

Chisholm, Frank P., Mrs. "Documents." (A letter confirming Hood's participation at the 1867–1868 State Reconstruction Convention in North Carolina) *Journal of Negro History* 5 (April 1920): 235.

Clayton, Joyce D. "Education, Politics, and Statesmanship: The Story of James Walker Hood in North Carolina, 1864–1890." Master's thesis, North Carolina Central University, 1978.

Cone, James H. *Black Theology and Black Power.* New York: Seabury, 1969.

———. *My Soul Looks Back.* Nashville: Abingdon Press, 1982.

Davis, Cyprian. *The History of Black Catholics in the United States.* New York: Crossroad, 1990.

Dickerson, Dennis C. "William Fisher Dickerson: Northern Preacher/Southern Prelate," *Methodist History* 23 (April 1985): 135–52.

Drago, Edmund L. *Black Politicians and Reconstruction in Georgia: A Splendid Failure.* Baton Rouge: Louisiana State University Press, 1982.

Drake, St. Clair. *The Redemption of Africa and Black Religion.* Chicago: Third World Press, 1970.

Du Bois, W. E. B. *Black Reconstruction in America, 1860–1880.* New York: Russell and Russell, 1963.

———. *The Souls of Black Folk.* Chicago: C. A. McClurg, 1903. Reprint, New York: New American Library, 1969.

Dvorak, Katharine L. *An African-American Exodus: The Segregation of the Southern Churches.* Brooklyn, N.Y.: Carlson Publishing, 1991.

Edmonds, Helen G. *The Negro and Fusion Politics in North Carolina, 1894–1901.* Chapel Hill: University of North Carolina Press, 1951.

Eighmy, John Lee. *Churches in Cultural Captivity: A History of the Social Attitudes of Southern Baptists.* Knoxville: University of Tennessee Press, 1972.

Eskew, Glen T. "Black Elitism and the Failure of Paternalism in Postbellum Georgia: The Case of Bishop Lucius Henry Holsey." *Journal of Southern History* 58 (November 1992): 637–66.

Faduma, Orishatukeh. "The Defects of the Negro Church." Occasional Papers No. 10. The American Negro Academy. Washington, D.C.: American Negro Academy, 1904. Reprint: *The American Negro: His Literature and Literature — The American Negro Academy Occasional Papers, 1–22.* New York: Arno Press and the New York Times, 1969.

Felder, Cain Hope. *Troubling Biblical Waters: Race, Class, and Family.* Maryknoll, N.Y.: Orbis Books, 1989.

———, ed. *Stony the Road We Trod: African American Biblical Interpretation.* Minneapolis: Fortress Press, 1991.

Fishel, Leslie H., Jr., and Benjamin Quarles, eds. *The Black American: A Documentary History.* 3d ed. Oakland, N.J.: Scott, Foresman and Company, 1970.

Fitts, Leroy. *A History of Black Baptists.* Nashville: Broadman Press, 1985.

Fleming, G. James, and Christian E. Burckel, eds. *Who's Who in Colored America.* Yonkers, N.Y.: Christian E. Burckel Associates, 1950.

Foner, Eric. *A Short History of Reconstruction, 1863–1877.* New York: Harper & Row, Publishers, 1990.

Foner, Philip S., ed. *Black Socialist Preacher: The Teachings of Reverend George Washington Woodbey and His Disciple, Reverend G. W. Slater, Jr.* San Francisco: Synthesis Publications, 1983.

Fordham, Monroe. *Major Themes in Northern Black Religious Thought, 1800–1860*. Hicksville, N.Y.: Exposition Press, 1975.

Franklin, John Hope. *From Slavery to Freedom: A History of Negro Americans*. 4th ed. New York: Alfred A. Knopf, 1974.

Frazier, E. Franklin, and C. Eric Lincoln. *The Negro Church in America : The Black Church Since Frazier*. New York: Schocken Books, 1974.

Frederickson, George M. *The Black Image in the White Mind: The Debate on Afro-American Character and Destiny, 1817–1914*. New York: Harper & Row, 1972.

Garraty, John A., and Robert A. McCaughey. *The American Nation: A History of the United States*. 6th ed. New York: Harper & Row, 1987.

Gatewood, Willard B. *Aristocrats of Color: The Black Elite, 1880–1920*. Bloomington and Indianapolis: Indiana University Press, 1990.

Gaustad, Edwin Scott. *A Religious History of America*. Rev. ed. San Francisco: Harper & Row, 1990.

Gavins, Raymond. *The Perils and Prospects of Southern Black Leadership: Gordon Blaine Hancock, 1884–1970*. Durham, N.C.: Duke University Press, 1977.

Genovese, Eugene. *Roll, Jordan, Roll: The World the Slaves Made*. New York: Vintage, 1976.

George, Carol V. R. *Segregated Sabbaths: Richard Allen and the Emergence of Independent Black Churches, 1760–1840*. New York: Oxford University Press, 1973.

Giddings, Paula. *When and Where I Enter: The Impact of Black Women on Race and Sex in America*. New York: William Morrow, 1984.

Gilmore, Glenda Elizabeth. *Gender and Jim Crow: Women and the Politics of White Supremacy in North Carolina, 1896–1920*. Chapel Hill: University of North Carolina Press, 1996.

Grant, Joanne, ed. *Black Protest: History, Documents, and Analyses, 1619 to the Present*. Rev. ed. Greenwich, Conn.: Fawcett Publications, 1974.

Gravely, William B. *Gilbert Haven, Methodist Abolitionist: A Study in Race, Religion, and Reform, 1850–1880*. Nashville: Abingdon Press, 1973.

———. "The Rise of African Churches in America (1786–1822)." *The Journal of Religious Thought* 41 (Spring–Summer 1984): 58–73.

Gregg, Howard D. *History of the African Methodist Episcopal Church*. Nashville: AME Church Publishing House, 1980.

Griffin, Paul R. *Black Theology as the Foundation of Three Methodist Colleges: The Educational Views and Labors of Daniel Payne, Joseph Price, and Isaac Lane*. Lanham, Md.: University Press of America, 1984.

Gutman, Herbert G. *The Black Family in Slavery and Freedom, 1750–1925*. New York: Vintage Books, 1976.

Hamilton, Charles V. *The Black Preacher in America*. New York: William Morrow & Company, 1972.

Handy, Robert T. *A Christian America: Protestant Hopes and Historical Realities*. New York: Oxford University Press, 1971.

————. *A History of the Churches in the United States and Canada.* New York: Oxford University Press, 1977.

————, ed. *The Social Gospel in America, 1870–1920.* New York: Oxford University Press, 1966.

Handy, Robert T., et al., eds. *American Christianity: An Historical Interpretation with Representative Documents,* vol. 2, *1820–1860.* New York: Charles Scribner's Sons, 1963.

Hardesty, Nancy. *Women Called to Witness.* Nashville: Abingdon, 1984.

Harding, Vincent. *There Is a River: The Black Struggle for Freedom in America.* New York: Harcourt, Brace, Jovanovich, 1981.

Harlan, Louis, et al., eds. *The Booker T. Washington Papers.* 14 vols. Urbana: University of Illinois Press, 1972–1989.

————. *Booker T. Washington: The Wizard of Tuskegee, 1901–1915.* New York: Oxford University Press, 1985.

Herskovits, Melville J. *The Myth of the Negro Past.* Boston: Beacon Press, 1969.

Higginbotham, Evelyn Brooks. *Righteous Discontent: The Women's Movement in the Black Baptist Church, 1880–1920.* Cambridge, Mass.: Harvard University Press, 1993.

Hildebrand, Reginald F. *The Times Were Strange and Stirring: Methodist Preachers and the Crisis of Emancipation.* Durham, N.C.: Duke University Press, 1995.

Hill, Samuel S., ed. *Encyclopedia of Religion in the South.* Macon, Ga.: Mercer University Press, 1984.

Hopkins, Joseph G. E., et al., eds. *Concise Dictionary of American Biography.* New York: Charles Scribner's Sons, 1964.

Hudson, Winthrop S., and John Corrigan. *Religion in America: An Historical Account of the Development of American Religous Life.* 5th ed. New York: Macmillan Publishing Company, 1992.

Hutchison, William R., ed. *Between the Times: The Travail of the Protestant Establishment in America, 1900–1960.* New York: Cambridge University Press, 1989.

Jacobs, Sylvia M. *Black Americans and the Missionary Movement in Africa.* Westport, Conn.: Greenwood Press, 1982.

Jeffrey, David Lyle, ed. *A Burning and a Shining Light: English Spirituality in the Age of Wesley.* Grand Rapids, Mich.: Eerdmans, 1987.

Johnson, Alonzo, and Paul Jersild, eds. *"Ain't Gonna Lay My 'Ligion Down": African American Religion in the South.* Columbia, S.C.: University of South Carolina Press, 1996.

Johnson, Clifton H., ed. *God Struck Me Dead: Religious Conversion Experiences and Autobiographies of Ex-Slaves.* Philadelphia: Pilgrim Press, 1960.

Johnson, Dorothy Sharpe, and Lula Goolsby Williams. *Pioneering Women of the African Methodist Episcopal Zion Church.* Charlotte, N.C.: AME Zion Publishing House, 1996.

Jones, William R. *Is God a White Racist?* Garden City, N.Y.: Doubleday/Anchor, 1973.

Jordan, Winthrop D. *White Over Black: American Attitudes toward the Negro, 1550–1812.* Chapel Hill: University of North Carolina Press, 1968.

Kalisa, Beryl Graham. "Let the Women Keep Silent in the A. M. E. Zion Church: Eliza Ann Gardner and Her Contribution, 1876–1922." *AME Zion Quarterly Review* 108 (October 1996): 31–38.

Koger, Larry. *Black Slaveowners: Free Black Slave Masters in South Carolina, 1790–1860.* Jefferson, N.C.: McFarland & Company, 1985.

Lakey, Othal Hawthorne. *The Rise of "Colored Methodism": A Study of the Background and the Beginnings of the Christian Methodist Episcopal Church.* Dallas: Crescendo Book Publications, 1972.

Latourette, Kenneth Scott. *A History of Christianity,* vol. 2, *Reformation to the Present.* Rev. ed. San Francisco: Harper & Row, Publishers, 1975.

———. *A History of the Expansion of Christianity.* vol. 5: *The Great Century in the Americas, Australasia, and Africa, A.D. 1800–A.D. 1914.* Grand Rapids, Mich.: Zondervan Publishing House, 1970. Originally Published in 1943 by Harper & Row.

Lerner, Gerda, ed. *Black Women in White America: A Documentary History.* New York: Vintage Press, 1972.

Levine, Lawrence W. *Black Culture and Black Consciousness: Afro-American Folk Thought from Slavery to Freedom.* New York: Oxford University Press, 1977.

Lincoln, C. Eric. "Black Religion in North Carolina: From Colonial Times to 1900." In *The Black Presence in North Carolina,* edited by Jeffrey J. Crow and Robert E. Winters, Jr. Raleigh, N.C.: North Carolina Museum of History, Division of Archives and History, Department of Cultural Resources, 1978.

Lincoln, C. Eric, and Lawrence H. Mamiya. *The Black Church in the African American Experience.* Durham, N.C.: Duke University Press, 1990.

Litwack, Leon F. *Been in the Storm So Long: The Aftermath of Slavery.* New York: Alfred A. Knopf, 1979.

Litwack, Leon, and August Meier, eds. *Black Leaders of the Nineteenth Century.* Urbana: University of Illinois Press, 1988.

Loewenburg, Bert J., and Ruth Bogin, eds. *Black Women in Nineteenth Century America.* University Park: Pennsylvania State University Press, 1978.

Logan, Frenise A. *The Negro in North Carolina, 1876–1894.* Chapel Hill: University of North Carolina Press, 1964.

Lovell, John, Jr. *Black Song: The Forge and the Flame.* New York: Macmillan Company, 1972.

Lynch, Hollis R. *Edward Wilmot Blyden: Pan-Negro Patriot, 1832–1912.* London: Oxford University Press, 1967.

Malone, Dumas, ed. *Dictionary of American Biography.* New York: Charles Scribner, 1936.

Martin, Sandy Dwayne. "The American Baptist Home Mission Society and Black Higher Education in the South, 1865–1920." *Foundations* 29 (October–December 1981): 310–327.

———. *Black Baptists and African Missions: The Origins of A Movement, 1880–1915.* Macon, Ga.: Mercer University Press, 1989.

———. "Black Churches and the Civil War: Theological and Ecclesiastical Significance of

Black Methodist Involvement, 1861–1865." *Methodist History.* 32 (April 1994): 174–186.

———. "Spelman's Emma B. DeLaney and the African Mission." *The Journal of Religious Thought* 41 (Spring–Summer 1984): 22–37.

Marty, Martin E. *Modern American Religion,* vol. 1, *The Irony of It All, 1893–1919.* Chicago: University of Chicago Press, 1986.

Mathews, Donald G. *Religion in the Old South.* Chicago: University of Chicago Press, 1977.

———. *Slavery and Methodism: A Chapter in American Morality, 1780–1845.* Princeton, N.J.: Princeton University Press, 1965.

Mays, Benjamin Elijah and Joseph William Nicholson. *The Negro's Church.* New York: Russell and Russell, 1933.

McMurray, George W., and Ndugu G. B. T'Ofori-Atta. *Mother Zion African Methodist Episcopal Zion Church: 200 Years of Evangelism and Liberation/The Birth Story of A Denomination.* Charlotte, N.C.: AME Zion Publishing House, 1996.

McPherson, James M. *The Negro's Civil War: How American Negroes Felt and Acted during the War for Union.* New York: Vintage Books, 1965.

Mead, Frank S., revised by Samuel S. Hill. *Handbook of Denominations in the United States.* 8th ed. Nashville: Abingdon Press, 1985.

Meade, Sidney E. *The Lively Experiment: The Shaping of Christianity in America.* New York: Harper & Row, 1963.

Medford, Hampton Thomas. *Zion Methodism Abroad: Giving the Rise and Progress of the A. M. E. Zion Church on Its Foreign Fields.* Washington, D.C.: H. T. Medford, 1937.

Meier, August. *Negro Thought in America, 1880–1915.* Ann Arbor: University of Michigan Press, 1963.

Miller, Albert G. "Striving to Reconcile the World: A Glimpse of the Life and Writings of Theophilus Gould Steward." *AME Church Review* 111 (April–June 1996): 38–53.

Miller, Floyd J. *The Search for a Black Nationality: Black Emigration and Colonization, 187–1863.* Urbana: University of Illinois Press, 1975.

Miller, George Mason. "'A This Worldly Mission': The Life and Career of Alexander Walters (1858–1917)." Ph.D. diss.: State University of New York at Stony Brook, 1984.

Moberg, David O. *The Great Reversal: Evangelism versus Social Concern.* Philadelphia: Lippincott, 1972.

Montgomery, William E. *Under Their Own Vine and Fig Tree: The African American Church in the South, 1865–1900.* Baton Rouge: Louisiana State University Press, 1993.

Moore, Moses N. *Orishatukeh Faduma: Liberal Theology and Evangelical Pan-Africanism, 1857–1946.* Lanham, Md. and London: American Theological Library Association and the Scarecrow Press, 1996.

Morris, Calvin S. "Reverdy Ransom, the Social Gospel and Race." *Journal of Religious Thought* 41 (Spring–Summer 1984): 7–21.

Morrow, Ralph E. *Northern Methodism and Reconstruction.* East Lansing: Michigan State University Press, 1956.

Moses, Wilson Jeremiah. *Black Messiahs and Uncle Toms: Social and Literary Manipulations of a Religious Myth*. University Park: Pennsylvania State University Press, 1982.

———. *The Golden Age of Black Nationalism, 1850–1925*. New York: Oxford University Press, 1978.

Nelsen, Hart M., Raytha L. Yokley, and Anne K. Nelsen, eds. *The Black Church in America*. New York: Basic Books, 1971.

Noll, Mark A., ed. *Religion and American Politics: From the Colonial Period to the 1980s*. New York: Oxford University Press, 1990.

Norwood, Frederick A. *The Story of American Methodism: A History of the United Methodists and Their Relations*. Nashville: Abingdon Press, 1974.

Outler, Albert C., ed. *John Wesley*. New York: Oxford University Press, 1964.

Painter, Nell I. *Exodusters: Black Migration to Kansas after Reconstruction*. New York: Knopf, 1977.

Paris, Peter J. *The Social Teachings of the Black Churches*. Philadelphia: Fortress Press, 1985.

Parrender, Geoffrey. *African Traditional Religion*. New York: Harper and Row, 1976.

Payne, Daniel A. *Recollections of Seventy Years*. New York: Arno Press, 1968.

Pelt, Owen D., and Ralph Lee Smith. *The Story of the National Baptists*. New York: Vantage Press, 1960.

Phillips, Charles H. *The History of the Colored Methodist Episcopal Church in America*. Jackson, Tenn.: 1925.

Quarles, Benjamin. *Black Abolitionists*. New York: Oxford University Press, 1969.

Raboteau, Albert J. *Slave Religion: The "Invisible Institution" in the Antebellum South*. New York: Oxford University Press, 1978.

Raboteau, Albert J. *A Fire in the Bones: Reflections on African-American Religious History*. Boston: Beacon Press, 1995.

Redkey, Edwin S. *Black Exodus: Black Nationalist and Back-to-Africa Movements, 1890–1910*. New Haven, Conn.: Yale University Press, 1969.

Reid, Daniel G., et al., eds. *Dictionary of Christianity in America*. Downers Grove, Ill.: Inter-Varsity Press, 1990.

Richardson, Harry V. *Dark Salvation: The Story of Methodism as It Developed among Blacks in America*. Garden City, N.Y.: Anchor Press/Doubleday, 1976.

Roundtree, Louise M. *An Index to Biographical Sketches and Publications of Bishops of the AME Zion Church*. Salisbury, N.C.: Copyright by Louise Roundtree, 1963.

Ruether, Rosemary R., and Rosemary Skinner Keller, eds. *In Our Own Voices: Four Centuries of American Women's Religious Writing*. San Francisco: HarperSanFrancisco, 1995.

Ruether, Rosemary R., and Rosemary Skinner Keller, eds. *Women and Religion in America*. 3 vols. San Francisco: Harper and Row, 1981, 1983, 1986.

Sanneh, Lamin. *West African Christianity: The Religious Impact*. Maryknoll, N.Y.: Orbis Books, 1983.

Scherer, Lester B. *Slavery and the Churches in Early America, 1619–1819*. Grand Rapids, Mich.: Eerdmans, 1975.

Schor, Joel. *Henry Highland Garnet: A Voice of Black Radicalism in the Nineteenth Century.* Westport, Conn.: Greenwood Press, 1977.

Sernett, Milton C. *Afro-American Religious History: A Documentary Witness.* Durham, N.C.: Duke University Press, 1985.

———. *Black Religion and American Evangelicalism: White Protestants, Plantation Missions, and the Flowering of Negro Christianity, 1787–1865.* Metuchen, N.J.: Scarecrow Press, 1975.

Simmons, R. H. "Rt. Rev. J. W. Hood, D. D., LL. D." In *Negro Stars in All Ages of the World.* 2d ed., edited by W. H. Quick. Richmond, Va.: S. B. Adkins & Co., Printers, 1898.

Simpson, George Eaton. *Black Religions in the New World.* New York: Columbia University Press, 1979.

Singleton, George A. *The Romance of African Methodism: A Study of the African Methodist Episcopal Church.* New York: Exposition Press, 1952.

Smith, H. Shelton. *In His Image, But . . . : Racism in Southern Religion, 1780–1910.* Durham, N.C.: Duke University Press, 1972.

Smith, Warren Thomas. *John Wesley & Slavery.* Nashville: Abingdon Press, 1986.

Snowden, Frank M., Jr. *Blacks in Antiquity: Ethiopians in the Greco-Roman Experience.* Cambridge, Mass.: Belknap Press of Harvard University Press, 1970.

Spain, Rufus B. *At Ease in Zion: A Social History of Southern Baptists, 1865–1900.* Nashville: Vanderbilt University Press, 1961.

Speaks, Ruben L. (Bishop). *Church Administration from the A.M.E. Zion Perspective.* Charlotte, N.C.: AME Zion Publishing House, 1996.

Spradlin, Mary Mace. *In Black and White,* vol. 1. Detroit: Gale Research Company/Book Tower, 1980.

Staudenraus, P. J. *The African Colonization Movement, 1816–1865.* New York: Columbia University Press, 1961.

Steele, Lillian Jane. "From Mount Zion Society to Soldiers Memorial African Methodist Episcopal Zion Church." Master's thesis, North Carolina Central University, 1986.

Sterling, Dorothy. *We Are Your Sisters: Black Women in the Nineteenth Century.* New York: W. W. Norton & Company, 1984.

Stuckey, Sterling. *Slave Culture: Nationalist Theory and the Foundations of Black America.* New York: Oxford University Press, 1987.

Sweet, Leonard I. *Black Images of America, 1784–1870.* New York: W. W. Norton & Company, 1976.

———, ed. *The Evangelical Tradition in America.* Macon, Ga.: Mercer University Press, 1984.

Swidler, Leonard. *Biblical Affirmations of Woman.* Philadelphia: Westminster Press, 1979.

Swift, David E. *Black Prophets of Justice: Activist Clergy before the Civil War.* Baton Rouge: Louisiana State University Press, 1989.

Synan, Vincent. *The Holiness-Pentecostal Movement in the United States.* Grand Rapids, Mich.: Eerdmans, 1971.

Thompson, Mildred I. *Ida B. Wells-Barnett: An Exploratory Study of an American Black Woman,*

1893–1930. Black Women in United States History Series, edited by Darlene Clark Hine et al. Brooklyn, N.Y.: Carlson Publishing, 1990.

Thompson, Richard K. (Bishop). *The Role of the Star of Zion in the African Methodist Episcopal Zion Church, 1796–1996.* Montgomery, Ala.: Alabama/Florida Episcopal District of the African Methodist Episcopal Zion Church, 1996.

Truth, Sojourner. *The Narrative of Sojourner Truth,* . . . Reprint, Chicago: Johnson Publishing Company, 1970.

Turner, Edward Raymond. *The Negro in Pennsylvania: Slavery, Servitude, Freedom, 1639–1861.* Washington, D.C.: American Historical Association, 1911.

Tuveson, Ernest Lee. *Redeemer Nation: The Idea of America's Millennial Role.* Chicago: University of Chicago Press, 1968.

Uya, Okon Edet, ed. *Black Brotherhood: Afro-Americans and Africa.* Lexington, Mass.: D. C. Heath and Company, 1971.

Walker, Clarence E. *A Rock in a Weary Land: The African Methodist Episcopal Church during the Civil War and Reconstruction.* Baton Rouge: Louisiana State University Press, 1982.

Walls, William J. *The African Methodist Episcopal Zion Church: Reality of the Black Church.* Charlotte, N.C.: AME Zion Publishing House, 1974.

Washington, Joseph R., Jr. *Black Religion: The Negro and Christianity in the United States.* Boston: Beacon Press, 1964.

Weisenfeld, Judith, and Richard Newman, eds. *This Far by Faith: Readings in African American Women's Religious Biography.* New York: Routledge, 1996.

Wharton, Vernon Lane. *The Negro in Mississippi, 1865–1890.* New York: Harper & Row, 1965.

Wheeler, Edward L. *Uplifting the Race: The Black Minister in the New South, 1865–1902.* New York: University Press of America, 1986.

White, Ronald C. *Liberty and Justice for All: Racial Reform and the Social Gospel (1877–1925)* . San Francisco: Harper & Row, Publishers, 1990.

Who Was Who in America : A Companion Volume to Who's Who in America. Vol. 1, 1897–1942. Chicago: Marquis Who's Who, Originally Published in 1943. Reprinted, 1962.

Willard, Frances E., *Woman in the Pulpit.* Chicago: Woman's Temperance Publication Association, 1889. Reprinted as *The Defense of Women's Rights to Ordination in the Methodist Episcopal Church,* edited by Carolyn De Swarte Gifford. New York: Garland Publishing, 1987.

Williams, Walter L. *Black Americans and the Evangelization of Africa.* Madison: University of Wisconsin Press, 1982.

Wills, David W., and Richard Newman, eds. *Black Apostles at Home and Abroad.* Boston: G. K. Hall, 1982.

Wilmore, Gayraud S. *Black Religion and Black Radicalism: An Interpretation of the Religious History of Afro-American People.* 2d ed. Maryknoll, N.Y.: Orbis Books, 1983.

———, ed. *African American Religious Studies: An Interdisciplinary Anthology.* Durham, N.C.: Duke University Press, 1989.

Wilson, Charles Reagan. *Baptized in Blood: The Religion of the Lost Cause, 1865–1920.* Athens: University of Georgia Press, 1980.

Wilson, Ellen Gibson. *The Loyal Blacks.* New York: Capricorn Books, G. P. Putnam's Sons, 1976.

Wiltse, Charles M., ed. *David Walker's Appeal.* New York: Hill and Wang, 1965.

Witherington, Ben III. *Women in the Earliest Churches.* New York: Cambridge University Press, 1988.

Wood, Forrest G. *The Arrogance of Faith: Christianity and Race in America from the Colonial Era to the Twentieth Century.* Boston: Northeastern University Press, 1990.

Woodson, Carter G. *History of the Negro Church,* 3d ed. Washington, D.C.: Associated Publishers, 1972; originally published in 1921.

Wright, Bishop Richard R., Jr. *The Bishops of the African Methodist Episcopal Church.* Nashville: AME Sunday School Union, 1963.

Yates, Walter Ladell. *The History of the African Methodist Episcopal Zion Church in West Africa, Liberia, Gold Coast (Ghana) and Nigeria, 1900–1939.* Hartford, Conn.: Hartford Seminary Foundation, 1967.

Young, Henry J. *Major Black Religious Leaders, 1755–1940.* Nashville: Abingdon, 1977.

Index